Dreaming Me

Dreaming Me

An African American Woman's Spiritual Journey

Jan Willis

RIVERHEAD BOOKS

a member of Penguin Putnam Inc.

NEW YORK

2001

RIVERHEAD BOOKS
a member of
Penguin Putnam Inc.
375 Hudson Street
New York, NY 10014

Library of Congress Cataloging-in-Publication Data

Willis, Janice Dean.
Dreaming me: an African American woman's spiritual journey/by Jan Willis.
p. cm.
ISBN 1-57322-173-2
1. Willis, Janice Dean. 2. Buddhists—United States—Biography.
3. Converts—United States—Biography. 4. Afro-American Baptists—
Southern States—History—20th century. I. Title.
BQ996.I44 A3   2001   00-042503
294.3'092—dc21
[B]

Printed in the United States of America
1   3   5   7   9   10   8   6   4   2

This book is printed on acid-free paper. ∞

Book design by Michelle McMillian
The title page art appears courtesy of The Thymes Limited,
Minneapolis, MN, and was created by Leslie Ross Lentz. The
title page art also appears on pages 1, 71, 131, 185, and 227.

In loving memory of my mother,
Dorothy Delores White Willis,
1921–1998

And for my father,
Oram Willis

And my sister
Sandra W. Williams

Family

Contents

PART 3: CHOICES

PART 4: BECOMING

PART 5: RETURN

Our deepest fear is not that we are inadequate.
Our deepest fear is that we are powerful
beyond measure.

—MARIANNE WILLIAMSON

PART 1

Birth

DREAMING ME:
THE TERROR OF LIONS

ༀ

When it began, I had just walked up the long wooden steps at the back
of my grandmother's house and entered the kitchen. In the darkened room, directly across from me, I saw the table and the broad back of my brother-in-law,
James. My sister, San, was standing at one end of the table. She glanced at me
as she reached into the cupboard and slowly brought down what appeared to
be a chocolate cake. I thought she was going to feed me. I sensed that I had come
here to eat; to be nourished in some way. But instead, she set the cake down in
front of James, and it disappeared behind his massive back. It was not for me.
I was deeply hurt; soulfully wounded. I determined to leave. I would go back
to our house. This was not the only place to get food. I would eat somehow. I
would not beg!

Just then, a dark and wispy shadow figure moved close to me. When it spoke,
I heard my mother's voice whisper threateningly into my ear: "You know it's
dangerous out there!" I immediately felt panicked, my knees buckled, and my
body developed a cold sweat. I sensed too that "outside" was fraught with dangers. Still, in frightened defiance, I turned and leaned out the door.

Next, I stood in a dry and very dusty place. The hot air that waffled and shimmered parched my throat. The dust was powdery under my feet. There were cages and wire coops all around me. Some of the doors to the cages stood opened. I looked toward one near to my right. When I did, suddenly a soft and plushy snake-like creature sprang out. The plushy creature was dirty white and spotted black. It jumped just in front of me, and I recoiled in terror as it came to rest limply on the powdery ground. I noticed that the other cages were all empty.

I found myself slumped down just outside the railings of a large corral. My head was touching one of its aged wooden slats. Inside there was a lion. He prowled the corral alone, circling in the heat, head down, his massive paws making the hot dust fly upward. His mouth was bloody. I was frozen in fear. I could neither run nor take my eyes off the beast. He was a magnificent creature: solid, firm, massive, powerful. In spite of the dust, his coat shimmered and gleamed. As he prowled, ravenous and near to me, it seemed that I could smell his awesomeness. In spite of my fear, I wanted to touch him.

The scene shifted and I was inside what appeared to be a barn. There were animal stalls here and hay underfoot. Another lion prowled anxiously, this time even closer. I gasped and turned my head away.

Then I was running. Running down a long red-dirt road in this arid country. I was running for my life. My only thought was "All the cages are open!" I knew the lions were after me. I didn't know how many, but I knew they were after me. I ran and ran, out of breath, panting through the hot air. I saw no one, no one to go to for help.

Finally I ran up to a town that looked like it was out of a Western movie. I scrambled up some stairs. A cowboy sat leaning against a building, his stir-ruped boots propped up against a railing. I screamed to him, "Please! Help me! They're after me!" But the man only rearranged his hat more securely over his eyes and leaned back again. I raced along the raised wooden walkway until I heard voices and turned through a set of swinging doors.

I found myself inside a bar. The place was packed and seemed somehow familiar—like an old New Orleans Cajun club I had once been in. I heard *the raucous sounds of zydeco blaring. My fear redoubled since I felt again like an intruder, a stranger, out of place. Still, I needed to find someone who would help me. Trembling, I was buffeted along from one sweaty body to the next. Desperate to get away from the lions, I pushed farther and farther in. Somehow, I moved through two long dark rooms, until I found myself in a back room, opened to the sky, with a few tables, and people scattered about and along a long bar.*

As I stood there, bent over and panting, a slim youngish white man came up to me. He reached into his shirt pocket and held out to me a clutch of money. As he did so, he made only one comment, phrased in the form of a question, spoken calmly and steelily: "Did you bring them?"

I knew he meant the lions.

Furious and deeply pained, I woke up.

I am a black woman from the South who teaches Tibetan Buddhism in a mostly white elite college in the Northeast. I have come a long way since leaving home. It has had its costs.

"WHITE GAL"

~❧~

This voyage that I am on,
This is a journey about what's basic:
A sense of place and of belonging,
Of safety and of being whole,
Of family, and home.

When I was a little girl, one of my mother's friends called me "white gal." It was the nickname I hated most of all. Other children sometimes taunted me with negative slogans: "Deanie Pie's daddy must'a been a white man." I was called "yella gal" more times than I can count; and each time it was a wound that pierced deep. I folded in, ashamed at the core. Both my parents were black. Even so, because of such mocking, I felt like a co-conspirator.

In the middle of my thirty-ninth year, just after my mother had had a very angry bout with my father, she turned to me and began nar-

rating the details surrounding my birth: the surprise, pain, hushed secrecy, and wrangling that soon erupted concerned my light skin and
sandy blonde curls. It seems it was the colored nurses' aides at Lloyd
Nolan Hospital (the company hospital that all of Birmingham's steel,
coal, and iron workers were required to use) who had first shattered my
mother's calm and relief following the birth of a *healthy* child.

They came in groups to my mother's bedside with secret warnings:
"Uh-huh. Girl, you done messed up now! Dat baby jes as sure white
as dat white daddy dat fathered her. You better look out from yo husband, if you loves life!"

Later, after seeing me for the first time, my mother, too, had apparently thought there had been some sort of mistake, some mix-up of
babies. Initially, she also worried. But soon enough, having come to
know that I was in truth of her womb and, therefore, also only of her
union with my father, she countered their attacks with a simple declaration. She said, "You should have seen *my* father."

My father was mum on the matter—at first. But even as I lay newly
arrived in Lloyd Nolan's nursery, my father's father, Belton, had begun
making suggestions to him about my mother's possible "illicit collu-
sions." My mother's hurt and sorrow in all this cannot be fathomed.
And while still a newborn, I believe I sensed this troubled welcome.

Subconsciously, it seems that I knew my parents fought over me.
Fought bitter battles of censure, hurled cosmic disclaimers: "It is not
mine!" and, even grander for a black child, "It is not of my race!" Perhaps my early sense of abysmal isolation and loneliness stems from
these first moments and days of life.

My mother explained that it was only after her father, Ellick's, visit
that the source of my fair coloring was grudgingly accepted by the two
male Willises. My grandfather's name was Alex, but most people pronounced it "Ellick." Ellick White (his surname was descriptive, as well
as Welsh) had come to visit my mother late one evening. They had not

seen each other for years, and whole worlds of experience and pain had found life in the time intervening. My father was working the graveyard shift down in Ensley's steelworks when Dorothy heard the thud of footsteps on the wooden porch and peered nervously through the front peep-hole to see the scraggily dressed old white man standing there. Hunched forward, he called her name in muffled tones: "Dorthay? Dorthay?" She leapt backward from the door in fear, grabbed me up in her arms, and ran on tiptoe back to the kitchen to summon Miss Chank, our neighbor, with anxious knocks through the wall.

We lived in a double-tenant frame house then, on Pleasant Hill Road in Ensley. Behind that street sloped the muddy trails that led down through the scrubs, across the tracks, and directly into the blast furnaces of the steel plant where my father worked. Often men would come up from the plant, like old hoboes, to forage for food or to nap on the porches of the black folks lucky enough to have company houses so near work.

We lived on one side of the house: my mother, my father, my older sister, Sandy, and me. Miss Chank occupied the other half of the house, and for reasons always unknown, she lived alone. My mother needed Miss Chank to come help or to go and get help, since she did not recognize the old white man hulking on the porch to be her own father.

"Miss Chank! Miss Chank! Wake up! Come help! There's some old white man out on the porch!" my mother began shouting as she knocked louder and louder against the creaky slats of the adjoining kitchen walls.

"What's dat you say, Dorothy? I's coming, honey!" was finally the response from the other side of the wall. And out she came, drawing her night robe up tight around her and calling up that deep, brusque voice of hers as she grabbed the heavy stick she kept poised nearby. Miss Chank bounded to her front door.

"What do you want up here, old man? And what're you doin' out here on our porch in da middle of da night?"

My grandfather fell back, startled by the sudden assault. He took off his hat, and, holding it in both hands, he explained:

"Ma'am, my name is Alex White. I'm looking for a Dorthay Willis, said to live here."

My mother, back at our front door listening, now slowly swung it open.

"*Daddy*? That really *you*?"

"Yes, Dorthay. It's me."

"Lawd, Daddy, we almost called the law on you! Come on in and tell me why you come after so long, and in the middle of the night." Miss Chank, too, made apologies, commenting on the dangerous times and how one couldn't be too careful. She wished Dorothy and her father a pleasant visit before, quietly now, fading back into her side of the double-tenancy and to whatever dreams my mother, in her desperation, had so abruptly shattered.

My grandfather, I am told, stayed with us for about two weeks after this rather shocking appearance. For the first time in his life he was without a steady job. The younger woman with whom he'd immediately taken up as soon as my grandmother, Sadie, had died had tired of him. He still had his good looks, though. He had twinkly blue-gray eyes, hair straight and soft as corn silk, and skin as white as any white man.

My father, and my grandfather Belton who lived just a few doors down from us in one of the biggest houses on Pleasant Hill, met Ellick then for the first time. After early suspicions retreated, the two showed him a cordial enough welcome. It was, no doubt, during this time also that they could see whence my own looks originated.

I myself saw my grandfather Alex only a few times. Seeing him left no doubt that he was at least half white. In fact, after another visit to us in Docena when I was about nine, I asked my mother why this particular white man came to visit us and why he called San and me his "little darlings." Though she told me that Alex was her father, my curiosity was not appeased.

I remember the first time I consciously saw "Alech," as I called him. He was a tall man. He wore a suit, brown as I recall, with thin blue pin stripes, a white shirt, and a tie. His pants were held up by suspenders, a mark of age as well as sophistication, I thought. I also thought he was very handsome; and kindly, too—for a white man. He would call us to him and have us sit on his knees. My sister and I liked to feel his hair, to run our fingers through its fine texture; and he let us play in it. He also seemed to know a lot about gardening; a good deal of conversation went on about the plot of vegetables and my special patch of strawberries we kept in our backyard.

As time passed and I grew, I became more and more the spittin' image of my father. Everyone agreed that Dean was sure enough her daddy's child! In time, my father too recognized it. Still, there's a funny thing about doubt, anger, and denial once unleashed: in spite of later correction and understanding, they are not so easily relinquished.

As for me, I became known as a moody child, one who was always thinking and brooding rather than playing. I was sensitive and reflective far beyond my tender years; and I am convinced that my behavior, at least in part, stemmed from my earliest mixed reception.

When I began working on my family's history later in life, I clearly remember the day that I became, literally, sick from having to look through white slave-owners' materials in order to trace my black kin. The more I stared at my scribbled charts, the sicker I became. It was not that I hadn't known there were white ancestors in my family's background. Given the contours of African American history and the system of slavery that so long dominated in the United States, hardly any black person in this country has avoided the forced mixture of the races. I knew my "light" skin came from somewhere, but it was much harder to own up to its having come from a specific some*one*.

I was following a thread of evidence indicating that my maternal great-grandfather was a Jewish storeowner named Mayer who lived in west central Alabama. But it became more and more clear to me that it didn't much matter whether or not this particular Mayer was my great-grandfather. Nor did it matter that he was Jewish. Most of my closest friends *were* Jewish; and whenever I thought of black-Jewish relationships, I considered us natural comrades, equally ostracized and discriminated against and—at key historical moments—working together to combat injustice. No, what mattered was that my maternal great-grandfather was *white.* That fact alone somehow made me feel dirty and polluted. Abstract ideas didn't produce such emotional turmoil; concrete examples, living flesh did.

As I was growing up in the sixties and seventies, the strong emphasis on Black Power and our African ancestry dictated that white ancestry should be kept in the closet. Its exposure gave us as a people no benefits. No matter how light-skinned, a black person in this society was *still black.* Of course, there was a whole subculture of blacks who prided themselves on their fair complexion. Indeed, a separate *class* of blacks, from the antebellum mulattoes and free persons of color to the social-climbing networks of the Bon Tons and Links, gave testimony to the benefits in terms of prestige and power that did operate among them. But I was not one of those blacks. For me, whenever my skin color had become an issue, it had always been a mark of embarrassment and shame. I was like the child who covers her eyes with her hands and thinks she is no longer visible. As long as I didn't look too closely at my own skin, I would not have to recognize the white blood that ran in my veins.

I had lived among different cultures and had developed what I thought of as a genuine appreciation of diversity. But this was somehow very different. The spectre of white blood, so generationally close, weighed extremely heavily on me. It made me neither accepting nor gracious. I did not wear proud shoes.

Once, when I was in Nepal, a distinguished Nepalese anthropologist began a conversation with me by saying, "Of course, your parents are *mixed,* are they not?"

I had denied the accusation loudly. "No! Both my parents are black!" I had responded, wounded even by the suggestion that they might not be. Over the years, other acquaintances had made similar inquiries. Always it was embarrassing, like an accusation impossible to defend against. I felt exposed, found out. Neither of my parents was dark-skinned, but both were black; and *I* was *black.*

Now, as I worked on this line of kin—I could not yet bring myself to say "*my* kin"—that old anger at being unrecognized and misunderstood resurfaced, together with that old shame. The pain I was experiencing had not so much to do with my earliest reception as with coming face-to-face with the fact of my white ancestry. My grandfather Alex's father was white. It was not frustration about *which* white man might have fathered him; it was the recognition that *some white man* had. The whole thing turned my stomach.

I had always hated the word *miscegenation.* Now I experienced why. Facing the fact of my white ancestry was like being given a diagnosis of cancer. There were white blood cells living inside of me that were out of the closet and out of control. They were eating my body and my soul alive, and I did not know if I could survive. What does one do when the oppressor's blood courses in one's own veins? How could

I run away from my own self? How to make peace with such horrific origins? Historically, I was both the victim and the child of rape conceived in terror. Everyone in the whole sordid history of slavery and racist oppression and all blacks are subject to its enduring legacy: black women unable to fend off white rapists; black men unable to protect their wives and partners. Given such history, the questioning of origins, though painful, was unavoidable.

Thus, from my birth, the history of blacks in this country became for me a very personal history. More than anything, I wanted my father's love and acceptance. As I grew older, I also wanted to be able to trust and to genuinely love others. To get beyond the pervasive sense of pain and suffering I carried, I knew I would have to find healing, to find that place of belonging that is so basic for us all: feeling at home in our own skins. And so, from my earliest days, my solitary quest became to find a way to accept myself, and to love *me*.

DOCENA

ᘒᓹ

Don't go too far!" my mother always reminded me as she pushed open the screen door and I rocketed forth, straight past her. I crossed the feeble new patch of Bermuda grass that was our yard, crossed the red clay that would later take on the semblance of a graveled road, and headed straight up the dusty alleyway that ran atop my grandparents' sloping backyard. My bare feet plopping up the dust so that it lightly coated my legs and chest assured me that this was the bliss and freedom of heaven. With complete and utter glee, I leapt and scampered along, my trusty bottle in hand, clothed only in the sky, the dust, and the white cotton panties we still-almost-babies were allowed to wear.

As a small child I romped through those alleyways with an excitement and eagerness possessed only by those too young to have judgmental eyes. Armed with my bottle, I minutely surveyed those dusty paths and mused on the further adventures awaiting me in the thick pine woods that surrounded the Camp and came right up to our backyard. For me, Docena was home and life was good. When we moved there, in 1950, I was two years old.

My parents had come to Docena, leaving the city security of life on Pleasant Hill Road in Ensley, Alabama, behind. They wanted a house of their own, even if this meant a return to the country. My father, however, continued to travel daily back and forth on the three-mile stretch of road into town to the Ensley branch of United States Steel. This fact later proved fortunate for us since by the time I entered school, the Docena mine had closed, and men whose livelihoods had depended on coal sat on their porches idle, poor, and despairing.

Docena, Alabama, was a tiny hamlet outside the city limits of Birmingham that, for as long as I can remember, was referred to simply as "the Camp." It had been created to house the white and black workers for the coal mine located there. I was well into adulthood before I happened upon a book that, describing the origins of certain place-names in Alabama, included Docena. From that book I learned that the mining camp in which I had been raised until I journeyed off to college had originally been named Booker, in honor of Booker T. Washington. That revelation filled me with a sense of quiet pride. First, because it suggested that as early as 1870, the black people of the Camp had had enough sense of community and pride to name their settlement after a black man of considerable power; and second, because the *fact* of their naming it indicated that, at least initially, blacks had had some power of their own. The book went on to explain that the Camp's current name was coined by a man named Stallingworth who had worked in Mexico as a railroad dispatcher and was later a train master in Docena. It was apparently he who had suggested the Spanish name—the feminine determiner *docena* meaning "twelfth"—for the nearby mine.

During all the time we lived in Docena, the commissary had been the Camp's only public building, serving both whites and blacks. It housed a grocery store as well as the sole post office, and it was there that, as a young child, I first saw the signs above the water fountains that read "white only" and "colored." Returning as an adult, I noticed for the very first time that above the building's entrance there was carved very large in concrete the solitary word *mercado,* or market, in Spanish. Perhaps the Spanish had had a longer hold on the Camp than we ever knew.

Still, I like to remember the meaning of the name my grandmother Jennie had told me when I was a small child. Grandmama had said that Docena was an Indian name and that, in the Choctaw language, it meant "the place where the mimosa trees stand upon the hills." I treasured this interpretation as a sacred trust, a private communication between my Indian-ancestored grandmother and me. And clearly, the description was true. Everywhere throughout the Camp, mimosa trees and honeysuckle vines thrived. Our front yard sported two gorgeous mimosas, and the air of Docena was filled with soft, pink cotton-balled trees and with the delicately sweet scent of honeysuckle.

I loved everything about the rural camp that stood on the other side of Village Creek from Ensley, nestled inside a verdant pine forest, clean-aired and fragrant. City folk called Docena "the country," but for me it meant forests and dusty paths and sweet smells. It meant the sounds of birds in the day and of crickets and frogs at night. It meant lightning bugs twinkling in the dark skies, and stars unobscured by city lights. The world was a natural wonder, perfect unto itself and completely joyous to my young heart. I loved it all.

Of course, by any external standard, we were quite poor. The four of us lived in three rooms: kitchen, living room, and bedroom. There was no inside toilet until I was almost five, and no extra bedroom for my sister and me until we reached junior high. Two double beds slept the four of us in one bedroom. In the kitchen the walls were painted with heavy coats of glossy light yellow paint applied directly to the wide wooden boards that bounded it. Wallpaper covered the wooden slats of the living room and bedroom. In the kitchen, my mother's pride and joy was the new electric range my father bought soon after we moved there. Before that, she had baked loaves of bread and light, tantalizingly fragrant biscuits in an old cast-iron wood-burning oven.

We used a fireplace in the living room for years, until a big oil-burning heater was installed. In the bedroom, a medium-sized coal-burning stove jutted out into the center of the room. During the winter, my mother liked to keep this stove glowing white-hot; and many a night my sister and I feared for our lives. My mother protested that we were just being silly. "There is no reason to be scared. The stove is fine!" she'd say.

My mother's name was Dorothy, and people called her either "Dot" or "Dor-thay." My grandfather Belton always called her "Doris." But my father referred to her as "Red," and it was certainly the most apt description of her character. She was an Aries, quick to anger, and she loved nothing better than having enough heat. She liked to see, not just feel, the fire. And so my sister and I lived with the fear that the coal stove would someday surely explode.

There was a single entrance road into Docena. The first two blocks on either side of the road housed blacks, and if, after the second block, one turned right, one entered into the bulk of the black section. There were six more blocks of black households. If one continued straight on the entrance road, after three blocks one ran into the white section. As blacks, we always turned right just after passing the first two blocks. To have continued straight would have been viewed as an intrusion into white territory that could have had serious consequences.

My family lived at the very farthest end from the entrance to Docena, the middle house of a group of three that alone formed First Avenue. Our address was 104 First Avenue. To one side of our house lived Dot and Bill Chambers and their three kids, Fred, Essie Mae, and Deb, who was born just after we moved there. On the other side of our house was a two-tenant structure that was inhabited by Jesse and Mae Eva Givins, Mae Eva's twin sisters, and a whole bunch of children, perhaps ten or eleven. My mom got along with both families, but she was closest to Dot Chambers the whole time we lived there. They were known as the two Dots.

My dad's father and mother, Belton and Jennie, moved to Docena a year or so after us, and bought the house that sat diagonally across the street from us. It was a corner property, at 100 First Street. Daddy's brother, Lamar, took the house next to theirs the following year. Consequently, there were three Willis households on that far end of Docena. This meant that Sandy and I had a set of grandparents and a lot of cousins nearby. All the Willis men continued to work at the steel mill in Ensley. It would later be my civic-minded father, and his father, who saw to it that there were street signs posted and a graveled road laid in the black section of Docena. My dad has always been a "Race man," and a man of pride.

I thought my sister, San, was beautiful and sophisticated, somehow always wiser than me, and savvy about the world. She did, however, like dainty things and paper dolls, for which I had no patience at all, preferring to build plastic models of Fort Apache or to shoot marbles. Still, throwing a sheet or blanket over the kitchen table, she and I would sometimes journey in our minds to far-off lands and camp out. We shared such a rich fantasy life that once we were absolutely convinced we had dreamed the same dream. When she eventually went off to school, I felt completely lost.

Though there was relative safety with all of us Willises living in a tiny cluster of houses at that farthest edge of Docena, my sister and I learned that there were threats to life and limb there. These were the threats that came to all black people living in the South in the 1950s and 1960s—they came from other human beings, those who had white skin.

Docena was a stronghold of the Alabama Ku Klux Klan. The Grand Wizard—or Grand Rooster, as black folks mockingly called him—made his home in Docena. It amazes me that black people have managed over the course of their long history on these shores to keep their humanity intact. For surely all the signs and signals around us told us otherwise; told us that we were less than human, a people cursed by God to live degraded lives; told us that we were lazy, stupid, and unfit for society.

Every so often, Docena's Klan reminded us blacks of our "proper" place. Their tactics were simple: they reminded us of who was boss by instilling in us fear of the consequences of ever forgetting it. None of the blacks who lived in Docena was spared the Klan's reminders. On a fairly regular basis, there were drive-throughs and cross-burnings in the Camp. This unimaginable psychic terror crippled my self-esteem and the self-esteem of many black people. I am a witness to our scars.

SNAKES

∾

Dot Chambers kept chickens. She sold the eggs to add income to her household. We regularly bought a dozen or so from her. However, the presence of eggs in such abundance also brought unwelcome guests, in the form of snakes.

I was *deathly* afraid of snakes. My parents kept a big garden out back, where we grew corn, beans, potatoes, carrots, peas, peanuts, watermelons, and strawberries. I loved seeing the seeds turn into little green shoots and then leafy green plants. We children were constantly reminded to keep a lookout for snakes when we were in the garden and to watch precisely where we stepped or put our hands. Our garden was visited by all sorts of snakes, big and small, long and fat. Some were an iridescent chartreuse; one, I remember well, was long, black, and shiny, with a triangular body. Owing to Dot Chambers's chickens and their eggs, we surely saw more of these creatures than most of Docena's residents.

Dot herself was something of a wonder woman in my eyes precisely because of her fearlessness regarding snakes. If we cried out "Snake!"

and ran for cover, Dot dropped whatever she was doing, grabbed her hoe, and came to our rescue. In one fell swoop, she would cut the snake in half. With a mischievous glint in her eye, she held it up before flinging it in a wide arc over the back fence. I can still see those arcs of snakes in the air; they give me the shivers.

I never learned to distinguish so-called harmless garden snakes from poisonous ones. I simply made a judgment that any slinking, earthbound creature had venomous fangs that could end my life.

One day Dot took it upon herself to help my mother solve the problem of my attachment to the bottle. I was almost three years old, and they'd determined that drastic measures were needed. My mother called me home, away from my gleeful scampering in the dusty alley across from our house. When I neared the house she motioned to me to go over to Dot's fence. "She has something to show you!" she said, before disappearing back into the house. I walked toward the fence happily, bottle still in hand. Dot Chambers walked toward the fence from the back of her house. With both hands she carried her hoe in front of her, and across its end lay the biggest snake I had ever seen. I froze. "You see this snake, Miss Dean Pie? If you don't drop that bottle, I'm going to put this snake on you!"

Sweat broke out on my forehead. My little heart raced like it might explode. My tender but reeling mind formed the thought to kill Dot. Slowly, my right arm unfolded. My fingers uncurled from the bottle that had for so long been my trusty friend. I felt its cool plastic slide slowly down my body and land silently in the fledgling grass. And then I ran, ran for my life, into the house and away from Dot Chambers and her snake. I never looked back, and to this day I've never gone back to look for that bottle.

Of course, this incident only intensified my fear of snakes. And because I am ever on the lookout for them, I invariably see them. In the heat of the California sun, I come upon rattlers basking in its warmth.

On my sole wilderness walk, I happened to choose to rest on a stone wall that was home to hundreds of them. And so it goes.

As a recently tenured professor, I was living in a fine, newly built house in Nepal when a huge snake decided to grace my establishment with its wealth-granting presence. My cook, Kanchi, made daily offerings of tinted rice to the water-colored image of the snake goddess that she insisted be tacked above the entrance of the house. It honored Lakshmi, the Goddess of Wealth, who in the form of a large serpent brought abundance to every household that worshipped her. I could understand the reasoning: snakes often came to farming households where large amounts of grains were stored, so the presence of one indicated that the granaries were healthy. But the ten-foot snake that took up residence in my yard was unwelcome, to say the least.

I knew there were other countries and cultures where the snake was revered. The Greeks had prized them. Our AMA had made it its symbol of health. But I did not want to have to creep into my yard each day on alert for a giant black snake. My desires, however, were ignored. The snake lay on my front steps. It crawled along my garden fence. One day Kanchi and I stood terrified together as we watched it slide silently up to the closed wooden door of the yardman's little house and, with its head, push in the door and slither inside. However, Kanchi could go home; this was where I lived.

Then one day, as I sat reading upstairs, the young boy who lived next door called frantically to me, *"Ma'am sahib! Ma'am sahib! Sarpa cha!"* "What do you mean, 'the snake is'?" I called back to him through the window. "The *sarpa* is coming up, Ma'am *sahib.* It's there, climbing up to the second floor!" The snake was winding its way up the large plant alongside my house. Looking timidly to where the boy's finger was pointing, I saw its head appearing just past the level of the upper patio.

It was then, between screams, that I called the yardman, Lakshman, and gave him the command to kill the snake. He seemed to be completely bewildered, as though he couldn't possibly be hearing me correctly. "Take the hoe from the shed and kill that snake! I don't care if it's good fortune or not. Kill it!"

The phrase "wouldn't kill a flea" takes on new meaning in relationship to Lakshman. Though he couldn't understand my fear and anger, he was willing to do what I asked. But he couldn't do most things. Lakshman couldn't build a fire, or shop very well, or do anything else Kanchi and I asked him to. Hired as a yardman, it was really for his cheery and eager demeanor that I had taken him on. Now I needed him, and I hoped that he could carry out this most desperate assignment.

The snake was now moving slowly along the top of the fence. Lakshman climbed up and, with hoe in hand, began cautiously following after it. "Go on, Lakshman. Use the hoe!" I urged. He looked back, sweating and grinning. Then it happened. Slowly, he raised the hoe above his head and then, swiftly, brought it down. But rather than strike the snake, the hoe crashed into the brick fence, and Lakshman almost fell several feet. The snake dove out into the air, straight as a board, its wide mouth agape. It was like living in a nightmare; that open-mouthed ten-foot shining black serpent stretched out and leaping through the air for what seemed like a full minute before diving into the adjoining field below. The image is etched indelibly in my mind.

There is no moral, or proper ending, to this story. I had ordered that snake's death. Lakshman was unsuccessful in killing it. The neighbors knew I was terrified but couldn't understand why I didn't welcome such a sign of prosperity. I continued to live in that house for a few more weeks.

I am ashamed and guilty about having such a strongly negative response to a living creature. Such hatred is not very becoming to either a Buddhist or a Christian. But I did want to kill that snake just as, when a child of three, I had wanted to kill Dot Chambers. Today, I know that what I *really* wanted to kill was the *overwhelming fear* that rose up and crippled me. Even now, I am still afraid of snakes. Dot, however, well . . . Dot is okay.

LIFE AT HOME

ѹ

What's the matter with you, you little devil? You think you know so
much! You just shut your mouth, you hear!" I swung my head around.
There was no one else at home; only my mother and me. Was she
screaming these terrible things at me? Her angry yelling continued,
"You, you . . . my Lord, where did you come from? You must be evil!" I was
her intended target. The room froze. My mother was yelling at the top
of her voice, *"You must be evil!"* I was five years old.

I had been attempting to help make up the bed. I was standing on
one side of it, my mother on the other. We were at the stage of pulling
up the cream-colored spread. What had I said just before? What had I
even been thinking? To this day, I cannot remember. What I remember only, in all its numbing virulence, is her rebuke, her utter con-
demnation. I was different, I was strange, I was smart—she often told
me—and now I was also evil. It was a weight that seemed unbearable.

I have asked my mother since about that occasion, and not unlike
any other parent, I suppose, who has been angered by a young child's
impertinence, she claimed not to remember the incident at all. When

I described it to her, she brushed it aside, first with denials and then with assurance that, anyway, she hadn't meant to hurt me. With uneasy laughter, she reminded me that with the mouth I had had even then, it's no wonder she had chewed me out.

From the moment my mother pronounced me evil for my smart mouth, I was determined to take a wholly new tack toward learning. It would be my personal, secret life; an act conducted privately and alone, against, and in spite of, disapproval. I was never going to be ignorant, even if it was evil to be smart, and even if—as turned out to be the case—it meant that I would have to shut my mouth for many years to come. If being smart meant making a pact with the devil then I would do it, and heaven help all those who would stand in my way.

I must have been quite a handful, really. All reports confirm this. I walked when I was just nine months old and, without losing a beat, proceeded to get into everything. I was always watching and thinking, judging and dreaming, and talking about things that either struck my parents with amazement or caused them to wonder where I'd come from. For my part, it seemed that my curiosity continually brought me trouble.

When I reflect back on my life at home, prior to my venturing off to school, what I envision is a sort of duel between my mother and my father, in which I was the contested territory. My father encouraged my intelligence; my mother seemed jealous of it.

Although I don't remember my father being around home very much, from time to time he walked into my life and dropped heavy questions on me. Once, he walked over to our bedroom light switch, clicked it on and off, and asked me, "Where does the light go when it's turned off, baby?" That question set my four-year-old mind to buzzing. It was an unfathomable puzzle; a problem so mysterious, deep, and weighty that I could not stop thinking about it for months. Years even. Soon after he first raised it, I was totally unnerved. I sweated over it. My thoughts circled around it as I surveyed the dusty paths. It was a worry that, for a time, consumed me.

Sometimes, when my father was home, I attempted answers: "It goes off, Daddy," or "It goes back to the power house that generated it." He'd comment, "Um-hum . . . maybe." I came to hate him as much for asking the question as I was determined to solve it. I am sure that my interest in science—and especially in physics—originated from that early query. But to this very day, in spite of my knowledge of physics, I have arrived at no answer that satisfies me. Nor do the lessons learned from Wittgenstein on the nonsensical formulation of the question provide me with solace. There was a challenge in that question that came not only from my father but also, it seemed, from the mysterious source of the entire universe.

My father asked me another weighty question during these early years. He'd been lying on the bed listening to gospel singing on the radio. It was a Sunday afternoon. I had sat through the last few minutes of the program with him. After turning off the radio, he got up to leave the room. But on his way out, with a sigh, he turned and asked, "Why is it, baby, that black folks sing so good?" Though it was a question that carried almost equal magnitude, unlike the query about the light, this one allowed me no handle whatsoever. Surely he knew that other people had voices, too, though I had to admit I enjoyed the singing he had just turned off much better than what we sometimes listened to on the white stations. When in later times he offered answers to the singing question: "Negroes sing from the depths of their sorrows," or "Black people have known the chains of slavery," I could not fathom the meaning of these ideas. Sorrows and slavery must be adult things; grown-up emotions and institutions. As before, the bewilderment brought on by the question both isolated and consumed me.

∽

By the time I was eight, I had concocted and blown up any number of volatile compounds in our backyard using a Christmas-present chemistry set and had peered into assorted varieties of leaves, skin, and butterfly wings with a tiny microscope. I had begun to amass vast collections of coins, stamps, and sea shells from around the world—to say nothing of two gigantic canisters filled with marbles of all sorts, booty I had personally won in games with the neighborhood boys. And since I was good at drawing, my mother bought me a real oil-painting set and an easel for my seventh birthday.

One of my earliest and fondest memories is of standing in the center of our kitchen at about age four, stick baton in hand, "conducting" symphonies by Dvořák and Rimsky-Korsakov. My mother had given in to my pleas for the 78 rpm. She thought the music completely unappealing and constantly yelled at me for turning the volume up, but I loved her without bounds for buying for me the ninety-eight-cent record.

For days and weeks, I was completely lost in the roaring sonorities of *Scheherezade* and in the somber strains of the *New World Symphony.* My head and arms sank and rose in waves and flurries as the music wholly enveloped me. I thought the *New World* particularly moving, somehow divinely captivating. Its sounds struck a deep, still, soul-place in me, though I did not and could not say why. It was only much later that I learned of Dvořák's interest in black spirituals.

I do not remember where I first heard classical music. Nor do I know how I could have known the names of particular composers. I suspect I first heard the music in movies such as Walt Disney's *Fantasia* or on television. How I ever claimed to comprehend the intricacies of musical notation and meter, I am not sure. Yet I was somehow drawn intensely and irrevocably toward this kind of creativity; and I marveled that in music, as in mathematics, there was a language that was universal. And so, for a time, while my father was toiling away at making steel in the fiery blast furnaces of the Ensley mill, I determined that if life were just, I would become a great conductor.

SCHOOL IN ALABAM'

ᘓᕼ

My parents encouraged me in school, yet I detected an underlying ambivalence. It takes abundant daring to say, "Well, world, I hope you're ready for her!" and such daring had been eroded for most blacks by centuries of racial prejudice. What were the chances of success for a black child from the rural South, and a girl at that, educated until college entirely in segregated schools, with little external encouragement?

For gifted black boys there was some hope. They could become preachers and sometimes even doctors. But what could a gifted black girl become? There were no examples of success in my extended family. I would become the very first to go to college; and, as the entire camp of Docena later mused and grumbled, not only would I choose one of those *snooty* Ivy League places but, what was worse, a northern school. Of the 234 students who graduated in my senior class, only four of us went on to college, and only I ventured northward.

Both my parents had been good students. But whatever dreams they might have had about higher education were either erased with time, as in my mother's case, or painfully dashed, as in my father's. He had attended the same high school as I did. And he, too, graduated valedictorian of his class. He liked science but excelled in debate and oratory. The gift of gab is accorded great respect in the black community. It appreciates nothing more than a man who can talk, whether this takes the form of preaching or of rap. My father also had a penchant for philosophy. I'm sure that if he'd gone on to college, he would have pursued this area of study with considerable interest. If he'd had the chance to go.

Never once, my father later told me, had his father or mother told him to keep studying, or that study was a good thing. In spite of this, he always loved ideas and books. Shortly after graduating with honors from high school, he ran away from home, hitched rides to Talladega, and camped out for a week's orientation at Alabama Agricultural and Technical College, the most eminent black college in the area. After dragging him home, his father, Belton, made it emphatically clear that college was not for him. He was to take the job that Belton had arranged for him at the Ensley plant. So it was that in 1939, at the age of nineteen and after such a promising beginning, my father became a steelworker.

I entered first grade in 1954, the year of *Brown v. Board of Education,* when the U.S. Supreme Court finally nullified the doctrine of "separate but equal" in education. That decision promised a much-needed antidote to black despair throughout the South. But in Alabama the Court's decision simply meant that the state's own courts went immediately to work to block the new law's implementation. Eleven years later I would graduate from a still-segregated, all-black school.

I had expected school to be a place where my spirit could run wild, galloping through new knowledge like so much summer grass. But it did not turn out to be like that. I had been reading my sister's books and doing figures for at least two years before I entered first grade, and often found myself bored and unchallenged. I learned later that some of my early teachers had been afraid of me and had admitted as much to my mother: "Lordy, Miss Willis, I was sure scared when Principal Jackson said that that little Dean was coming to my class!" "Little Miss Know-It-All," I was called. Terror to classmates and teachers alike.

My inner silence and secrecy regarding things intellectual no doubt date from the time my mother pronounced me evil for being too smart. However, I know I must have spoken up throughout my elementary, middle, and high school years, since I quickly came to the attention of my teachers and was one of the chief prides of both of my schools' principals: Mr. Jackson of Docena Elementary School, and Mr. Ware of Westfield High. My sights had been set, for years, on going to school in a way unknown to my parents. To them I simply wanted to follow my sister, Sandy, to whom I was devoted, who left home every morning for some place to which I could not accompany her. For two years I had been in visible agony whenever she headed up and over the graveled road and disappeared. But I also wanted, for myself, to get on with learning.

Almost everything seemed to block my desire. In Docena, there was no kindergarten for black children. I was not allowed to enter first grade until the fall of the year in which I turned six years old. Since my birthday fell in February, this meant that I turned seven halfway through the year. My folks had made a number of valiant attempts to argue with Docena school officials that, being quite ready, I should be admitted even though I was only five. Their efforts were to no avail. I suspect that nobody then really understood the depths of my desire to enter a place where learning was the primary activity; where knowledge was respected and even revered. To me it represented the place where someone strange, moody, and smart-though-evil might be appreciated.

I got my comeuppance in the form of boredom and boredom's child, mischief. I already felt too old to be in Miss McCall's first-grade class. Besides, who cared to see Jane run? Or Dick run? Or Spot run? They showed only blonde and blue-eyed children engaged in the stupidest adventures.

I was much more interested in what was going on with the others in the class. Restless, I wrote notes and squirmed constantly. I talked a lot, too. And once I made the fatal mistake of chewing bubble gum in class. That day, Miss McCall had had it. She'd told all thirty-five of us to take a rest: "Heads on desks!" I don't know what pushed me to keep fidgeting and whispering to my classmates. I just couldn't stop myself. All of a sudden, Miss McCall's voice went up several decibels.

"Little Missy. Who gave you permission to chew gum?" I fell silent then, but I didn't think she could possibly be meaning me. I was, after all, Deanie Pie, the smartest kid there. Her second booming pronouncement left no doubt:

"You! Little Miss Deanie Pie!" Her voice had become a pointed finger at the end of a gigantic arm that reached all the way from her desk up front to my head. I felt the buzzing breeze of it.

"Yes, I mean *you!* Come up here."

My body got shaky all over. Miss McCall was a big woman, very light-skinned, with that soft, wavy "good hair." She weighed a lot but was also soft-bodied and, I thought, cuddly. But she was known for inflicting great blows on a child's knuckles with her heavy wooden ruler. That day, the punishment Miss McCall decided upon was, for me, much worse than swollen knuckles. She had everyone raise their heads and made me stand before them as she announced, "Some of you here need to know who's in charge! Now, as for you, Miss Deanie Pie, you are to spend the rest of today standing in the cloakroom. You are not to come out until *I* say that you may. Now go."

It could not have been worse. Before the entire class she had

brought me down a peg. I was banished. A number of students snick-
ered. I wanted to die. But the ordeal did not end there. When I peeked
out from the cloakroom hoping that she had softened, I was greeted
with that booming voice, "Did I tell you you could come out, young
lady? Get back in there!" I could hear the rest of the class going on
about their work, but I could not participate. I began to scheme about
ways that a seven-year-old could avoid ever setting foot inside a school
again. I had thought Miss McCall would be a friend in the great adventure of learning. That day in the cloakroom I listed her among all
those who would be my lifelong enemies.

From the beginning, my teachers relentlessly compared me to my
sister. This always troubled me because I loved her so deeply. I cham-
pioned her whenever I could, to many a teacher's displeasure. Then
came the fateful day when, with respect to San, I committed a deadly
mistake.

In third grade, Miss Sanders was my teacher. I felt shy and tried to
keep a low profile, since I knew of no surer way to lose potential
friends than to participate in that fatal game of being teacher's pet. To
avoid peer derision, at lunchtime I usually tried to find my sister and
her best friend, Mandy. One day at lunch break, I searched and
searched among the others for her, but she was nowhere to be found.
I nearly panicked. In desperation, I decided to check her homeroom.

Turning into Miss Fisher's room, I saw Sandy and Mandy standing
at the blackboard. They were being kept in until they could correctly
solve a math problem dealing with fractions. Relieved to see them, I
rushed over to the board and blurted out, "You sure gave me a scare!
What are you doing in here?" Sandy motioned me to shush and explained that neither of them could work their problem. In an instant,
I said, "Ah, that's easy!" and scribbled the answer on the blackboard.

Sandy motioned me to turn around. Sitting at her desk was Miss Fisher herself. She had been guarding the two and had seen the whole thing. This time I had really done it. Not only had I embarrassed my sister, but I'd done it in front of her teacher and her best friend. All I had really wanted was for them to be able to come out for lunch.

Instead of censure from Miss Fisher, the event engendered a special meeting between her and Principal Jackson about my being skipped a grade. If I could already do fifth-grade work so easily, why make me sit through fourth grade? Unbeknownst to me, the die was cast; and the first day of classes the following year, Mr. Jackson walked into Miss Stimpson's fourth-grade classroom, took me by the hand, and led me down and around the hall into Miss Fisher's class. He made a brief speech to the students there about the rewards of study and then motioned me to take a seat.

I must have felt a bit elated. But as soon as class started, I began to sense that old familiar feeling of isolation and loss. Now I would have to try to make friends with students who, I supposed, already resented me.

At home, news of my being skipped got a completely different reception. When I tried to tell my mother about it that evening, she exploded in anger. I had not quite figured out myself what the day's events had meant. I remember that I could only manage to fumble out the details of what had happened: "Mr. Jackson came and got me out of Miss Stimpson's fourth-grade room and took me to Miss Fisher's fifth." It soon became very clear that my mother didn't like it. I had no way of knowing that she might be concerned about how my sister and me being so close in grades—Sandy was entering the sixth grade that year—would affect my parents' ability to afford higher education for us. I decided that her anger must have to do with her "too much learning is evil" idea. And I knew that I was completely defenseless to fight that one with her.

Later that evening while I sat brooding, as only a child of nine can do, I heard my mother's voice. She was talking with Dot, across the back fence. They were discussing me. "I hear Dean's got skipped to the fifth grade. I know you're proud of her!" And then my mother said, "Oh, yeah! We're proud of her, all right!"

The words sounded genuine, and my heart leapt so high that my body jumped straight up. In less than an instant I was racing toward the back door to embrace my mother and receive her absolution. Flinging open the back screen and bounding off the porch, I was stopped dead in my tracks by my mother's ice-cold glare. "What do *you* want? I'm talking to Dot!" were the only words that came from her mouth. I sank into an abyss from which it would take years to extricate myself.

Fifth grade presented no major problems, though I quickly found out that despite being able to read anything, spelling was not my strong suit. A stout, older woman who wore thick black-rimmed glasses, Miss Fisher was a strong disciplinarian. Every day she required each of us to stand and recite a Bible verse, a practice that I did not appreciate at the time.

One day, soon after I'd been skipped, Miss Fisher asked us all to stand along two sides of our classroom. She announced that she was inaugurating a spelling bee and that these were to become regular, weekly events in her class. I stood sixth or seventh in line. Until me, everyone had spelled their assigned words correctly. When my turn came, Miss Fisher said, "Spell 'wealth.'" My mind went completely blank. I asked her to please repeat the word. "Wealth," she said again.

"W-e-l-l-t-h," I whispered.

"Try again, young lady. And this time, speak up."

"W-h-e-l-t-h," I stuttered.

"Incorrect. Take your seat."

I returned to my desk, the very first student to be asked to do so. Some of the students still standing laughed aloud. "See . . . she ain't so smart!" went around the room. As always, my hurt was mixed with anger. I could do nothing but sit and stew over the incident, until the spelling bee was over. All the while, I thought to myself, "Why *that* particular word? How should I, or anyone else standing there, know anything about wealth?!"

The only thing that salvaged life for me in Miss Fisher's class was that there, for the first time, I made friends. Ella Doris Lee was my first. Ella lived on Sixth Street, just across the street from the front of the school. She was a bright girl who talked a lot and who seemed always to be happy. Sensing my uneasiness at being among this new group of students, she embraced me. We became fast friends, buddies from then on. Now I had a friend in my own class. No need to hunt out Sandy.

My second fifth-grade friend was Norris. He was a dark-skinned, smiling boy, with huge eyes and long eyelashes. He wore his hair very short—we called it a "skinny." I thought him the cutest boy I'd ever seen. Of course, besides my boy cousins and those whose marbles I had won with my keen shooting, he was the first boy I had ever really looked at. Norris liked me, too. He was the class prankster and the best dancer at the school. I had never learned to dance, but because he liked me, Norris said he'd teach me so we could dance together. And he did, and we did; and for a time, we were quite the couple on the dance floor.

Docena's segregated school did provide me with a great dual education. Though our desks were hand-me-downs and our library almost nonexistent, many of my teachers were truly fine educators. Miss Fisher, Miss Craig, Miss Hardy, and others were all top-notch teachers who struggled to give us children what we needed to know—for the world and for our own spirits. When we studied world literature, we studied black literature alongside it; when we learned history, we heard about the blacks who participated in it. Whenever we sang the national anthem, we followed it with the Negro national anthem. We were schooled in the memorizing and performance of black poetry. Even now, when I recite James Weldon Johnson's "Creation," I stretch out my arms and stamp my foot at key points in the poem. Many of my black peers today, educated at the same time, make exactly the same gestures.

In 1962, on the day that I turned fourteen, John Glenn orbited the earth. The fact that he did so on my birthday made the event seem all the more important to me. From that moment, I was completely enamored not only of math and science in general but of the Space Age. I read anything related to space. I decided for a time that I would become the first black woman astronaut. Then I determined that theoretical physics was the place I wanted to make my mark. No one told me that such dreams were extravagant for a young black girl living in a mining camp in the Jim Crow South of the 1960s. They might have thought so, but as well as I can remember, neither my parents nor my teachers ever discouraged me. If they did, I didn't hear them.

While still at Docena Elementary, a guidance counselor conducted I.Q. tests, and my score came back "two points shy of Mensa status." I didn't know, or care, what Mensa was, but from then on news spread around the school that I was some sort of genius-child. With all that I was taking in at the time—teachers brought me special books, some took me aside for advanced mathematics—I hardly took notice of the national groundswell of sentiments and actions pushing for a more integrated and just society. Besides, in Docena, blacks remained firmly under the suppression and watchful eyes of whites. Racism there showed no signs whatever of losing strength.

There was a most painful exercise that smart black children at school in Alabam' were required to perform for white school superintendents. When these superintendents visited Docena Elementary, I was usually the student singled out to answer questions. On one such visit, when I was ten years old, the slim, bald-headed visitor decided to pose questions regarding the various layers of the atmosphere. I could eat this stuff up, but I did not want to have to answer him. My teacher peered at me with pleading eyes. I shook my head in defiance. I would not answer his questions. I would not take part in this demeaning game.

"What is the layer of atmosphere that lies above the stratosphere?" he asked. "Doesn't any one of you know the answer?" I hated these men, with their smug airs. My teacher continued to plead, silently, with her eyes. Finally, I stood and blurted out the answer.

"The ionosphere," I said, and slumped back into my chair.

"Well, Principal Jackson, I see you have a smart one in here!" the old man said with feigned delight. He might just as well have said, "a smart *pickaninny.*" I was more than angry.

Just after he left, my teacher called me up to her desk.

"What did you say to him?"

"Ma'am? I said 'ionosphere.' "

"How do you spell that word?"

It was then that I realized she had not known the answer. I slowly spelled out the word for her and, utterly disheartened, returned to my seat.

So much for my early intellectual life—the good, the bad, my father's questions, school, and the ambivalence in society about a black girl's proper education. My mother would take a different tack—making sure my evil soul was saved.

THE HOLY OPENS ITS ARMS TO ME

ᢙᢖ

Get outta this house," my mother said. "And don't come back here a sinner before God's eyes!" She was sending me off to Docena's annual tent revival. She meant for me to join the community of the faithful, to become a good Baptist, and finally, at age fourteen, to join church.

Years of gentle cajoling had done no good. I was always ready with some argument about the preacher's faults: his greed, his hypocrisy, something. Often enough I feigned illness hoping to avoid Sunday school even though, owing to the fact that Docena had only one black church, Baptist Sunday school came around only every two weeks. On alternate Sundays, St. Matthew's Baptist Church became St. Paul's A.M.E. Zion in order that Docena's black Baptists and Methodists could both be accommodated. Apparently, neither congregation had funds enough to build a separate structure. My evasions became even more desperate when my sister and I were judged old enough to stay for regular services.

It was not really so much the preacher I minded, though I certainly had no love for him. Rather, it was the unease that the services stirred up in me each Sunday. Each week the congregation was swept up in a mysterious spiritual frenzy that began gradually but soon rushed ahead uncontrollably to its cathartic end. Quite simply, nothing scared me more than black women engaged, as good *feeling* Christians, in the activity known as "shouting."

Since Mama and Daddy always had some active part to play up front—both sang in the senior choir, and Daddy was usually asked to lead the congregation in prayer—my sister and I had to scour the pews alone for some safe place to sit. Safe meant somewhere away from the hefty women who, when shouting, would jump up and flail about, flapping their gigantic fleshy arms and screeching, "Oh yes, Jesus! Oh yes, Lord!" A swat from certain spirited arms could knock a person out cold. We had seen this happen, even to some of the big male ushers.

It always struck me as strange that the phenomenon of shouting was called "getting happy," for it seemed that the acrobatics that we children observed were much more akin to the kind of behavior that warranted straitjackets. People's bodies became stiff as boards. They jerked as if they wanted to bolt and run. They fought with the ushers, who were there to help them. All this was accompanied by shouts and wails, "Praises to Jesus," and choruses of "Amen"s and "Well!"s from the surrounding faithful. Nobody seemed particularly happy to me.

For me the only fun part was the early few minutes prior to the sermon proper. First there was the sheer pageantry of people in their Sunday best. Anyone wearing something new or especially nice had to find a way of getting their outfit shown off to the entire congregation. They did this either by waiting until the collection plate had passed their row, requiring them to march down the aisle alone and up to the offering desk so the entire church could see them; or they volunteered to read the announcements in lieu of the secretary; or they led the church in an additional prayer. Such splendid show!

Then, from the choir stand, came the organ roll that signaled the choir's entrance; and all heads turned to the rear of the chapel. This for me was real pageantry, and I enjoyed it more than any other part of the service. The choir members assembled in the foyer. With the sounds of the organ, the doors to the chapel were swung open by the white-gloved ushers. By twos, the choir marched in. They came not solemnly, but stepped with a gait that echoed, "I'm bound for glory!" and with smiling faces that beamed, "Don't you want to go?" My own spirit leapt at such an invitation. "Yes!" my racing heart would cry in silence. "Yes! I've got on my traveling shoes!" Like an army of angels, the choir's procession continued down through the central aisle, around the main podium, and up into the choir stand. In twos they filed past the pews, their robes swaying with each step and each beat of the organ. If there was a proud, confident, and joyous moment of the service, for me it was when those honey-voiced angels in the Lord's army came marching in.

Once the choir members were stationed, each before his or her seat, a final chorus was sung: "We're marching! Marching! Marching up the King's highway!" The preacher stood, flanked by his deacons, and pronounced a solemn "Amen." "Amen"s echoed and everyone sat down. The serious part of the service was about to begin.

Black preaching is marked as much by delivery and cadence as by message. In all the Sundays I attended services I never heard one in which the preacher's opening remarks were not exactly the same. He began with apologies for some minor illness he suffered, whether a cold or simply hoarseness. He then asked for the congregation's prayers and forbearance on this account. Next began the familiar refrain: "I praise the Lord that I'm able to stand here before you this morning, one mo' time. For there is nothing guaranteed about life here on this earth of ours. There are many who were amongst us last Sunday who have gone on now, who have been called on, before us." These slow and earnest remarks were punctuated at regular intervals with "Yes,

Lord!" and "Sho' is the truth, Reverend!" from the deacons, the Amen corner, and the always trusty wing of matrons.

The preacher then called upon the secretary of the church to read the names of the "sick and shut-in," after which he designated a member of the congregation to come forward and lead the others in prayer. These formalities finished, he stepped up to the podium proper and began his sermon. It was at this point that my sister and I started to squirm; for once he got rolling, we knew shouting would soon erupt. The various members of the congregation all had their own individual styles of shouting; and usually, a characteristic lead-in gesture, too. My sister and I had studied these in order to protect ourselves. For example, there was Miss Mae, a very skinny lady who always sat at the end of a certain pew. As the preacher's cadence rose and fell, a gentle smile came across her face, followed by a chuckle. When her shoulders started to move with the chuckle, we knew her shouting bout was under way. She'd start to clap her hands in quick succession. It was time to move out of this woman's way. She was little and skinny, but her flailing arms packed a wallop.

The ushers in their white gloves and the woman dressed in white who carried the little bottle of smelling salts would slowly move down the aisle from their stations at the back and come to rest at the side of Miss Mae. Sensing their nearness was her cue that it was now all right to let go completely, and so she did. Her hat went flying. She went stiff as a board. Two or three ushers tried to wrestle her into sitting back down, or relaxing, or not killing herself—or them, we were never quite sure. But it was already too late to stem the mounting tide.

The preacher was at the height of his sermon. He was leaning over, crouching, and slapping his thigh. His sentences were short, breathy, and punctuated with "Hah!"'s: "And then the Lord God Almighty, hah! That made all heaven and earth, hah! That same God, hah! Called down unto His servant, Moses, hah! He said, 'Moses!' Hah! Moses!"

In quick succession, the rest of the congregation let loose its pent-up feeling, too. Miss Mae was "happy." So were they. The preacher had caught fire. The Spirit of the Lord was here and present. The God of Israel had saved His children. He would save them, too. Praise the Lord! Hats and wigs went sailing through space. Ushers grabbed for eyeglasses to prevent people from doing themselves harm. In the choir stand, too, someone was getting happy. One and then another. Legs, thighs, garter belts, and underwear. All were seen, as large bodies flapped and went limp in the ecstasy of the Spirit.

The preacher was energized. His sermon was working and his congregation was with him. The hard week of troubles they had bottled up inside them wanted release. Disappointments had been pressing in on them, weighing them down; and they needed relief. Sunday was the time to testify and be relieved. Praise the Lord! Shouting was just the medicine that the Doctor, Lord Jesus, had ordered; and none too soon.

Some people just whimpered to themselves or cried softly (like my mother), and a few tears fell; but they never lost their composure. But sometimes people got hurt. They jumped up and fell hard over the smooth wooden pews. High heels got caught and ankles got twisted. People drunk on the Spirit. If enough people cried and shouted, the congregation was satisfied that the preacher had done a good job. If not, there were muffled mumblings about him all week.

Now my mother wanted me to join church. Did she want me to "get happy," too? She was tired of being responsible for my sins. The Baptists said that one becomes fully responsible for one's own sins at age twelve. Why, Lord Jesus was already preaching to the elders by then. At fourteen, she had been carrying me for two years; and she did not intend to keep doing it, either.

Docena's tent revival had been going on for the previous three days. Tonight was the final gathering for the year, and this, my mother declared, was my final chance to make amends. I left the house more worried and frightened than I was angry. There was no getting around it this time. I walked heavy-hearted but resigned, down the graveled road.

When at last I reached the grassy field and the big open-aired tent, my entire body was trembling like a leaf. The tent was spilling over with people. Everyone in the Camp, I thought, must be here. Almost all the folding chairs were occupied. There were even some white people there. We never joined together at any other time, but they liked to hear good old-fashioned preaching, too. I quickly scanned for a safe chair and luckily spotted one on the outside and near the back. Almost faint, I sank into the seat with a sigh, and thanked God for it. It was almost evening, and being summer, hot as anything. Everywhere, thin cardboard fans were trying to do battle with the intense heat. The matrons were out in full force, leading the songs and waving their fans. One of them, seeing me, motioned me to move up a few rows; but I shook my head and said, as respectfully as I could, "No, Ma'am. Thank you." I was drenched in sweat. "Please save me," I prayed to someone up there, "from having to do this!"

A song ended and a hush fell over the audience. The reverend from St. Matthew's stood to introduce the guest preacher. As usual, the pastor reminded us, guest ministers were invited in from outside to lead revivals. This particular guest preacher was famous in the area for his many successful campaigns. He was a hell-destroying, fire-and-brimstone exhorter, recognized as having received the call at a very early age, and we were extremely privileged to have him with us. There followed a rousing round of "Amen"s as a young man of about sixteen or seventeen years stood up and stepped to the center of the podium.

I was afraid to look directly at him at first, knowing that I would have to give myself over to him. When I did look up, I saw that he was a well-dressed boy, in suit and tie, and he did not seem to be sweating at all. He had large eyes but usually kept his head reared back, as if resting delightfully upon some invisible but divinely fluffy pillow. His smiling face was serene and seemed to be enveloped in a sort of radiance. His first words were spoken softly: "Friends, won't you join me in a good old song?" Then he began the tune himself:

> Amazing Grace, how sweet the sound,
> That saved a wretch like me.
> I once was lost, but now I'm found,
> Was blind, but now I see.
> 'Twas Grace that taught my heart to fear
> And Grace my fears relieved. . . .

The song went on for a long time, with its lilting strains and gentle encouragement. It was one of my favorites; and for a while I almost forgot the fears I had come with.

"Amen"s circled the tent at the end of the singing. With a soft voice he began: "You're not the only sinners the Lord God has seen, friends. He's seen many a sinner over the long course of His days! But don't you want to rest in Jesus, now? Don't you want to rest in Him?" His remarks were begun gently; but it was not long before the Spirit entered into him and the "Hah!"s started to echo. As the pitch and intensity of his sermon mounted, so too that of the congregation. If Sunday services were serious, then this was a thousand times more serious. This was revival; nothing short of our very souls was to be won, or lost.

All around me people were shouting, fainting, and falling out. My mind was reeling; my body felt like jelly. I was hot and cold at the same time, sweating profusely. When the young preacher began to wind things down, he offered the invitation. It was the cue I had been waiting for; the time when I would have to stand and be counted. Softly, he said, "Now is the time. For all those who want to be right with Jesus. For all those who want to take a seat on His right side. Come up, now. The doors of the church are open. Won't you come, to Jesus, right now?" Without a moment's hesitation, the matrons took up his cue and began to sing softly:

> *Come to Jesus! Come to Jesus!*
> *Come to Jesus, right now!*
> *Right now!*
> *Come to Jesus! Come to Jee–e–e–sus!*
> *Right now.*

Their voices were feeble, high and straining, but the message was what was important. As they continued to sing, the young preacher stepped down from the podium and walked through the tent, his hands and arms outstretched. "Won't you come to Jesus, sister? Now's the time." He looked, I thought, in my direction, but then turned to a man seated on the other side of the tent. "Aren't you tired of being a sinner, brother?" The man stood up and began to move forward. I knew it was now, or no going home. I stood up, too. A number of us were now wading through the crowd of already saved onlookers.

Seeing people standing up in response to the preacher's invitation fueled even more shouting. By this time all my strength had left me. Trying to make my way to the front, I stumbled and fell over onto people. They each caught me and buoyed me up with arms that said "Well done!" and proud faces that said "It's time. Praise the Lord!"

I started to cry, and then the floodgates opened. Someone took my arm, carried me forward, and sat me down facing the congregation. Along with a number of others, I sat now on the "mourner's bench." It had all been too much for me. I sobbed and sobbed, completely and uncontrollably. And the more I cried, the more the onlooking Christians shouted and praised the Lord. To them my tears meant I was truly repentant. One more lost sheep was found!

After some minutes, the young preacher approached each of us on the mourner's bench. He asked us our names and whether we were truly ready to abandon our sinful past and accept the Lord, Jesus Christ, as our Savior. Through sobs, I managed to blurt out a "Yes, Reverend," and with my hand in his, he turned to ask the church formally: "Are the members of St. Matthew's Baptist Church willing to accept this young lady, sister Janice Dean Willis, as a candidate for baptism into its fellowship?" Through my sobs, I heard several voices respond to the question with the standard reply: "Yes, Reverend, we the members of St. Matthew's Baptist Church are willing to accept her, and do so gladly, in the name of Jesus."

The hot night seemed to stretch on interminably, but at last the revival service was ended. People rushed forward to congratulate the preacher and to offer those of us who had "declared" the hand of fellowship. A group of people who lived up in my direction accompanied me part of the way home. When I reached our front door, my mother swung open the screen with anxious eyes. She asked me some questions but I don't remember all of them. Yes, I had joined church. In a week, I would be baptized. And now, all I wanted to do was sleep.

I had declared my intention to join Christ's fold on a Friday evening; and my baptism would be held on Saturday of the following week in order to make me a full-fledged member of the church by next Sunday's services. During the ensuing week, the older folk in the community smiled when they saw me and reminded me that this week's interlude was a dangerous time. Miss Virginia, my grandmama's oldest friend, one day expressed the danger explicitly: "Don't let ole Satan change your mind now, child. Keep vigilant!"

The neighborhood kids poked fun at me. As I walked home from school they chided, "Dean's gonna get dunked! Don't you drown in there now, Deanie Pie!" Drowning was a genuine fear. I could not swim and wasn't anxious to have this fact verified during my baptism.

On Saturday morning all my old fears—and some new ones—had rolled themselves up into a rock-hard boulder that balanced itself right in the middle of my chest. My mother's excited wake-up call left no doubts: "Get up, Dean. Today's the day. Get up and bathe down good." She had cooked a big breakfast of eggs, bacon, and biscuits. The mood in the house was cheery, like Christmas.

When I asked what I was supposed to put on, Mama came in and handed me a long white terry-cloth gown. It was scratchy.

"Just this?" I asked, dissatisfied. "Just this," she answered, "and some good underwear!"

"But won't I be too cold?"

"You'll be all right. Now hurry up! We can't be late. A lotta folks, I hear, gettin' baptized today."

"Well good then," I thought. "Maybe if we're late, I won't have to drown!" (As it turned out, Mama was wrong. Later, I thought I was going to freeze to death.)

For Baptists a whole universe revolves around the ceremony of baptism. A sprinkle on the forehead just will not do. Lord Jesus had appeared before John and waded out with him into the blessed River Jordan to be baptized; no mere sprinkling of water could substitute for that. In the yard to the side of the church was a deep tank. It measured eight feet long by six feet wide and was about five feet in depth. For baptisms it was filled with slightly over three feet of water. There were concrete steps leading down into it.

That Saturday morning my father had already gone off to work at the Ensley steel mill. But the three of us—my mother, me, and San— headed up to the church at a clip. Sandy carried towels; my mother, a change of clothes for me. I was flanked on either side. Escape was impossible.

When we reached the church, there were throngs of people there, and, to my surprise, a lot of them were wearing white gowns like me. At first view, all of them looked younger than me. I moaned. "Out of place, again!"

"Shush moaning and carrying on!" my mother swiftly chastised me. "This is a blessed and a joyous occasion! Go on now and stand over there with the others." My will was looking for a backdoor but came up empty.

It was then that I noticed Mr. Sledge. He was wearing a white gown, too. Mr. Sledge was the Camp's old drunk. He could be seen wandering through the streets mumbling to himself, with a bottle in his hands or stuck in his back pocket. He worked as a miner when Docena's coal mine was open, but since it'd shut down he'd taken to sitting on his porch staring off into space or wandering the streets mumbling. People said that the Klan had gotten after him, I didn't know for what. They'd taken him off and beaten him up bad; and he'd just been no good since. People kept coming over to congratulate him, saying that this was the right step to be taking and that they were proud of him. I was glad he was there, too. It meant I was not the oldest candidate.

Reverend Moseley came out of the church in his long gown. The throngs of people pushed for a place close to the edges of the tank. The line was ushered over.

One by one we went down. When my turn came, I balked. The steps were wet and cold to my bare feet. Two deacons took each arm to lead my trembling body down. I looked up in desperation, wanting to flee; but among all the wide-eyed faces my eyes settled on my mother's stern expression. It said silently but firmly, "Go on, young lady. Get in there!"

The water was dark, murky, and cold. The bottom of the tank was gritty. My teeth began to chatter. When the deacons let go of me I waded over to Reverend Moseley, reaching for his hands. I thought I was going to fall, but just then, he caught me. And so the thing was under way. He turned me around and put one of his arms behind my back. He closed his other big hand over my mouth and nose. I knew I was going to die. Then, raising his voice and saying, "Lord, we baptize this young sister, in the name of the Father, the Son, and the Holy Ghost," he bent me over backward and dunked me into that dark water. My feet came off the bottom. I was floating. I was drowning. I seemed to be held under for a long, long time. Then it was over. My feet found the bottom of the tank. Murky water was flowing off me. It was in my ears and in my eyes. For a few seconds I floundered about. I wiped my face as I lunged for the steps.

Then something wonderful happened. I couldn't see anything very clearly, but from all around the sides of the tank, arms and hands were extended down, reaching out to me, for me. Hands welcoming me into the community of the faithful. Into the community. Reaching out for me. Joyously welcoming me. I had a new home now. A much bigger family.

Maybe this was what Jesus had felt when the dove appeared in the sky above Him. These hands were wondrous things. They were like the Holy opening its arms to me. There was more love there than I had ever felt; and it felt bigger precisely because it was extended not just to me. This love, in a flash, dissolved all fears. These hands took me completely beyond myself. They reached out with equanimity toward all. Toward any and everyone reaching back, up to them. For the first time, I felt that I belonged to a family as big as humankind itself; and yet even bigger than that, taking in all creatures who breathed and cried and struggled and sang.

Of course, the next day things would return to normal and I'd find myself again in a divided camp, with whites on one side and blacks on the other. This spiritual connection with all things did not erase the racism of the everyday world I inhabited. And it would take many years and a trip halfway around the world before I again experienced anything like the grace and serenity of that joyous immersion into community. Before I felt so at home again.

Nevertheless, on that day, though my teeth were still chattering as I walked home, my spirit—like that dove's—was soaring.

THE TALK

෨ఴ

During the entire time that my family lived in Docena, there was no door-to-door mail delivery. We had to go to the commissary to pick up our mail. The drinking fountain for "whites only" stood prominently at the front of the store just past the two check-out counters; the colored fountain stood at one of its farthest corners, almost hidden. I learned from my mother to honor these signs, on threat of some frightful, though unvoiced, consequence.

When I was deemed old enough—around eight or nine—getting the mail on Saturdays became one of my chores. To get to the commissary from where we lived, I had to walk down a long hill that came to an end at Fourth Street before turning right and veering up and past our church. The church was a sort of demarcation point; it stood at the end of the black section of town. After that, I had to cross the street diagonally and, just briefly, enter a corner of the white section.

A little white girl lived in the house at the corner. I often saw her playing outside. She was younger than me, perhaps four or five years old. She was in her backyard, barefoot and clothed only in some skimpy top and panties. Her legs were usually very dirty, spotted or smeared with dried mud. She had thin, stringy white-blonde hair and big bright blue eyes. Invariably, just after I'd crossed over from the church side, she would start yelling at me: "Hey, where're you going, you *dirty nigger*?"

It was my tears about the little white girl's taunts that prompted my father one day to give San and me the infamous talk about our being "just as good as the whites." It is a talk that is inevitably given, at some point, to young black children. What he said to us, as near as I can remember, went something like this:

"Now, it seems that you girls and that little white girl are different, doesn't it?"

"Yeah, Daddy. It sure does," I chimed in.

"Well, she's not *any* different, not any *better,* than you two."

"No, Daddy. She *is* better; she's white!" I argued.

"Wait now. Listen to me. That little girl has five fingers . . . see? . . . just like you!" he began again.

"But she has blonde hair, Daddy. That's *better!*"

"It's only different, not better. She has two feet, too, just like you . . ."

At some point, I just stopped listening. My father meant well, I know. But I also knew that that little girl made me feel dirty when she called me "nigger." There was something in her voice that touched my deepest place and that also seemed to echo other whites' opinion. If the talk had to be given, it was already too late for me to hear it.

I happened to be visiting San in the 1980s when I overheard her giving this same talk to her two boys, Michael and Jason. Some taunt had been yelled at Michael, and he was getting ready to go back and fight the other kid. I heard Sandy speaking softly but firmly to her sons in their room. In her den, I paced, hardly able to contain myself. Ultimately, I called to her to come out. She yelled to me, "In a minute, Dean," and stayed to finish her talk.

When at last she joined me, I blurted out, "Sandy, why do you tell them these things? Don't you realize what it does to their self-esteem?"

San was calm and steadfast. "I tell them because I love them, and because I want them to live."

"But how can they feel okay about themselves if you're telling them on the one hand that they can accomplish anything they want to; and on the other that they have to be careful of the whites who hate them? I mean, it's contradictory—they can do any and everything; but there are some things they can't do! Which part are they supposed to believe?"

"They're supposed to believe both, because both are true. My sons are bright boys. I believe they can achieve whatever they set their minds to. But they live here, Dean, not up North." That was a dart aimed at my haughty, Northern thinking; we both knew that racism was alive in both regions. "And here, they have to know that there are people who hate them and want to do them harm just because they're black."

To that, all I could say was "Well, I think it's a big mistake!" She was right, of course; and she was doing what any loving parent must do—respond to their children's individual wounds.

But I couldn't help thinking back to how that talk had made me feel. Far from building my self-esteem, the fact of its being given at all had only confirmed that there *was* a difference between blacks and whites, and that that difference had hateful and possibly dangerous consequences. I have never been a parent, and Lord knows, black parents have their hands full, especially in this regard. But I would rather children be told *every day,* from the time they can understand the language, how special, bright, talented, and all-around wonderful they are. Then the child would gain a good solid image of himself, built up over time, continually. This way, when hateful words are hurled, there is a buffer already in place, as well as a context. Then the parent could explain simply, "Well, too bad for that hate-filled person. The problem is theirs, not yours!" And the child could see—and understand—that though the world has some crazed, hate-filled, and frustrated people, their craziness and hatred, their threat and menace, is not all there is. And a specific episode wouldn't seem so overwhelming. Possessed of a strong, healthy self-image—like armor—even a young child could fend off hateful and ignorant attacks. The child might even come to view the attacker with sympathy.

In my particular case, I feel that the talk came too late and too abruptly, without my having the benefit of previous, sustained, armor-building confidence in place. So the talk was as wounding as the little white girl's taunts. The tragedy is that it ever has to be given. For at least in my case, and probably in the cases of lots of other young blacks, rather than calm fears and give confidence, it has just the opposite effect.

MARCHING ON TO
FREEDOMLAND

ॐ

Inside Daddy's big car, Daddy, Mama, Sandy, and I are dressed in our Sunday clothes. It is hot inside and there is no air.

"Mama, why do we always have to keep the windows rolled up?"

"Because mean white men like to throw acid in little black children's eyes. Just use your fans, and stop squirming so much!"

I was perhaps nine or ten years old when my mother offered this explanation of why we had to sit hot and sweating in our best clothes. Many black children had been blinded by acid or hot lye thrown through open car windows.

A few years before, young Emmett Till, a fourteen-year-old boy visiting from Chicago, had been taken by a mob of whites and lynched in Money, Mississippi. Closer to home, children in Montgomery, Alabama, had begun to go missing, only to be found dead later. In 1957 the Civil Rights Act had been signed into law. Blacks hoped the right to vote regardless of color would soon follow. But the stepped-up violence against black children seemed an attempt to destroy us before we reached voting age. Blinding us would certainly keep us from getting an education.

My father remembered his high-school teachers holding special classes back in 1939 so that he and other bright students would be able to pass the rigorous and unlawful tests administered to blacks in the South who wanted to register to vote. He described for me his own test. He had literally to stand before a registration board comprised of three seated whites. They had fired questions at him for an hour: "How many *words* are there in the U.S. Constitution? Who was president of the United States in 1920? Who was governor of Alabama in 1930? Lieutenant governor in 1929?" They required him to recite the Constitution of the State of Alabama. He had then been dismissed and told that he would learn, by mail, whether or not he had passed. Two weeks went by before he received the notice that he had. My dad's summation: "Finally, joy, relief, and exhilaration overshadowed the stress we had all endured. What a price we paid for a privilege that was already ours!" Soon after my father passed his registration test, Alabama passed a law that voters would have to pay a poll tax in order to vote. In 1939, when my father passed, the tax was $1.50, a tidy sum at the time; and though it should have been free, my father thought it well worth the price.

By the spring of 1963, things got personal. All around the tiny hamlet of Docena, the civil-rights movement was exploding. A wave of sit-ins at segregated lunch counters began in Greensboro, North Carolina. Within two weeks, sit-ins had spread to fifteen other cities in five Southern states. College students from Alabama State began sit-ins in Montgomery. News of these events was discussed at church. Martin Luther King, Jr., had decided that it was time to focus his campaign on Birmingham, the city he described, truthfully, as "the most segregated city in the South." King's drive against racism in Birmingham began on April 3. Though he continued his advocacy of non-violent demonstrations, Dr. King determined that it was necessary to put black children on the frontline in Birmingham. The struggle for our rights and for our long-promised freedom had come home. All across the city, black students mobilized to march.

In 1963 I was fifteen, a tenth-grader at Westfield High, a county school located some miles from downtown. As King's Birmingham campaign loomed nearer, one day at school an announcement aired on the intercom: "This school will remain open. Classes will continue to be taught. Students are not officially excused from classes. Yet absences during this time of crisis will not be held against anyone." Those last words were all that we needed.

The few students with access to cars came to the high school and loaded up before heading downtown. Sometimes, the school bus drivers would tell us they were going there and we were welcomed to come along. I joined the marches as often as I could get a ride. It never occurred to me that I shouldn't go or that it might be dangerous to do so.

Birmingham's infamous police commissioner, Eugene "Bull" Connor, had Dr. King arrested on April 12. Then Connor ordered the use of the hoses and police dogs to halt student protesters. For many students, classmates of mine and others, it became a badge of honor to be able to say that they had been arrested. Hundreds of young people crowded the city jail. They spilled over into its cafeteria and hallways. With room only to sit or stand, they sang freedom songs the whole time.

Dr. King wrote, in his famous "Letter from the Birmingham Jail," that during those turbulent days the children had been brave. But it was not that we were brave. It was just that, at long last, we could actually *do* something that might help to change things. I was never arrested; and I certainly did not feel brave. I was especially afraid of Bull Connor's dogs. Once, the water cannons caught me with tremendous and unexpected force, and I marveled that water could *burn* so. But we were larger than our individual selves; we were part of a movement for change. As we marched singing freedom songs, we became part of that great family of blacks who had "brought us thus far." Because we knew we were morally and spiritually right, we were physically energized. And we began to believe that we would triumph.

On some days, my dad and I would march together. At one of the biggest marches, the one often depicted in histories of those days when Connor's ferocious German shepherds were out in full force, snarling and attacking, our whole tiny family was there. Keeping to the sidewalks, we were marching in twos. Dad held my hand tightly. Mom had Sandy's hand right behind us. I became almost paralyzed as we neared an angry group of policemen with their dogs leaping and snapping. Daddy's grip tightened. "Keep walking," he said calmly. "Just keep walking." But as we reached the group, the police released their dogs on a tall, slim man right in front of us. They cornered him. One vicious dog went for the man's backside, ripping his pocket; another dog in front of him was yelping at his face. Suddenly, the man pulled out a knife from his pocket. For a second, there was a bright glint from the knife's blade. Then the man brought it down and slashed the dog's neck. Blood spurted everywhere as the dog's yelp became a whimper. I wanted to run; but my dad's deep voice said, "Be calm." Several policemen then moved in on the man, all of them wielding their billy clubs. They pounded that poor man mercilessly right in front of us and then picked him up by his arms and legs and carried him off, face-down, to some unknown destination. The march continued.

I have several times seen photographs of that man being attacked. It's the famous picture we've all seen. And at least twice I have remarked to my father, "We were *right there,* Daddy. *Right there!* But we're not in any of the photos I've seen." His response has consistently been "Yeah. We were right there. But we *weren't* there to have our photos taken!"

The specter of Bull Connor's violent response to youthful, non-violent marchers brought our long-standing plight before the conscience of the nation. On May 10, after five and a half weeks of marches, a biracial agreement was announced in Birmingham to desegregate public accommodations, increase job opportunities for blacks, and provide amnesty to those arrested. A massive sigh of relief and joy went up from Birmingham's blacks.

But white segregationists could not stomach the agreement. On May 11, a bomb was exploded at the home of Dr. King's brother. A second blast shattered Dr. King's own headquarters at the Gaston Motel. Some blacks rioted in response. Two hundred and fifty state troopers were sent downtown to keep the peace. White racists' maliciousness continued to smolder. Eventually, the eyes of the nation would be brought once again back to Birmingham when, on September 15 of that same year, four little black girls were killed in the bombing of the Sixteenth Street Baptist Church, and Birmingham came to be known as "Bombing ham."

The spring of 1963 changed me fundamentally, not just because I had marched together with King and Abernathy, Arthur Shores, Fred Shuttlesworth, and so many more of my own generation. It was also that I had *stood with* and, therefore, *stood up for* myself and for my people. White people no longer held my spirit in chains, no longer bent my body low. By marching, I had talked back. And I had learned to do so with a new attitude, unafraid of the consequences.

If being brave means doing a frightening thing in spite of the fear, then perhaps we children were brave, without knowing it. For at the time, there was much pride as well. With our spirits high and our joyful songs, we were marching on to Freedomland.

"TROUBLE ALONG
THE CABLE"

০৩৫

I am amazed by the number of black faces that appear on American television nowadays. Especially on commercials. One sees black babies' bottoms being pampered, black entrepreneurs renting Jaguars, beautiful, dimpled children trying on parents' shoes and joyfully scuffing hardwood floors, a young black brother and sister discussing the content of their breakfast cereal, whole black families piling into luxury minivans. It's taken for granted that black people are a recognizable and accepted part of this society. But in my lifetime, it was once impossible to see any black face on television. When I was a child in the Jim-Crow South, it was not that black people were invisible; black people were completely nonexistent on the airwaves.

Somehow, in the mid-fifties, my father got the money to bring a television into our house. It was one of the first TVs in the black part of Docena. After Sandy and I had finished our homework, we were allowed to watch the big black-and-white console. We did so with glee, racing to view Gabby Hayes and Hopalong Cassidy, Roy Rogers and Dale Evans. On Saturdays, there was Howdy Doody, and on special

Sunday evenings, "The Ed Sullivan Show." We felt blessed. But though we could watch singing cowboys and talking wooden puppets, we could not see black people. For all my days in Docena, never was there a black person's face on that TV. Not once did we see ourselves.

We knew, of course, that black people did things in the world. There were great black boxers, for example. My dad listened to their fights on the radio. There were black entertainers, too. Nat King Cole and Sammy Davis, Jr., were big stars at the time. Sammy Davis was so big, in fact, that he often appeared on television—though not for us. How clearly I remember one Sunday evening when my whole family hugged the console waiting for Davis to sing and tap on "The Ed Sullivan Show." We leaned in close as stiff-necked Ed began his introduction. But just as Sullivan threw wide his arms to greet Davis—like so many times before—the card came on, with its message of denial.

One of the clearest memories I have from childhood is of that card. I can draw every line of the man depicted on that placard, wearing baggy patched pants, a floppy cap, and carrying a large gashed-in cable with star-shaped chunks of stuff exploding out of it. To the side of the cartoon were written the words "Trouble along the cable." Every time a black person appeared on television, we saw only this card.

Now, for all the black people (and we never knew how many) that we, as blacks, were not allowed to see on TV, we were never left out of viewing the grand conventions of the KKK. Today I wonder how widely broadcast these events were in their day. We Southern television viewers were treated to two- and three-day-long spectacles that reminded us that the Ku Klux Klan was strong; that white supremacists were all-powerful and fully in control. It would seem that such racism tied into the airwaves of the media would have been impossible, to say nothing of illegal. But I am a witness.

Owing to my various scholastic achievements, a Northern television station took an interest in me and actually came down to Docena to do some filming. By the time I was to graduate from Westfield, I had received offers of fully paid four-year scholarships from several Southern, Northern, and Ivy League schools. It was 1965. Northern schools were eager to do something for the cause of advancing civil rights. I found myself, along with a few other hand-picked black high-school seniors from the South, a prime catch.

Someone, somewhere up North, decided that a documentary featuring three or four of us bright blacks, soon to be entering the nation's best colleges and universities, would make a good story. I was chosen to be one of those filmed. The one-hour documentary included interviews with four of us, three boys—one of whom was also from Birmingham—and me.

Cronkite, who would anchor the program, did not come down himself. But another anchor whom I'd seen on television came, accompanied by three others who formed his production crew. Those men carried huge cameras and light gear and big recording instruments. They spent a day with me, filming me at home, in the language lab at Westfield, and on a staged walk from the school bus stop at Docena Elementary to my home. I remember that the crew asked me to redo the last part of the walk home. I am convinced, in retrospect, that they wanted to make sure to get shots of the house that stood next to ours, with its run-down foundations, teeming with kids hanging over the banisters. I still have regrets about the blatant exploitation of those children.

This documentary was never aired in Alabama. Relatives of ours who lived in Chicago saw the program, and my sister's friend Mandy Simmons watched it on TV when it was shown in whatever Northern city she had gone to for nursing studies. But none of us ever saw the film that would eventually stir up such trouble. I have never been able, even today, to get a copy.

One day in the mid-1980s, I got a call from Wesleyan's public relations office. A good friend there had discovered an old clipping from a 1965 issue of *The Wall Street Journal* and suspected that the piece might be about me. He sent over a xeroxed copy.

The piece was about me, and several other black Southern high schoolers. But—like the 1960s TV documentary—neither I nor any of my family had ever seen it. The article had appeared on the front page of the September 23, 1965, edition of the paper. Its headline read, "Interracial U., Northern Colleges Seek to Draw More Negroes from Schools in South," and its subheading was: "Janice Joins the Ivy League."

By the time I read through the three-column article written by staff reporter Paul P. Martin, I had been a college professor for more than ten years. Seeing it now, my emotions quickly ran the gambit—from delight at the find to utter embarrassment at my own sentimental and corny statements to rage at the tone of the piece that seemed to glorify the Northern schools while clearly suggesting they'd lowered their standards in order to admit blacks.

The piece began:

"Janice Willis, James Lewis, and Myron Thompson are in the ranks of the freshman forces mustering at Ivy League colleges this month. But chances are no one will pay an inordinate amount of attention to them.

"For the three young Negroes are being joined by enough others of their race so that, unlike in past years, their presence isn't especially noteworthy. In fact, Negroes this year account for about three percent of the acceptances at the eight Ivy League colleges and their seven sister-schools. Not a whopping percentage, admittedly, but almost twice the rate of last year and a far cry from the one or two Negroes that had been a staple for many years at most private colleges in the North."

It continued:

"The Negro applicants to the Ivy League face the same rigorous standards as other applicants. However, some other colleges, notably Antioch in Ohio, have lowered admission standards to enable more Negroes to attend. . . .

"Under the program, the college gives tutoring and guidance to the Negro students before they enter and while they are freshmen. But from then on the students are expected to meet the ordinary school requirements. 'We anticipate relaxing our admission standards but not our graduation standards,' Mr. Bush says."

Specifically about me, Martin wrote:

"Miss Willis, for example, the seventeen-year-old daughter of a steelworker who lives in a Negro area near Birmingham, Ala., was accepted by Cornell University, Bryn Mawr, and several Southern schools.

"The girl was a prime catch. She ranked first in her high school class, was treasurer of the student council, and winner of a host of honors and awards. She is typical of the type of Negro the colleges are seeking, in contrast to a few years ago when the competition was pretty much limited to the football captain. 'Now the all-state quarterback often sits on the bench while the all-A student becomes the college's first draft choice,' says one college admissions officer."

I felt like I stood—again—on the auction block.

I was quoted in the piece. Though I had never even met Martin, my comments had apparently been passed along by Charles McCarthy, a recruiter who had come down to Birmingham to talk to a bunch of us "bright ones." In the article, there was all this religious talk coming from my mouth. What was *that* about?

"Adds Janice Willis: 'I'm very humbled by the whole thing. I don't think there is anything as important today as obtaining the very best education possible. My scholarship to Cornell has given me this opportunity. But it has also given me a great responsibility—not only to my parents, the university and my teachers, but to God as well. I can't let any of them down.'

"Janice says that 'after reading the scholarship letter from Cornell, my parents grinned, cried, thanked God, and began to grin again. The cycle pretty much continues, even today.'"

So much for a piece of Americana rediscovered. It might just as well have remained buried.

News of my scholarship offers had been appearing throughout my senior year in the four-page local black newspaper. I knew the whites in Docena saw these papers, too, and I worried that there might be trouble for my family because of my growing conspicuousness. It would not be long before Docena's Klan had its say.

Growing up in Docena, where black men sat all day on their porches, glassy-eyed, not only because they were without jobs but because each had had at one time or another his own fateful encounter with Klan members, hearing of Klan beatings was a fairly normal occurrence. I had heard the Klan night riders going through Docena honking their horns to frighten us. But as a child, I had run into these folk only once before.

They were after Joey Williams but I didn't know that at the time. I knew only that a group of white men dressed in hoods and robes barged into my classmate's birthday party, yelled obscenities, broke a boy's arm, and said, "How dare you niggers play loud music and have fun!" The boy's parents could not protect him.

Docena was noted for its high Klan membership. Long before church burnings came to America's attention in the early nineties, the Ku Klux Klan had burned crosses and started fires at our one black church on a regular basis. Going back to the fifties and early sixties, grown white men had doused black children with acid indiscriminately. I often wonder, where was the rest of America then?

Sandy and I had been warned by our parents not to go anywhere in the Camp after school except home, but this was a birthday party and so we'd disobeyed. I liked the boy, liked being asked to his party. He lived only a block or so behind our elementary schoolyard, so we thought we could safely drop by—just for a little while. By the time we arrived, the party was already well under way. Kids from inside had spilled out onto the high porch of the wooden frame house. They were blowing balloons and party horns. Some carried little bowls of ice cream.

Just as Sandy and I approached the yard, two or three carloads of white-robed and hooded men pulled up. They shut off their engines and charged up the stairs of the house. One of them yelled, "Whose loud damn party is this, anyway? Where's the nigger that's having it?" The scene turned into slow motion as I watched the men push their way through the kids and disappear into the house. There was shuffling and screaming. Then two of the men brought Derrick out onto the porch. They shoved him and twisted his arm behind him. He cried out, but everyone else seemed powerless to help him. Where are his parents? I wondered. Can't anybody help him? After a few minutes, the hooded men filed down the stairs, still cursing that the music was too loud, and shouting at the rest of us, "Niggers don't deserve parties!"

I don't remember much of what happened after that. Derrick was taken off to some faraway emergency room. The party was ended. Sandy and I ran the whole of the seven blocks home.

It was much, much later that I learned—from Ella Doris, Joey's cousin—the full story behind that frightening day. It went something like this: Derrick's younger sister, a few days before, had gone on foot to Docena's commissary to pick up her family's mail. We were always cautioned not to cross the street that separated the black and white sections of the Camp too soon. Derrick's sister had, apparently, not heeded this advice. Rather, she'd crossed early and so, for the last few steps, walked on the edge of the lawn of an old white woman who lived there on the corner. The woman, seeing her, had yelled obscenities at her, which she'd later repeated to her older brother, Joey.

Now, Joey was a teenager, and he had had enough. He'd gathered a bunch of his friends together. They'd collected a cache of stones, and from the other side of Miss Virginia's house, a vantage point they thought gave them anonymity, the boys had thrown the stones so that they landed on the white woman's tin roof. But the white woman had run out, and although she couldn't identify all of the boys, she had spotted Joey. And so it was that on the day of Derrick's birthday party, the hooded men had come looking for Joey. They wanted to teach Joey a lesson. But they'd found only Joey's brother, Derrick, and so they broke Derrick's arm.

As fate would have it, when Docena's Klansmen came to visit us, my father was not at home. He was working the graveyard shift, eleven to seven. Only my mother, Sandy, and I were there, sleeping. A caravan of cars, horns honking, was making its way through the town. All blacks knew what this meant though we didn't—as yet—know who was being targeted.

The Klan made several circuits around the black section of the Camp. Then, peeking through the bedroom window, no lights on inside, we saw the cars come to a stop, one by one, on the street in front of our house. My mom had already grabbed her .22 caliber pistol. "Get on the floor; try to get under the bed," she whispered. I was glued to a corner of the window. I could not take my eyes off what I was seeing: a crowd of enrobed whites—men, women, and *children*—was amassing.

Some men set up a cross in the alleyway right across from our house and lit it. I was amazed that their uniforms were not all the same color. There were purple satiny robes and red ones and white ones. Sandy whimpered softly. My mom took up her station, her tiny pistol in hand, by our front door. We held our collective breath. We were alone.

In my frozen panic I found myself completely awed by the spectacle. I thought of our closet, where Daddy kept his shotgun. But I knew I couldn't shoot it. Nor, strangely, did I want to. What I *wanted* was to talk to these people. To convince them that they were making a mistake; to show them that we were a family, *just like them*; that we were *human beings, just like them*. I wanted to *teach* them. I wanted them to know what I knew about the community of creation—what I'd experienced at my baptism. But my body and my lips were numbed in fear.

The minutes stretched into eternity as we waited for a bomb. But cross ablaze and garbled speeches delivered, the Klansmen and women and their enrobed children got back into their cars and trucks and rode away. For whatever reason, that night our lives were spared.

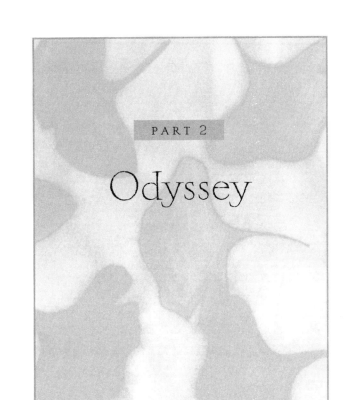

PART 2

Odyssey

DREAMING ME, II

～

The lions were inside the house. It was my house, though not my actual, present one; and the lions were a miniature pair, a male and female couple, a bit smaller in size than, say, a golden lab.

I was anxious about the lions being so close. They roamed on their soft paws downstairs while I nervously awaited their arrival upstairs, where I stood in the bedroom. I had closed the bedroom door, but the small lions had no problem pushing it open. I froze, heart thumping as they did so, and could only watch as the two creatures padded around the bedroom, heads lowered, sniffing.

To my right, the bedroom window opened out onto a steeply sloping green pasture. There was a soft rain falling, and a breeze blew through the room, floating delicate white curtains up and about. The air felt damp but was more refreshing than cold. Soon, the female lion made another circumambulation and left the room. Out of the corner of my eye I saw her bound playfully up the sloping pasture.

The large-maned male lion approached me. With a nudge of its head, it pushed me over backward onto the Tibetan-carpeted floor. With a soft grunt, the *miniature lion plopped down next to me, pinning me with its soft but weighty right paw. I could smell its strong animal odor. It slept.*

It got darker. The lion was not going to hurt me, but neither was it going to let me go. I would have to spend the night this way, pressed down by this diminutive beast.

I awoke the next morning tired. I felt a depressed cavity on my chest where the lion's paw had lain, heavily, all night.

CORNELL

⟲

After an interminably long bus ride, I arrived once again in Ithaca. I was sweaty, hungry, and completely exhausted. I had thought I could handle the ride a bit better than the year before. Then, I had been selected to come to Cornell for the special summer program held there each year by the Telluride Association. That particular trip had marked my first visit to Cornell and my longest journey anywhere away from home. It had taken almost two full days; I left Birmingham in the predawn darkness and arrived in Ithaca quite late the next evening. In between there were countless stops, long hours of waiting for connections, and some mechanical repairs. But by far the worst part of that first trip had been the fact that—in 1963—I could not sit down and eat at any of the lunch counters on the way. Even though that spring I had marched with King in Birmingham, the Supreme Court had not yet agreed to uphold the Civil Rights Act that prohibited discrimination in public accommodations. As far north as Scranton, Pennsylvania, I could not sit in the bus station's cafeteria to have a sandwich.

My sense of loneliness on that first trip and my fears about what awaited me have blotted out most of the individual details of that journey. But what stands out in my mind is the sense that I did have a traveling companion, though no one else saw Him.

Since I did not consider myself to be overly religious, it still strikes me as strange that wherever that Greyhound traveled, a clear vision of Jesus glided along, just outside my window. I can only assume that I must have prayed during those long hours—prayed for safety, for food, for a welcoming place. And my prayers were answered: I was not traveling alone. Jesus floated there, with me. And whenever I doubted or felt particularly afraid, I had only to glance to the window to see that He was still there, riding the wind currents, a holographic epiphany, life-size, reclining, gently smiling Jesus.

My mother and I, it was said, had been born with cauls over our eyes. This meant we saw things that other human beings did not. My mother told tales of having seen men grow as tall as trees right before her eyes and then suddenly disappear. But I always thought these stories were like those my grandmother Jennie told about "hants," the spirits of long-dead folk who returned to guide the living or, as she often said, to tell the living something important, like where gold was buried. But I did not normally have such visions. Nor had I ever seen any portrayal of Jesus that looked like this one, with His body lying down, His head supported by His right hand. Later, I would see this exact position on depictions of the Buddha's passing away, His so-called Complete Nirvana posture. But then, I knew nothing about Buddhism. I only know that Jesus rode with me on that first bus ride to Cornell and that His gently smiling eyes comforted me throughout that journey.

On my second trip to Cornell, no Jesus. Just fatigue. To make matters worse, my luggage was not on board. It had gotten misplaced during all the bus changes. I didn't have a single change of clothes with me. In this state of utter beleagueredness, I took a cab to Telluride House, the only familiar place I knew on campus.

I learned that I had been assigned to Mary Donlon Hall, a dorm for first-year women students. It was one of the newest buildings at Cornell, an impressive, six-story modern structure, triangular in shape. All the rooms in Donlon were doubles. I had arrived worried and timid. Not having any clothes only added to my sense of insecurity. I boarded the elevator for my room, hoping against hope not to see, or be smelled by, anyone. I couldn't imagine how my situation could have been any worse.

Fortunately, it didn't get worse. When I turned the key and pushed open the door to 618, my roommate was not there. That she'd arrived was clear from her partial unpacking. I fell onto the bed nearest the door and slept the sleep of the dead. I awoke later that evening to a girl's husky voice saying, "Well, hello there!" It was Cathy, a tall, blonde, blue-eyed beauty. I introduced myself and, trying to hold back tears, narrated the tale of my ill-fated bus trip and lost clothes. She smiled a deep, dimpled smile and said, "Well, until your clothes get here, you'll just have to wear some of mine. You're welcome to do that." That was certainly a nice offer and I had little choice but to accept. But Cathy was 5′10″ and I was 5′4″. Until my bags were found and delivered to Donlon—some four days later—I walked around campus feeling even more awkward than I might have in clothes that dwarfed me and made me look like a child who had been thrown away; like "Aunt Hattie's child," black folks would say.

Cathy and I were okay together; but we had different schedules and, as it turned out, completely different reasons for being at Cornell. Already educated at the best schools, Cathy had come to Cornell to find a mate. That first year she dated every captain of every sport's team at

Cornell. She was outgoing and popular. I saw her vulnerable and teary only once when, at the end of our first year, she confided to me that she hadn't yet met a single boy she would consider marrying.

One has to wonder whether there's any attention paid to the pairing of students during their first years at college. Cathy's father was the chief executive officer of Exxon in Europe; my dad was a steelworker. Her home was in Summit, New Jersey; mine was a mining camp in Alabama. Perhaps putting the two of us together was some sort of plan to foster diversity; it would certainly be hard to imagine a more dissimilar pair than we.

Randy Fingerhut, from Syosset, Long Island, was a straight-shooter from the beginning. On the very first day that classes began, she walked right up to me and said, "Hi." She asked, "Hey, do you know how to get to Goldwin Smith Hall?" And having been at Cornell the previous summer, I did know. It struck me immediately that she did not have "race" in her eyes. There was no hint of that positive discrimination that says, "Oh, there's a black person. I'll make her feel good by talking to her." About my height, with light brown hair and freckles, Randy spoke in staccato bursts, with a strong Long Island accent. Without feigning kindness, with no awkwardness or guile, she had asked me a question about something I knew. And with that simple exchange, I began to feel that I belonged there, too.

During that first semester, Randy and I became fast friends. It turned out that she lived in Donlon, too, and on the same floor as me. Rand was a chatterbox, direct, opinionated, and a real live radical, a card-carrying member of SDS, Students for a Democratic Society. What she wanted to know most from me was whether it was really as bad for blacks in the South as she and her friends up North thought it was. Now, I was happy enough for the attention and for the instant bond I felt with her, but I had come to Cornell with a brooding, quiet, and mostly silent manner. It was hard for me to tell anyone how bad things really were. That first year, Randy and I spent many an hour together, on the floor of Donlon's lounge-cum-kitchenette, talking about all sorts of things. I know that she got me to talk more than I would have otherwise; and perhaps she learned from me how sometimes to accept silence.

It was Randy who introduced me to the world of whites who were not racist. She also introduced me to the stirring music of Bob Dylan. In Dylan's raspy and haunting tunes, the civil-rights movement, the folk movement, and the anti-war movement all came together. He sang about James Meredith and Medger Evers, people I knew; and about situations I knew. And I fell in love with this young poet, activist, and musician. For me he joined the ranks of no lesser immortals than Stevie Wonder. I bought a second-hand Yamaha guitar and began learning some chords. It was the beginning of a watershed year.

The world began to open up for me. One may say that this is typical for anyone's freshman year of college. But I had been snatched from the jaws of despair and given a respite from poverty. Even Cornell's campus was paradisiacal. Its hundreds upon hundreds of acres overlooking Cayuga Lake and the gorges that dotted and crisscrossed them gave the place an air of being a wonderland. For the first time in my life, I was free to think, to explore, and to question. I began to feel truly blessed.

The only downside of living in Ithaca, its ferocious winters, I had yet to experience. When winter later arrived, it caught my attention, for never in my life had I experienced snow or cold like that. Yet I somehow managed to make it through four years at Cornell without ever learning that one could shield oneself from such harsh conditions. I was so modest that I never asked, and no one ever told me, about thermal underwear. I weathered Ithaca's winters with only my thin corduroy jeans, sweaters, and jackets. In hindsight, I am amazed that I never lost any digits to frostbite.

When I went to Cornell as a freshman in 1965, the school boasted 14,500 students. Though there were almost 250 African students there, studying mostly in the graduate schools of International Relations, Agriculture, or Hotel Management, there were only 8 of us home-grown blacks, and we quickly found each other. There were, in fact, 7 African American men and myself. Like me, the boys had all been drawn from Southern states.

Of the seven African American men, one in particular stood out for me. His name was Melvin Brady, but everyone called him "Mack." Mack had come from Lynchburg, Virginia. He had a laid-back, never-flustered manner, and he was really funny, the life of the party. In Lynchburg, he had earned money for college by caddying for white golfers on courses where no blacks were allowed to play. Still, he told me, he had developed an appreciation for the game; and the money was good. He also liked to shoot pool. At some point in the year, we discovered that Willard Straight Hall, the huge gothic-style student union, had several tournament-size pool tables on its top floor. On many a day after classes, Mack and I would meet there for pool. The game appealed to my mathematical proclivities, and Mack had grown up around pool halls. I liked to pop the balls, making them smash and crash before entering the pockets. Mack, the master, attempted un-successfully to teach me the soft-touch approach.

When it came to choosing classes, I was much more conservative and prudent. While Randy ventured widely, taking classes in astronomy, physical anthropology, economic history, and Greek, my first semester at Cornell I enrolled in physics (the field I planned to major in), French, sociology, English, and philosophy, all at the introductory levels. I found the workload difficult but doable. To my surprise, the course I found the most challenging—and the most fun—was the philosophy course.

That year, the philosophy department had a visiting philosopher named A. L. Stewart from England. Perhaps unfamiliar with the typical introductory philosophy class with its survey of key thinkers and ideas, what Stewart presented was a detailed investigation of Wittgenstein's *The Blue and Brown Books.* I was immediately drawn to Wittgenstein's thought. Cornell was one of the leading institutions for studying analytic philosophy and boasted a number of such philosophers, most notably Norman Malcolm, who had actually studied at Cambridge under Wittgenstein. I bought Malcolm's memoir of his days with Wittgenstein and read and reread it, like a new Bible. It was Wittgenstein's *method* of teaching that so intrigued me. He had persuaded Cambridge administrators to let him teach his courses in a little hut. His students, most of whom were advanced graduate students or already teachers themselves, were not allowed to be late. Wittgenstein would sit next to a window or to his little stove and simply think aloud while his students scribbled furiously to record his words. After pushing himself to his limits, Wittgenstein usually retired to the local movie house where he had a reserved seat in the very front row, making it impossible for him to see anything on the screen. Here, I thought, was a serious philosopher, one thoroughly committed to the search for truth. Now, having been introduced to Wittgenstein through my very first philosophy course, I was determined one day to study at the feet of the great old man Malcolm. I decided to become a philosophy major.

Cornell's philosophy department was called the Sage School of Philosophy. I thought the name was embarrassingly presumptuous, even though it came from a past president and donor to the school and was not, I think, originally intended to suggest the Greeks. Still, it was a thrilling place to be in those days. Becoming a major was like joining a club, and we philosophy majors, forty-four of us when I was there, considered ourselves to be quite special people. We were the select few in the Liberal Arts College who were the really smart ones, the thinkers. We had our own lounge and chess room in Sage Hall, where there were continuous chess games going all hours of the day and night along with nonstop discussions and debates, arguments and counterarguments. Following Wittgenstein's method of analytic, or critical, philosophy, the catchphrase around our department and the chess room was "What does it mean to say . . . ?" Our shared and constant endeavor was to check up on how we as students and others were going about doing this thing called philosophy. Our professors stopped by from time to time to drop pearls of wisdom or to begin a line of reasoning that was open to debate. The philosophy chess room at times sounded like a *yeshiva* or, as I would later learn, like the evening courtyard of a Tibetan monastery—people gathered in small groups, some animatedly engaged in arguing points and refuting them, others intently listening. The groups usually discussed or debated new ideas that came up in our classes, but sometimes there were also stories told about our esteemed teachers. Even though I was quiet and shy, I loved the sheer energy of the place.

One of the most famous tales circulating in the chess room concerned Malcolm and his long and close relationship with Wittgenstein. It was said that one day a student arrived late to one of Malcolm's classes. There was a guest lecturer that day, but the student had arrived too late to hear the introduction. After observing the lecturer, the student leaned over and asked a classmate, "Hey, who's that guy acting so much like Malcolm?" It was, of course, Wittgenstein. Apparently Malcolm had not only been Wittgenstein's very first American student; he had studied so closely with him that he had adopted most of Wittgenstein's mannerisms.

There were a lot of other things going on at Cornell at the time. The war in Vietnam was heating up, so anti-war groups formed and demonstrated on campus. My first year there was a lengthy student hunger strike against the war and a lot of rallies. Every night on the evening news, we watched as Buddhist monks and nuns set fire to themselves, with prayers for peace on their lips. I wondered how those peace-loving people could continue to endure the constant terrors of air and chemical warfare, the relentless bombing assaults, the day-to-day hell—and still hold on to loving-kindness and peace. In Birmingham, we civil rights marchers had been given instructions on how to meet violence without striking back, but I found it hard to hold my anger in check. Because of the war and the way Vietnamese Buddhists were dealing with it, my interests gradually turned to Buddhism. I became determined to learn more about it.

One of the first books I read was Alan Watts's *The Way of Zen*. Next, I read whatever I could find by D. T. Suzuki. Something about the teachings struck a deep chord in me. They seemed pristinely clear teachings that offered a sophisticated analysis of suffering and, more important for me, a method for overcoming suffering. By my second year at Cornell, I had decided that what I needed most was to go to a Zen monastery in the far northern reaches of Japan and meditate. The austere life of a Zen renunciate seemed my calling.

I had maintained my contact with the Telluride Association and House members and sometimes I went to the House for special lectures and dinners. As I attempted to navigate my way through college life, this group of highly intelligent folk continued to feed something in me. One night it happened that a senior at the House told me about the year he had just completed in India. It was from him that I first heard about the Wisconsin Program. He'd suggested, "Why not go to India and study Buddhist philosophy there?" India? I had no interest whatever in India. I knew nothing about the place; and besides, I had set my mind on studying Zen in Japan. Still, I put the suggestion in the back of my mind for safekeeping.

With so much new and exciting stuff going on, it's hard to see how that phenomenon known as the sophomore slump ever caught up with me. But somehow it did. One day Randy and I walked out of an English class together, looked at each other, and said, "That's it. Let's get out of here!"

It was then that I mentioned to Randy what my Telluride friend had said about India. We decided to give it a shot. Interviews for the Wisconsin Program were being held in New York. We cut our classes that day and drove down to the city in funky blue jeans. We parked somewhere near the Biltmore Hotel, where the interviews were taking place, went into the hotel lobby's ladies' room, changed clothes, and took an elevator up.

In order to be accepted for the program, one had to successfully pass two interviews: one with Joe Elder, a Wisconsin sociologist of India, and another with a campus administrator. One by one the group of nine or so students filed in, first into one room, and then into the second, closing the doors behind them. At the end of the day, Randy and I sat together in the waiting area. The Wisconsin administrator walked over and said to Randy, "We're sorry, but we can't accept your application to the program. Last year, we had some problems when one of our students got involved in demonstrations in Delhi. We simply can't chance that happening again." It turned out that the Telluride friend who had told me about the program had been, in fact, the troublemaker in Delhi. Never one to keep her political views secret, Randy had told them about her involvement in SDS, and that had apparently blown it for her. To me the administrator said, "We will consider your application, however. You should be hearing from us in a few weeks."

"That's okay," I blurted out. "If she doesn't go, I'm not going either!" It was my stab at being defiant.

On the ride back upstate, I repeated to Randy, "Well, bump India! I never wanted to go there anyway." I meant it. Surprisingly, she was not upset at all. She said to me in a calm voice, "Don't give up on it so quickly. If they take you, you should go. It will get you away from here and—who knows?—you might like it."

Randy's sentiments were echoed by most of my teachers. Not that the trip would get me away from Cornell, but that studying in India might be a wonderful experience for me. A few weeks later a letter arrived telling me that I had been chosen for the program. The accompanying materials gave fuller details about the additional requirement of summer study and about the stipends participants would receive. In India we would each be given a free bicycle and 250 rupees per month. We would have the additional support of a Wisconsin House in each location, and best of all (I thought), each of us would receive a free round-the-world ticket. I began to think that I could put up with some months in India if I knew that afterward I could go to Japan and find my mountain monastery.

I knew that convincing my parents such a trip was a good thing for me would be the most difficult part. After all, just going up to Cornell had seemed to them like going to the ends of the earth. Now I wanted to travel, literally, halfway around the world. But I had begun to turn my mind that way. A Buddhist saying goes, "Mind decides, body and speech follow." After some weeks of pleading and explaining, my parents reluctantly gave their blessing, and I went to India for my junior year. As things turned out, I never got east of India.

INDIA!

〇〇

It was in the predawn hours that our Air India plane set down on the tarmac outside Delhi. The heat and humidity were already apparent. After jostling with luggage and making our way through customs, we flooded out onto the noisy street in front of the airport, lined with fuming buses and auto-scooters. But it was the smell of the place—something akin to warm pee—and the bustling crowds that almost overwhelmed us. We twenty-five Wisconsin Program folk spent a day and a night in Delhi, camping around the Wisconsin House on the edge of the university, and getting last-minute orientation details and information. That first evening we were treated to scrumptious Indian food at Moti Mahal's in Old Delhi, a super restaurant. The next day, nine of us would fly on to Banaras.

The crowds, noise, pollution, and smell had left me exhausted. I was not sure at all that I wanted to remain in India. Nor was I alone in my hesitations. The Delhi experience had not jibed well with the image of India I carried in my mind. But landing in Banaras changed all that. In Banaras there was no tarmac. The smaller plane simply cruised down onto a grassy strip. From the windows, I saw women in *saris* stand up, appearing suddenly from the tall grasses. They'd been stooping till the plane's engines stopped. Outside the fence of the airport, in a wide paved road, camels and elephants, mounted by lone riders, padded slowly along. "This," I thought as my heart leapt, "*this* is the real India!"

Now that we had arrived, I could think back on all that it had taken to get here—from the first letter arriving from the Wisconsin Program to the actual plane trip. Before journeying East I had had to travel West. I was now one of twenty-five juniors selected from colleges and universities around the country to represent the program in India. To do so, all twenty-five of us first had to go through an intensive ten-week period of summer school studies in order to prepare. For my program in '67–'68, the summer classes were held at the University of Illinois's Urbana campus. From Cornell, this meant that I had to travel westward, to study language, Indian philosophy, and a full round of orientation classes.

At our first group meeting, I found myself again in a familiar position: I was the only black student in the program. Still, this was a new and interesting group of people. All were there because they wanted to go to India, and none of us had the slightest inkling of how much the trip would change our lives.

We learned the proper way to greet a person, that is, how to give *anjali,* a greeting with bowed head and cupped hands. We also learned how to eat with our right hand—there is quite an etiquette involved, since allowing food to reach below certain joints of the fingers is considered very poor style. And we practiced the ritual of squatting so as to be able to handle the holes in the floor that would soon serve as our only toilets.

I had also made a few new friends. The first was an Antioch student named Elea Mideke. A small olive-skinned girl with large eyes, Elea was an artist. In Washington, D.C., where her father worked for the Labor Department, she'd had shows of her sculpture and pen-and-ink drawings since she was twelve. Her love, however, was for the horses she raised and cared for on the family's place in Virginia. In Elea's eyes, I saw a sadness. When we became close enough friends, she had told me that she was in mourning for a wondrous horse of hers that had recently died, in spite of her desperate attempts to save it. I loved Elea immediately because it was evident that she loved so deeply.

She also traveled *very* lightly. She'd brought a bicycle with her to Urbana. She liked to go riding in the cool evenings. When we all left for India, her baggage was the lightest of anyone's. She took only a drawing book and a Rapidograph pen, a tiny—and ancient—Kodak camera, and one skimpy dress that could be easily washed and dried, saying that the people in India wore clothes so surely we could get those there.

Another new friend was Jim Duncan. He had a sophisticated prankster mentality, and broad grins came easily to his lips. Jim and I liked the same kind of music: folk, soul, and heavy doses of Stevie Wonder.

Those who were going to Osmania University in the South studied Telegu. The rest of us studied Hindi, whether first- or second-year, and each of us enrolled in an elective course related to what we thought we might wish to study in India. The ten weeks were challenging and fun. Then the summer program came to an end. We were given a last weekend off and told to gather again at Chicago's O'Hare International Airport. Amid teeming families of Indians with their huge suitcases and massive bundles wrapped in cloth and burlap, we twenty-five boarded the giant iron bird, beginning an unknown and magical spree.

Our first stop was London. After several hours of waiting in the international transit lounge, we were informed that our plane was disabled. Engineers were trying to fix the problem. Not the most auspicious start. Finally, on another plane, we took off from London headed for Moscow. Our route also had been changed.

Landing in Moscow was an eerie experience. We were greeted by military police who ordered us to turn over our passports before herding us into a tiny, sparsely decorated room. Through the few windows opening onto the rest of the airport, we could see Russians. I was surprised that our stereotypes seemed to be confirmed here. The people moved slowly and, it seemed, broodingly. There were a number of old women sitting, all wearing black clothing and dark scarves. There were soldiers with guns. The scene was somber. It occurred to me that next we might be loaded onto trucks and driven away to some prison, never to be seen or heard from again. Things were not helped by our chaperon's uneasy and ineffective pleas for the return of our passports.

Then Jim went into action. He decided to steal the framed picture of Lenin that was the sole wall decoration in our detainment room. Maybe this was Jim's way of breaking the ice, but it threw the few of us who knew about his scheme into an extra panic. "Don't, Jim! Not even in jest!" we pleaded. "Look, man, these soldiers are serious!" Jim made clucking sounds with his teeth and gave us winks as he eyed the picture. Hours went by. By the time the soldiers suddenly ordered us to reboard the bus that would take us back to the plane, we felt like dishrags. And Jim had *not* gotten the Lenin picture.

Now, at last in Banaras, we were divided into pairs and loaded onto rickshaws, our suitcases or backpacks resting beside us or under our feet. It was the first time I had ever had a skinny, shabbily dressed man pull me and another person and our bags by pedaling. I instantly felt that we were all too fat and too heavy. On the other hand, traveling by rickshaw gave us the time to look at things and to see where it was that we were; to begin to see this strange and dusty, this hot, magical, and enchanting place.

We had a pretty strict regimen: we met each morning at the Wisconsin House on the campus of Banaras Hindu University. There, we ate breakfast together—usually *chapatis,* or dry, wheat-flour crepes, presoaked fruit, and jam—before adjourning to other rooms in the House for our Hindi classes. Then we went to our respective university classes. We also had to begin planning our individual field projects. There were to be two week-long gatherings of the entire group, one at Christmastime and one at the end of the program, and we were not to leave our respective campuses until those times.

I didn't take well to rules and could sometimes be persuasive in my rowdiness. The nine of us had not been in Banaras for a whole week when I convinced my new friend John to join me on a sight-seeing trip. John was a tall, straight-laced, and ruddy-faced mid-Westerner. He was quiet, conservative, and had as his ambition becoming a Christian missionary in India. He was not exactly my type, but I knew that a male traveling companion was a good idea. Single women traveling alone in India were prey for derision, or worse. John and I snuck off to the Banaras train station, stood in interminable lines to get tickets, and finally boarded the "13 Up" headed north to Delhi. The "13 Down" ran south and east, all the way to Calcutta. We were jostled by hordes of staring crowds, some friendly when we tried out our fledgling Hindi, others menacing and glaring. At Delhi we made the appropriate connections and, a few hours later, arrived in Agra. John and I wanted to see the grand Taj Mahal.

It is rare in life when an experience far exceeds expectations. Seeing the Taj Mahal was such an experience. Constructed as a mausoleum for the Turkish empress Muntaz Mahal, the white marble building was begun in 1632. It is said that it took twenty thousand laborers and twenty-two years to complete. The finest stonemasons, carvers, and engineers were brought in. The marble is delicately inlaid with precious and semiprecious gems from India, China, Tibet, and Baghdad. Sitting at the end of an elegant canaled walkway, the light playing off its marble, the Taj is ethereally luminous, at once simple and majestic, immense and fragile, a true wonder. But our trip had been a "no-no"; and thereafter we were effectively grounded. John and I were satisfied. We had begun to appreciate the varied richness of this land.

What the program folk had not succeeded in doing back in Urbana was to get me to give up smoking. The habit ultimately forced me to leave my residence at the Women's Hostel on campus and to move to International House, where married foreign students lived. I welcomed the move for the single room and the added freedom it gave me. The smoking habit also greatly strengthened my bonds with various rickshaw *wallas.*

Rickshaw *wallas* typically smoked beedies, tiny dried aromatic leaves wrapped around a few pieces of tobacco and tied with thin thread. Beedies were the poor man's cigarette, and I often shared my own smokes. Traveling this way, I got a wholly other, and much more intimate, view. With their typically frail bodies, the rickshaw *wallas* worked extremely hard from sun-up till sunset, carrying heavy burdens long distances for a few pennies, or *paisa.* They ate very little, preferring to send their earnings home, back to their families in various villages. Consequently, though each tried to maintain a sense that their efforts would be successful, their life spans after entering the profession were usually no more than seven years. For days on end, I would ride with a few of them. I asked them to give me tours of Banaras, of their special places, and still feeling guilty about being pulled along by another person's labors, I paid them in rupees.

The rickshaw *wallas* taught me to speak Bhojpuri, the dialect of Banaras and its surroundings. Bhojpuri is quite different from Hindi. All the tenses of the verb "to be" are completely collapsed. For example, riding along and passing a wedding tent, the rickshaw *walla* would say, "*Shaadi ho.*" Now, *shaadi* is the word for "wedding," but this simplified phrase can mean either that a wedding was about to happen, was happening, or had happened. It is impossible to know if one doesn't know already.

Banaras, also known by its ancient names, Kashi and Varanasi, is revered for its three-mile stretch of seventy *ghats,* all leading down to the most sacred of waters for any Hindu. Indeed, for Hindus, Banaras is *the* holiest city because here there is the confluence of three separate sacred rivers: the Varuna, the Asi, and the Ganges, the latter being known as *Ganga Mataji,* the great Goddess Ganga, Mother-source.

I spent countless hours roaming along the *ghats.* I especially liked to watch the early morning activities here: Brahmins praying and doing their ablutions, men and women *dobhis* washing clothes, women bathing and managing to change their *saris* without exposing their bodies, flower-garland sellers sitting among mounds of flowers, naked *sadhus,* or holy men, walking or seated, praying the whole time.

It was along the *ghats* that I witnessed two scenes that made indelible impressions on me. During the first, I noticed a group of young boys playing and chatting together. One of the young boys was animatedly relating a narrative. When he'd finished, three of the boys laughed, pushed, and patted him on the shoulders. A fourth young boy stood motionless, his face showing no emotion. Puzzled by the seeming and sudden exclusion, I took the chance to ask them, in Hindi, what had just occurred. With no guile whatever, the storyteller and one other boy chimed in together. The first boy had been telling a certain joke. The three boys who laughed were of similar castes and so could enjoy the joke; but the fourth youngster was of a lower caste. Therefore, he knew he could not participate in their merriment.

I witnessed the second scene early one morning near Asi Ghat. I sat on a flagstone near the water. I was marveling at the thought of this murky and polluted river being venerated as the purest water on earth. Every Hindu wanted to be cremated along these *ghats* so that his ashes might be sprinkled into this purifying source. My eyes focused on a certain Brahmin wearing his sacred thread. He was perhaps in his mid-fifties, white-haired, and big-bellied. Standing waist-deep in the water, he turned as he prayed to face the four directions. Occasionally, he squatted down completely so that his body and head disappeared momentarily into the brownish water. He was clearly a devout Hindu. Suddenly he, and as a consequence, I, noticed a form floating in the water. It was a small body, wrapped in white cloth and tied around the neck, waist, and feet. It bobbed and moved, untethered from its rock-mooring. The man interrupted his prayers, spat in disgust at the corpse, and then continued praying. India possessed abundant riches, but it also had a grim side. After these encounters I felt pretty low. Two joyous discoveries brought me back to life: the music of India and meeting the Tibetans.

Music was everywhere in Banaras. There were often all-night concerts held at the Hanuman Monkey Temple not far from BHU. Music was also a part of my curriculum, for in addition to Hindi, Buddhist philosophy, and a research project on contemporary Hindi poetry, I had enrolled in an extra course in music. Three evenings a week I met with other students at the circular-shaped music building with its open central courtyard to study sitar and tabla. Our classes were taught individually, as tutorials, but first we all came together in the courtyard to sing India's national anthem as the sun sank down.

I enjoyed sitar, once my two left-hand fingers developed the deep grooved calluses necessary to play the instrument. I had first to suffer through three or four weeks of painful and bloody finger seasoning, continually pressing and pulling on the superthin steel wire. There were many fine musicians studying at BHU at the time. One such student was Ravi Shankar's nephew, Ananda. He played passionately but must have been under a lot of pressure, given his uncle's great renown. In terms of sheer technique, two women students were best, though they showed no intensity or even love for the music. They played along, chewing gum and looking totally disinterested. Still, both graduated with honors, ahead of Ananda, who finished third.

But for most of the students at BHU at that time there were larger, more pressing issues. During 1967–68, there were Hindu/Muslim riots in the city and a growing anti-English campaign on campus. Students marched and demonstrated against English-language textbooks and exams; they wanted their textbooks in Hindi. It seemed to me to be a reasonable enough desire. But converting the old colonial system and developing new curricular materials were well beyond the financial means of the school or, I suspected, of the Indian government. What such political unrest meant for us Wisconsin folk was that often there would be no school. Classes were canceled or halted due to student unrest. Sometimes, if we were off campus when a big rally started, we found ourselves blocked from getting back in. At such times, I was aided by my friendships with various rickshaw *wallas* and with an African man named Cletus Semiono who was a medical student at BHU. Cletus, a young man from Tanzania, had a nice apartment not too far from campus and a wonderful stack of great soul music.

The whole world was in an uproar; change was in the air, and I was beginning to turn away from the vision of Japan that had led me East. It was a trip to Sarnath, where the Buddha Shakyamuni delivered his first sermon, that would change my life forever.

Sarnath lies about seven miles north of the center of Banaras. To get there one has to navigate through the throngs of people in the tightly packed areas of the city. I enlisted the services of one of my rickshaw *walla* friends for the day.

On the outskirts of Banaras, space opened up. The breeze actually blew. The road seemed to widen; bustling ceased. Going to Sarnath was like going to another world. I spent hours walking through the park, surveying the giant *stupa,* circumambulating it, or slowly making my way through the museum. I enjoyed just sitting at one or other of the tea stalls, where some shade from the blistering sun was available. I liked watching the Indian art of making tea: throwing globs of sugar and milk into vats of boiling water, all the while singing the familiar chant: *"Chai, chai, gurum chai,"* "Tea, tea, hot tea!"

Burgundy-colored monks often stopped at the tea stalls on their way to do errands or to catch a rickshaw into town. These were among the first Tibetans living in exile. I don't remember how I first connected with some of these monks, but somehow I found myself being invited into one of their monasteries. After a short walk, we turned off the dusty road into a green courtyard that opened onto a two-storied white structure. The monastery was a little oasis of religious activity. I saw monks studying. I could hear them chanting. I found the atmosphere very pleasing.

Perhaps it was because of my genuine interest in Buddhism, and the fact that this was my main BHU course, that I was so readily accepted and taken in by the Tibetans. Perhaps it was just because these gentle people actually practiced what the Buddha had taught, and so radiated compassion to all beings. But especially after my two negative encounters on the *ghats,* this place became a haven for me, a home away from home. My sojourns here became more regular, and another level of appreciation for India opened up. I found a warmth and acceptance here that somehow, so far from rural Alabama, made me feel at home. Still, even in the midst of this idyll, that other home had a way of rearing its ugly head.

WHAT CASTE ARE YOU?

❀

Just outside the gates of Banaras Hindu University stood the little town of Lanka. On one side of its single street were laundry shops, called *dobhi* stands, and assorted vegetable stands; on the other stood a vast array of textile and dry-goods shops. The street teemed with people, bicycle rickshaws, and free-roaming cows, goats, water buffaloes, and other animals. It was strewn with large piles of fresh cow or buffalo dung, steaming in the sun's heat. To get into or out of BHU, one had to navigate this one-street town. In the evenings, when the sun's heat had cooled, various groups of students poured into Lanka, whether for business or promenade.

Two of the little stands were favorites of mine. One was a *dobhi* stall I visited with some regularity. My newly tailored Punjabi-styled dresses and pants outfits, called *salwa kamises,* were washed by being pounded upon the rocks of the creek that ran just behind the line of stalls. Good *dobhis* washed and pressed clothes and returned them to customers in neat stacks tied with a cord. But an unscrupulous or careless *dobhi* could easily destroy one's entire wardrobe of thin cotton clothes. One had to find, usually through trial and error, a good one. Having found such a one, I stuck with him.

I also had a favorite dry-foods stall in Lanka. Every couple of days or so I stopped here during my evening stroll or bike ride to purchase little bags of salted crackers that reminded me of Ritz crackers in miniature. The owner, or *jamandaar,* of this particular stall was a stout Punjabi Sikh. He wore his hair knotted atop his head, tucked beneath a tiny white coverlet. He had a white beard, too, that he kept tightly rolled to his face with a sort of fine black net. The man usually sat on the platform of his stall, one leg tucked in, and swatted away the flies that buzzed around his myriad glass jars containing peanuts, cashews, crackers, and rock candy. Sweets and salty snacks were his goods, and he seemed to do a brisk business.

The *jamandaar* began to recognize me and before long greeted me with a gentle smile whenever I approached, asking only what size bag of crackers I wished that day. Actually, the question came in terms of weight: "How many *tolas"* or grams, did I wish? One day, after I'd been at BHU for about two months, the *jamandaar* took the occasion of my visit to ask me a question that, he explained, he had been pondering for some time. "Would it be all right," he queried, "to ask you, madam, a personal question?"

"Well, that depends on what it is," I said. With this half-consent, the *jamandaar* proceeded.

"Madam, what *caste* are you?"

For a moment, I was completely taken aback.

"Caste?" I responded to his question with a question. "Well . . ." Thinking that he might mean which country I came from, I finally said, "I am an American."

"But, madam, you don't look like the other American students here at BHU. Your hair is different . . . and your skin—"

"I *assure* you," I interrupted him, "I am an American. We

don't have castes in America," I began to explain. "I am a black American."

To my amazement, the *jamandaar* next said, "Oh . . . American Negro. So sorry, madam. I am so sorry."

This declaration, offered so directly and with such sympathy, left me speechless. Here in this one-street town of Lanka, some ten thousand miles away from the United States, this Indian *jamandaar* was empathizing with me about my unfortunate caste. Here, amid cows and dung and washermen and every manner of sentient being, I felt completely and utterly exposed. Worse, I was even pitied. As the old folk back home used to say, "You could have bought me with a ha' penny."

I had thought that India offered a refuge for me, a respite from concerns of race. That evening's chat with the *jamandaar* abruptly changed all that. What struck me in particular was the *jamandaar's* knowledge about the world. He sat in his tiny stall in Lanka but he was a man who had a much broader view of things. On any number of subsequent discussions with people in different parts of India, I found this same wide-ranging knowledge, whether about American literary classics, Bette Davis movies, or international politics. They were much more cultured than Americans. *We* seemed to be under the mistaken impression that the United States was the only place worth knowing about.

I was forced to confront the whole notion of caste—both the system in India and my own denials about the existence of caste in America. The term used to denote caste in India is *varna,* and *varna* literally means "color"; it is cognate with the English word "varnish." When the Aryans (formerly from areas in southern Europe) had invaded India between 2000–1500 B.C., they had set up the *varna* system. It was intended to distinguish them from the darker-skinned indigenous peoples of the Indus Valley civilization whom the Aryans conquered and whom they referred to both as *dasyas* (servants) and as *dracus* (dark-skinned). Clearly then—all claims to the contrary by some prominent African Americans that India is a wondrous land of brown-skinned rulers and people without discrimination—the original meaning and present-day use of the *varna* system is as a color- and racially-based form of social and economic discrimination. One's *varna* still determines one's occupation, making the term, strictly, more akin to "class" than "color," though the two concepts are intimately linked. On that score, the *jamandaar* was right. Saying that I was a black American did mean that my class status was lower than most other Americans. There was no way of denying that.

After I licked my wounds and braved it enough to return to his shop, the *jamandaar* told me in subsequent talks that I looked to him more like the people of Assam, who were round-faced and fair-skinned. As he had wondered about my origins, this had been his earliest speculation. Now that actual origins were out, he and I began a series of conversations about race, societal structure, and politics in the United States. India and I were meeting; we were making contact.

BLISSED-OUT AT
SWAYAMBHUNATH

൭ഗ

The Wisconsin Program was over. The twenty-five of us each made our plans for travel to Asia. My friend Elea and I decided to visit Nepal together. Traveling there was an adventure in itself, as we sat huddled amid folk and animals alike on an overcrowded bus that wound its way ever so slowly up from the blistering heat of the *terrai* plains and climbed thousands of feet into the ever-greening countryside of this remote mountain kingdom. We had heard it said that "India is like the sun; Nepal like the moon." We found the analogy perfect. The terraced hillsides of Nepal sported verdant fields of rice. The white-snow peaks of the Himalayas, or "Abode of Snows," could be seen in the distance. From the hot, crowded intensity of India, where few people smiled, we found ourselves in a place of lush, green spaciousness, where smiles came easily. It was better than a vacation; it was like arriving in paradise. Then, too, it just so happened that Elea and I found ourselves in Kathmandu Valley during a very special time for Buddhists. At Swayambhunath, a three-day celebration in honor of the Buddha's birthday was already in progress.

Kathmandu Valley is the site of two of Tibetan Buddhism's most famous reliquary shrines, or *stupas*. The first is Swayambhunath, located atop a green hillock to the west of the city's center; the other is Bodhanath, a mammoth *stupa* situated amid a bustling town of shops and monasteries in the flatlands of the valley lying north of the city.

For two entire days before Elea and I ventured up to the top of Swayambhunath, hundreds upon hundreds of devout Buddhists had been circumambulating not just the *stupa* on top but the very base of Swayambhunath hill itself. They made this much lengthier circuit slowly, many carrying huge stones upon their backs as a form of penance. Some made the bottom circuit by doing full body-length prostrations in the holy dust. As Elea and I approached the entrance to the shrine at the bottom of the tree-dotted hill, I was deeply moved by the sincere outpouring of love and devotion evidenced in the faces of these Tibetans.

After the first few flagstone steps upward, we encountered three brightly painted stone Buddha statues, each roughly ten feet tall. People had made offerings of flowers and even of cooked rice grains that they stuck onto the Buddhas' lips.

Slowly, we climbed the almost three hundred steps up to Swayambhunath. Often we, like many others, stood to the side or squatted to take a rest before continuing the long climb. The path became steeper, and for the last fifty or so feet, the steps were so steep that I was forced to hold on to the long metal railing cemented into the center of the steps and pull myself up.

Having made it to the entrance, I leaned my body against the giant, ten-foot-long *dorje* that greets all pilgrims. A huge gilded replica of the "thunderbolt" or "diamond scepter" wielded by tantric masters, this gleaming *dorje* at the terrace entrance to the *stupa* became my resting place. Elea, less winded than me, scurried off to have a look around.

In the rarefied air of the place, my senses began to focus on the sounds all around me and the thousands of folk up there. The Tibetans and the Newari Buddhists—men, women, and children—were making their way around the *stupa* in a clockwise direction. As they did so, they each turned the bottoms of the brass prayer wheels that were inset all around the *stupa*. I listened to the *prattle, prattle, prattle* of the turning prayer wheels. In the four cardinal directions of the *stupa* were little altars. At the top and center of each altar there was a tiny bell. As each pilgrim came to that altar, he or she briefly paused, silently prayed, and gently touched their foreheads to the bell. I heard the *ting, ting, ting* of the bells and knew that each represented the touch of a human head. Too exhausted to move, and still resting upon the golden *dorje,* I was transported to a realm of heavenly sounds—*prattle, prattle, ting, ting, prattle, prattle, ting*—at a place where heaven and earth seemed to meet. Then, Elea reappeared.

"You should go over there," she said, motioning to a raised doorway to my right, "and look right."

I responded, "El, I don't know if I can make it over there!"

"It'll be all right. If you *never* do anything else, it will be worth it!" was her reply.

Somehow, I willed my body up and away from the *dorje.* In the doorway was a crush of people. I managed to squeeze myself into the right-most corner. For balance, my right knee pressed into the back of a monk who was sitting on the floor facing away from me. This was the entrance to a small temple. Immediately, I noticed the fifteen-foot gilded statue of Maitreya, the future Buddha, known as the Buddha of Love. It stood in the very center of the tiny room and towered above everything else. For a fleeting moment I caught sight of Elea. She'd followed me in, and I saw her disappear behind the statue.

Elea had told me to look to the right. As I began to do so, I noticed, just out of the corner of my eye, two shaven-headed Tibetan monks. Their cheeks filled with air as they forcefully blew into their long horns, each perhaps twelve feet long, resting on the floor. I saw the monks blow into their horns, then sit back, straight up, in meditative posture. Then, their mouths completely removed from the horns, the sound issued forth, came around in back of the great Maitreya statue, rounded the room, and gently struck my left ear, pushing me over and causing me actually to look toward the right. As I looked at the figures seated on the floor, I saw six chanting monks facing me. Another six sat even closer to me, their heads facing the other monks. My knee was pressing into the sixth monk's back. Everything began to move in slow motion. The monks were conducting special chants in honor of this unique occasion. The Tibetan temple paintings, or *thangkas,* usually kept concealed from public view, were, for this occasion only, completely unveiled.

I looked into the eyes of those six monks facing me. They were gone completely to some other place. And when I *saw* them, *they took me along, too,* wherever they were. I felt completely and utterly gone, and completely and utterly blissful. I had never felt as happy, as light, and as overjoyed as I was then.

I have no idea how long I remained in this blissful state. The next thing I remember feeling was Elea tugging on my shirt.

"Jan, it's getting dark," she said. "We have to go; to get down from here."

"No," I whispered. *"I'm never going to leave this place!"*

I don't remember how we got down and back into town that night, but we did. I knew that I meant what I had earlier said to Elea: *I'm never going to leave this place.*

Nothing could top the beginning of our sojourn in Nepal. Still, there were some other spots we wanted to visit. So, two or three days after my Swayambhunath experience, Elea and I went out to the great *stupa* at Bodhanath. In those years, Bodhanath *stupa* was striking. As we approached, the gigantic whitewashed mound surmounted by huge

mysterious eyes that faced all the four directions rose up from the verdant green of rice paddies. It towered over the roofs of the buildings
encircling it.

Elea and I wandered into all the little shops inside the circular compound and watched the life that unfolded on the broad-bricked walkway that served as the path around this massive structure. During the
warmth of the day, people laid out thick mats there, upon which they
dried grains or chili peppers. Groups of men played dice games. There
was a brisk activity of trade in the air as tourists entered and floated out
of shops, after being served tea and bargaining for ancient Tibetan
treasures and modern curios. During the evening hours, the cobbled
path became a teaming thoroughfare. People took their promenades
there. They met and conversed with each other, telling their prayer
beads as they went. Some folk walked alone and silently spun the
stupa's inset prayer wheels. A mass of people, as individuals and in
groups, living their social and religious lives seamlessly.

Elea and I went into a Tibetan woman's dress shop. In the tiny
shop, the woman sold jewelry and a large selection of Tibetan *chuba,*
or dresses. Suddenly, a group of perhaps five or six Tibetan monks
came in. It was hard for everyone to fit into the small space. The tallest
monk in the group was also the most striking in appearance. His forehead was very broad, his skin very fair, and his eyes were beautiful. He
seemed also to be the one in charge. The monks peered at Elea and me.
We smiled and said *"Tashi delek,"* the Tibetan greeting we had learned.
The tall monk approached me, looked directly into my eyes, and
pointed at me with his finger. In a gentle but authoritative voice, he
said, surprisingly in English, "You should stay here and study with us."

The regal bearing of this monk, and then his utterly charming manner of speaking, melted my knees before I heard what he'd actually
said. It was as if, in Stevie Wonder's words, "the love bug bit me." I
would agree to anything he proposed. When words finally formed and

issued from my mouth, I heard myself saying, "Why, yes! I'd love to!" But then something jolted me, and I quickly added, "But . . . but . . . my mother says I have to come home!" I had been gone nine months. Cornell and Alabama, school and civil rights, seemed so far away.

Every day of our last two weeks I made it my business to go out to Bodha and see the charming monk. His name was Lobsang Chonjor. He was perhaps in his late twenties and had been enrobed since he was seven. He was at the Gelukpa Monastery, just across an alley on the back side of the *stupa*. It was the monastery with the most monks, about sixty in all. Lobsang Chonjor always greeted me respectfully, had tea prepared for me, and made time to talk. Like thousands of other Tibetans, Chonjor and his fellow monks had fled Tibet in 1959 when the Chinese invaded their country. It was from him that I first really began to learn about how Tibetan Buddhism was practiced and about how life for these refugees was progressing.

Lobsang introduced me to the abbot of the monastery and to a whole host of other monks there. Happy faces and hot tea greeted me daily. It was a very active place, especially its kitchen, where all community-related business was carried on. Lobsang was at the time the "keeper of the keys" of the monastery. He was its general manager.

When the time came for Elea and me to leave Nepal, Chonjor and several of the other monks escorted us to the airport. They draped us in the traditional white silk scarves that Tibetans give to both arriving and departing friends.

I returned to the States, to my senior year at Cornell, and to my old friend Randy. But during all of my senior year, I corresponded with Lobsang. Following the tumultuous events of that next year, I would see him again.

TOO GULLIBLE?

৩৩

While I had been in India and Nepal, Randy had hooked up with a guy named Robbie. I had never met him. When I returned to the States, she was waitressing for the summer at a hotel in the Catskills, and I went there to see her. As we talked in the tiny little cabin she shared with three other girls, there was a tap on her door. It was Robbie, a tall guy, lean and lanky, with long flowing curly black hair that reached halfway to his waist. Though Rand introduced me, he said nothing, simply giving me a silent nod. He was the head busboy at the hotel that summer, and that's where the two of them had met. As Rand whispered to me "He's the king around here," Robbie took out a cigarette. His only comment was "Hot, isn't it?" He took off his shirt and walked back out onto the little porch. He reared back his head and shook out his hair. Then he lit the cigarette and took a long-legged leap from the porch. Rand and I watched as he ran up the grassy hill that stretched upward from the cabins, waving his arms in the air. A soft rain was falling. Robbie's tall frame and long dark hair, galloping up that verdant hill in obvious enjoyment of the cooling mist, actually cut a handsome figure. But I turned immediately to Rand and said, "This stuff makes me sick! I think you need to leave." She smiled and shrugged it off. "Look, Jan, I like him a lot. True, the living conditions aren't the best here, but I'm making money and I'm *not* leaving." And that was that.

She did like Robbie a lot. And some time later, she announced that they were getting married that summer. I still thought of Robbie as just a hippie, a guy who hadn't even spoken to me, who had just come in, loosened his hair, and gone galloping off into the rain. But Rand was my friend. I went to the wedding.

Randy's folks had planned a big Jewish wedding out at their home in Syosset. There were about fifty guests. The rabbi who was to perform the ceremony was coming in from the city. He wasn't familiar with Long Island and, while trying to find their house, he got lost. As everyone anxiously awaited him, two separate groups of wedding guests began to form. All of us young folk, Rand and Robbie's friends, clustered outdoors on one side of the house, while all the older folk were either inside the house or gathered out back on the bricked patio.

The wedding was a story in itself because Rand's parents were getting a divorce at the time, and her father actually left the house for good that night after the wedding. So Rand's mom and dad were not speaking to each other but were still trying to entertain the guests while everybody waited for the rabbi. Then there was Robbie's diabetic father, who just needed to eat something. Among those of us outside, joints started passing around, while all the older folk started to engage in heavy drinking. It was quite a scene.

From time to time, various older folk would come up to me and say, "Oh! *You* must be Jan, Randy's friend!" And I'd say, "Why, yes! *How* did you guess?" Not only was I the only person there wearing a gold lamé *sari* and so clearly Randy's friend just back from India; I was also the only black person who wasn't carrying around a tray of appetizers in my hands.

By the time the rabbi showed up, all of us were either stoned or drunk. But the wedding ceremony, at last, took place. Robbie ritually crushed the glass. They were married. People could eat. And Rand's dad left the house. In the wee hours of the next morning, a number of us curled up in sleeping bags on the floor.

After that, the three of us continued to do what the two of us (Rand and I) had done before. And throughout everything that followed, these two people became my closest friends. My initial dislike for Robbie was soon forgotten when I came to know him better. Rob was quiet, almost withdrawn, and liked to draw, whereas Rand and I were verbal, always chattering away. Whenever the three of us were together, Rand and I would be animatedly involved in some discussion, while Robbie would be off somewhere in a quiet corner with his drawing pad and pen. But when we paused and asked Rob what he thought about the issue, he'd always be right there. His response might be short, just a word or two, but if we looked at what he had been doodling while we were ranting on, his drawings captured exactly the essence of the topic, deftly epitomized in lines of flowing dark ink. Rob's most enduring qualities were that he was genuinely gentle and nonjudgmental. Though he was as political as we were, I never heard him say a derogatory thing about anyone.

Rob had grown up in Brooklyn, 1084 New York Avenue in Flatbush. He and his young cronies had lived a fast and wild life. For fun, they hung out on the roofs of their apartment buildings, smoking and listening to music and, sometimes, taking daredevil leaps from building to building. At other times, a group of them would play chicken in the subway lines, sneaking into the stations and standing on the tracks, waiting until the last possible moment before jumping out of the way of an oncoming train. Sometimes, he told me, they had only enough time to fling themselves up tight against the blackened walls before an advancing train roared by, feeling the great wind gusts whipping their hair about as they screamed. Of course, these were things that their parents were never told. They were Brooklyn kids—young, tough, inner-city hippies.

Rand and Rob got their own apartment in Brooklyn, and it became a sort of regular affair for the three of us to visit Rob's folks, Walter and Mickey, in their second-story walk-up in Flatbush. The tiny, cramped apartment was clearly too small for their family. Robbie had an older sister and two younger ones, a younger brother and a twin brother, Alan, though they were not identical and not very much alike. Alan eventually enlisted and went off to the Navy; Robbie managed to get a 4-F during his induction physical. He would have run away to Canada if he had passed. He wanted no part of fighting a war in Vietnam he didn't believe in. Rob was the first child to actually leave home, and by the time he did he was sleeping on the couch in the living room. They were a close and happy family, a good thing given such tight quarters.

What immediately struck me upon entering the place was its two floor-to-ceiling cupboards that flanked either side of the doorway. Each was stuffed to the gills with sweets—cookies, candy, cream-filled Ho-Hos, Mallowmars, Hydrox, you name it. Robbie's dad was a salesman for such goodies, and though he couldn't himself enjoy them, being a diabetic, it was clear that everyone else in the family had a giant sweet tooth. The three of us would file in, Rob would grab a bag of cookies from one of the pantries, we'd all turn right, into the tiny kitchen where Walter and Mickey sat, and milk was immediately brought out. It was like a ritual. Their tiniest of kitchens had barely enough room for the table and six chairs that were crowded around it. Clotheslines on rollers stretched out from the single kitchen window over to the next building's walls. It was a classic neighborhood tenement. Rob's mom, Mickey, smoked cigarettes, and that made her, for me, an instant friend. The five of us crunched around the table began our conversations, which were usually casual and chatty, over milk and cookies and smokes. I felt welcomed and included.

When Robbie's folks moved to a larger place, a row house in Carnarsie, the three of us went over to see them. Just before we visited, Carnarsie had suffered a huge racial incident, covered in all the papers. It had involved a black kid and a Jewish man, and the neighborhood was still tense. But we weren't thinking about that when we took the train to Carnarsie; we were just dropping by to see Rob's folks in their new place.

It just happened that on the Sunday afternoon we chose, Rob's folks were having guests. They were entertaining another Jewish couple. As usual, Rob entered first, and I could hear his folks greet him happily. Next, Ran went through the door, and they said, "Hey, kiddo!" And then I walked through. The whole room instantly went silent.

The heavy silence let me know immediately that it was about me; my presence had embarrassed Robbie's folks, and they were ashamed before their guests that their son had brought his black friend home with him. Both Rob and Rand realized with me what had just happened. Robbie moved into the kitchen, nervously inviting Rand and me in there. But the set-up in Mickey and Walter's new house was different, and there was only a half counter separating the kitchen from the spacious living room. The three of us could still be seen by the four people who sat in there, speechless. Their conversation had abruptly halted at the instant of my entrance, and the embarrassed silence hung heavily in the air.

I couldn't stand it, but I couldn't speak. I turned and ran out of the place. I ran, sobbing and overcome with rage, all the way to the nearest subway stop. That summer I had a job in the city. I caught a train back to Manhattan and up to my own place. The roar of the train barely muffled the sound of my sobs. For the whole trip, I was shaking. I was uncontrollable and inconsolable.

Not long after I reached my apartment, Rob and Rand knocked on my door. They tried to make apologies. Robbie said he wasn't going to stay "for that kind of shit," so they'd come to be with me. These two were really my friends. They didn't try to make excuses for a racist world. They regretted what had happened and wanted me to know that. They wanted to see how I was doing and to be with me; to stay, and to stand, with me.

But what I hadn't been able to yell at Rob's parents, I screamed now at them, and at the top of my lungs: "Robbie, your parents or not! If I had had a machine gun, Rob, I would have blown them away, all of them! Blown them away, I tell you! And the reason I would have blown them away is because *no other black person, no other human being, should ever have to feel the way they made me feel; feel that hated, that despised, just because of the color of their skin!* I would've killed them, Rob! I would've killed them!" They let me scream. And my body shook and shivered; and I cried and cried, and crushed myself into a ball on my bed. Because I had *meant* what I said.

For the whole of two days my body quivered. I was sick with rage. My heart, I was sure, was going to explode. My head was all crazy. I was feverish and had chills at the same time. I could not eat. I could not sit or lie still. My mind turned around a single thought: murder, slaughter. That was the first time in my adult life that I came to know from my own experience how truly dangerous and destructive anger is, how mentally and physically sickening it is for the person who suffers it; how wholly afflictive and harmful it is, not only for others at whom it might be directed but also for the one experiencing it.

Randy and Robbie stayed with me those two days. Though they both had jobs and lived somewhere else, they knew how upset, how enraged I was; and they knew *why.* They stayed to comfort me because they had come to understand the depths of my agony and their folks' part in its creation.

On an earlier trip to Cornell, both of my parents had met Randy, and they liked her. They knew that she was a good friend of mine. But at home in Birmingham, I had sometimes heard them say, in conversation with other relatives, almost embarrassed themselves, "Well, Dean thinks some white people are okay; she thinks some whites can be trusted." Their comments made it clear that they thought I was, in general, too trusting in this regard, too gullible. Relatives had said, "Well, she does live in another world, but white people are pretty much the same everywhere." Whenever I'd tried to explain that I thought I had *genuine* white friends, friends who were not racists, inevitably I had been cut off with that frustratingly stereotypical question: "Yes, baby, it's good to have good friends, but would they ever invite you to their homes for dinner?" "Dinner?" I'd said. "Yes, dinner and more! Not all white people are racist. Some people in the world are actually like me; they see people *just as people!*" But my response was always met with incredulity. My family members just shook their heads. I could hear them saying silently, "Poor Dean! She just doesn't know yet." Now, after Carnarsie, I was left wondering whether my folks might have been right.

For years I had been living in a white world. I knew that lots of whites only paid lip service to the notion that all people were equal, even the most liberal ones who flattered themselves for their open-mindedness, who made it their life's struggle to bring about a level playing field. I had seen my share of two-faced whites. But I thought I was wise enough to tell the difference.

I knew some whites for whom I was the exceptional black person; not like the majority of blacks whom they didn't and couldn't trust. Randy's father, Mel, was like this. Mel ran a small business in a rough section of Queens. He'd once been attacked as he headed to work by a black man who had tried to rob him. Since then, Mel thought all the blacks around there wanted either to cheat him or to rob him. He thought they hated him. He didn't trust any blacks on the street. He was afraid of them; they made him uptight. I was Mel's exceptional black. He'd told me himself that I was nothing at all like most of the blacks he daily encountered. "Jan's different. She's smart; she's not like all the others." It was an attitude shared by lots of white people. And, of course, those exceptional blacks are the most like them; they're usually light-skinned, have gone to their schools, can speak their language. I liked Mel, in spite of his fear of blacks. I saw him as a well-meaning though biased man, shaped by his upbringing, his experience, and his fear.

I had encountered other whites within our nation's institutions of higher learning who, despite claims to the contrary, were racist at their cores. When I was applying for a Danforth Fellowship for graduate school in Buddhist Studies, I had to be interviewed in New York by a Fordham professor. He was a fairly young man, a philosophy professor, who sported a long wispy beard. It seemed that for most of the interview he kept trying to get a rise out of me. I watched his intensity build in contrast to my usual calm distance. We were discussing those all-night musical concerts in India. He remarked that he couldn't see how anyone could sit through one of them. I told him that enjoying the music made the time fly by. Without warning, he suddenly flung all his papers into the air and shouted, "I just don't *believe* you're really this calm! I mean, most of the blacks I see on the streets every day want to slit my throat! I know they do!" At that outburst, I gathered up my things and started for the door. My parting comment to him was "Well, you've got a real problem there. But it's definitely *your* problem." I got the fellowship anyway. And at the first gathering of new Danforth recipients, I met a whole host of genuine human beings, black people and white people, whose primary focus was not race; people who recognized its existence and knew its heavy weight but who were committed to fostering, through their teaching, an appreciation for diversity along with genuine humanistic values. People who were people. Those folk I trusted.

Still, what could I do with this Carnarsie experience? I couldn't talk with my own folks about it. It would only have confirmed their suspicions. And I knew it was too presumptuous of me to gainsay their lived experience. I suspected that I would not last long living under the day-to-day burden of overt racism and the countless little indignities of racism that came along with it, which they knew only too well from living their entire lives in the South. But I also knew that not all whites were the same.

My folks couldn't be right about that. Rand and Rob were true friends. So were Vera Schwarcz, Elea Mideke, Ed Dirks of the Danforth Foundation, Bea MacLeod, who'd made it possible for me to go to Cornell that first time, and any number of great teachers I'd had while there. These folk were whites I trusted. So, for the time being, I was left to stew alone about the pain I had suffered in Carnarsie. I refused to believe that I should give up on all whites, and I decided, after my anger subsided, that I would much prefer to err on the side of trust, to remain open to people as people, than to live the rest of my life angry and closed off. At the time, I was completely unaware that only months later I would be faced with this decision again. And the next time, I would have a gun in my hands.

GUNS ON CAMPUS

❦

J an?"

"Yeah . . ." I answered the phone groggily, trying to place the girl's voice.

"Most of us are in the Straight. Can you get here? If you need a ride, call the House." I peered across my room trying to make out the time. It was around 4:00 A.M.

"Uuh . . . okay . . ." was all I could manage. The receiver slid from my hand, and my head dropped back heavily to the pillow. *"Holy shit!"* I thought. "They're doing it. *We're* doing it! The Black Student Alliance is making good on its threat to take over the student union. Holy shit!" The phone rang again. This time Mack's voice was on the other end:

"I'll be there in fifteen minutes." Mack didn't ask any questions; he gave me no choice. His voice told me, "Get up and get going, girl. This is the real deal."

"Right! Okay."

The day before, a large group of us BSA members had marched into

Willard Straight Hall, Cornell's student union, and held a rally in the lower dining hall. We had done that because the day before *that,* someone had burned a cross on the lawn of a house where twelve black women students lived. The BSA wanted answers from the administration concerning what it planned to do about the cross burning. We also wanted to know how the university planned to respond to our repeated requests to have a Black Studies program inaugurated. The rally had been much more heated and insistent than any before. There had been a lot of demanding speeches by the newly elected leaders of the organization. They called for immediate action by the administration, *or else.*

It was parents' weekend at Cornell, a warm mid–April one, in 1969. Thanks to being a senior, I had the privilege of living off–campus, and I had joined with three other girls in renting a beautiful house right down on the lake. But this meant that I was about seven miles from campus. After Mack's call, I dressed quickly in the pre–dawn darkness, crept downstairs and out the back door, and climbed up the hill to the road. Not long afterward, Mack's car appeared.

As we drove toward town he gave me a catch-up report on how things had developed overnight. We two had a special mission: first, to scout out the town, and then to make a run or two to the airport.

"To the airport?!"

"Yeah. There may be some people from outside coming in to help us."

Mack seemed clearly to know lots more about what was going on than I did.

When I'd first come to Cornell, there had been only 8 of us, but now there were some 260, mainly from urban, inner-city schools in the North, and, as Mack told me on our ride, most of these were inside the Straight, "except for us, and a couple of people who're at the House." The "House" was the Black Studies House. It was not an official housing for a Black Studies program, but more of a cultural-interest house.

With Mack at the wheel, we made a couple of circuits around Ithaca and its environs. To my amazement, as we cruised by some houses, we saw townspeople loading rifles and shotguns into the trunks of their cars. These folk were coming to campus to get us "uppity" kids. Now I was really scared. This whole thing seemed to be whirling out of control.

When we arrived at the House, a young black woman was sitting on the steps out front. She sat with her face in her hands, whimpering; she seemed dazed. Mack and I proceeded up the steps past her. He opened the door and went in. Then I came to the doorway. There, on the floor, guns of every description were scattered all over. I caught my breath.

"Where did all these . . . these guns . . . come from?" I finally managed to ask. From a back room, a boy's head surfaced and said, "From all around here, though it was tough to find a shop where there were any left." He motioned for Mack to join him in the back. I could only stare. A few minutes later, Mack touched my shoulder and said we had to make an airport run. I was glad to get out of there.

At the Syracuse airport we picked up two men and carried them back to the House. As Mack was filling them in, I came to hear the whole history for the first time. While I had been in India, the BSA had become much more militant. New black students were on campus who were more aggressive in their demands. They'd thought there might be an armed confrontation and had begun planning for one.

Back at the House again, these men, Mack, and two others went into counsel. I found myself once again in the front hallway, with all the guns. After a while, one of the leaders and Mack came up to me and said, "Okay, Jan. We have to get some of these over to the Straight now. June has her car out front. You two have to drive them over and take them in through the lower Straight door. Someone will meet you there to help."

"No," I stammered. "You can't be serious!"

"Look, no one will suspect you two girls. Don't worry. Just get going!" I turned toward the porch. June was still sitting there on the steps, weeping softly. Something about her timidity made me feel bolder. A few years before, my sister and I had waited, frightened and breathless, in Docena while my mother stood by our front door with a tiny .22 in her hands, prepared to defend us from a Klan attack. Today we weren't just going to wait. We were going to take action.

"Come on, June. Get yourself together. We can do this. We have to do this!" I said, peering into her eyes and shaking her by the shoulders. She began slowly to calm down. Then, cautiously, on alert to guard against onlookers, the four of us loaded eight weapons into the back of June's car. She drove, and except for the guns, I was her only passenger.

A large group of students and professors had gathered at the front entrance of the Straight. Townspeople were also arriving. Nothing like this had ever happened at Cornell. Some in the crowd were there to offer us support; others simply wanted to know more about what was happening. Many, especially some fraternity boys, were threatening to go in and kick us out. They'd come when news got out that parents on the upper-floor hotel of the Straight had been rudely awakened and ordered outside by BSA members wielding pool cues.

On the backside of the Straight, things were quiet. From Triphammer Road, a block below the service entrance to the building, June drove her car up onto the paved walkway and slowly steered it up to the lower back door. Our approach went undetected. The door opened and several boys hurried out to carry the guns inside.

I could hardly believe the scene in the two adjoining dining halls. They had been completely transformed into bomb shelters. Mattresses from upstairs rested atop most tables. Tall trash cans filled with paper stood next to all the doorways. About 150 black students were gathered in the back dining hall. In the front one, male students patrolled the tall gothic windows, like sentries. The 8 guns we'd brought in were distributed to 6 of them. A pump-action shotgun was taken by a bandoleered student who'd transferred from West Point the year before and who was placed in charge of the makeshift militia. Ed Whitfield, a brilliant student who was the president of the BSA, was given the last gun. Other students had brought machetes in with them. A table of organization was assigned, and students became "ministers" of defense, health, safety, and so forth.

In addition to several cafeterias and, hence, freezers stocked with food—one of the administrators bemoaned the fact that we "could probably eat for six months on the food stockpiled in there!"—the student union also housed the campus radio station. A group of boys had been working on getting the cables linked up so that they could monitor calls from the administrative offices. Such calls were then sometimes aired through the large speakers that hung from the corners of each dining hall. As desperate as things were and as frightened as I was, I was still proud of the intelligence, ingenuity, and abilities of those boys.

Randy and Robbie were returning from a cross-country trip when they heard about the Cornell takeover. By the first evening, they had arrived and begun attending meetings with Cornell's Students for a Democratic Society. They were trying to determine how best to support us. Some of Cornell's professors, too—Dowd, Bishop, and others— were meeting with SDS and with the administration in attempts to help calm the situation.

As the hours went by, the stand-off only intensified. Twice, fraternity boys attempted to storm the building, using hammers to crash through the windows of the radio station. Two black boys got hurt and came with bleeding faces down to the dining hall for first-aid. Perkins, Cornell's president at the time, issued a number of radio statements that first day, reassuring parents and calling for order. He insisted that there would be no police summoned to the campus.

The stand-off lasted into the afternoon of the second day. It was then that we were all called together in the back dining hall. The former West Point student told us that he had overheard Perkins requesting the National Guard to get us out of the building "by force if necessary." Panic and shudders echoed through the hall. The main coordinating body of BSA had decided that we would preempt this plan and grab the upper hand by announcing that *we* had decided to end the takeover and leave the building. First, we had to do a quick sweep of the place. This meant that we had to dismantle the fire-starter trash cans and do a number of other things that left no evidence of any untoward intentions on our part.

Then we had to prepare ourselves for our departure. A group of us women went up to the game room and brought down armfuls of pool cues. Back in the dining hall, we broke these in half and pushed the heaviest end up our coat sleeves. We went through quick practice sessions on how to let these drop down into our hands so that we could use them as weapons.

It was announced over the public address loudspeakers that in an hour we were coming out of the building and would march as a group over to the House. After clean-up, we all began amassing in the front hallway of the main entrance. We were formed into a makeshift platoon, with unarmed women at the center, pool-cued women encircling them, macheted-men flanking us, and those few with guns surrounding us all. We were reminded that at the doorway, we would have to squeeze in a little to make it through, but were cautioned to keep together and to move as a group. There were to be no stragglers; we were to maintain movement as a unit.

It was dark in the hallway, and hot. When the big gothic doors were finally swung open, light and air at last poured in. But we had no way of knowing what would happen to us next, when the campus and the world saw us for the first time: students wielding guns.

Whitfield, the former West Pointer, and Skip Meade took point. With weapons raised they led us out. Camera lights flashed. As we inched forward and through the massive doors, some of those gathered outside cheered. Others softly clapped. Still others shouted angry taunts. We kept our band of bodies close-knit and made our way slowly out of the building, up past the libraries and through the quad, across Triphammer bridge, past the Lodge, and over to the House. It was an extremely tense march. For the first time since the takeover, we were all exposed. Anyone could have fired upon us. Fortunately, no one did.

At the House, we continued our march until everyone was safely inside. Then a few of our leaders and the two outsiders we'd brought in went back out to the porch, and a brief news conference was held. Inside the House, crammed tight with students, emotions were beginning to spill over. Some students wanted to leave campus right away; others wanted to go to their dorm rooms, get a shower, and take a nap. It was decided that no one should leave.

About twenty of us were called to an upstairs room. It was time to institute a new table of organization and a plan for the next few days. All seven of the senior men with whom I had first entered Cornell were given assignments for the new conditions that now prevailed. I was made Minister of Women's Safety. A young, fiery woman from New York City protested my selection. She wanted the job. She shouted as much, huffed and puffed, and had to be physically restrained before acceding to the will of the group. My appointment stood.

It was not a job I relished. We knew how hard it would be to keep everyone calm, orderly, and safe. We knew that there were townspeople as well as white students now roaming the campus with rifles. We spent that first night crowded and crammed into every inch of the House. During the next days, small groups of blacks were allowed to return to their dorm rooms for necessities and report back immediately. Solitary trips anywhere were forbidden. Library study trips were made in groups. We stayed together this way for almost two weeks.

Evenings were especially tense. Fraternity boys and others regularly called and threatened to burn us out of the House. Campus policemen came to the door, grudgingly, and sneered at us. A phone line was set up so that we could call home and let worried relatives know that we were okay. When my turn to call home came, I talked to my mom and dad and, to my surprise, to my grandmother Jennie. When the phone was handed to her, she asked sweetly, "Baby, you all right?"

"Yes, ma'am, Grandmama. We're okay." Then, I said, "Grandmama, I had to be here."

"I know, baby. You keep safe now."

My eyes welled up with tears. I pulled myself together only by glancing up to see Mack, sitting across the room from me, chewing gum and playing poker. He was, as always, calm under fire.

In spite of being told by the campus administration that we could all go home and that we would all pass our respective courses, most of us stayed on campus until the semester ended. Those of us blacks who were graduating wanted especially to take part in this year's commencement ceremonies.

After all that had happened that spring, the administration had ordered the procession marshals to keep the precise location of the beginning of the line a carefully guarded secret. While parents—my own included—waited inside the large domed gym, the two thousand graduates of '69 assembled outside on the quad. All students were arranged by college or school, but no one knew in which order we were to make our procession past the president, deans, and other university officials who stood on a platform atop Olin Library.

Mack and I marched together. In a remarkable end-of-the-year coup, he somehow managed to learn where the head of our Liberal Arts line would be. The two of us took up that position. And when, with a sudden wave of the chief marshal's hand, the signal to turn and march was finally given, Mack and I turned in place, *at the head of the line*. In our black graduation gowns, past open-mouthed administrators, we marched with our fists held high.

DECISION TIME:
A "PIECE" OR PEACE?

⟨⟨⟩

I had already made up my mind to return to Nepal after leaving Cornell when I picked up a copy of *Time* magazine and read the story about Fred Hampton's tragic death. As they slept in an apartment at 2337 W. Monroe Street in Chicago, he and another of his comrades had been shot to death. The pictures of the room showed blood-splattered walls and bodies lying in disarray. I had personally met Fred Hampton earlier that same year when he had given a talk at the University of Wisconsin. Now, that young warrior was dead. The photos churned my stomach. Against guns, we had no chance.

During the summer and early fall of 1969, I had had to make the most important decision of my life: whether to join the Black Panther party or return to the Tibetan Buddhist monastery in Nepal. After the experience at Cornell, I was convinced that as a thinking black person in this country, I was left no choice but to join the party; to lay my life on the line for my beliefs and for my people's freedom. Making the choice troubled my every waking moment and invaded my nights.

After graduation I had agreed to a job as a teaching assistant for a philosophy course at Cornell. It was a way to earn income and a place to live after school. I took an apartment just at the edge of Cornell's Collegetown. As summer's end approached, I met one of my former professors to say good-bye. He asked about my future plans, and I told him they weren't decided but that I was considering the two alternatives of Panther party or Nepal. In a matter of days, he had arranged a luncheon for me with my thesis advisor, himself, and the dean of the college. At that meeting, the three men made me a unique offer: if I chose to, I would be admitted to graduate studies in philosophy at Cornell *and* I'd be granted my first year there, *in absentia*. In short, I could return to the monastery in Nepal at Cornell's expense, with a University Traveling Fellowship.

Before that, however, when I'd participated in the Straight takeover, one of the men brought in from outside had given me the name of a key contact with the Panther party in Oakland, California. If I was serious about my commitment to revolution, he'd said, I had better have a meeting with this man. I felt that I had to follow through and check out this path, this choice, as well.

At summer's end I hitchhiked across the country with Rand and Rob. On the way, we stopped off to visit other hippie and politico friends. One of our stops was at the University of Wisconsin in Madison. There we were told to check out the campus lecture one evening that was being given by Fred Hampton, the head of the Chicago Black Panthers. Flanked on either side by my friends, I marched into the lecture hall proudly sporting my tall Afro. The three of us were strangers there, and we could tell that among some of the students, there was speculation going on about our identity. At such moments, I felt proud that I might actually be thought already to be a Black Panther. Several students moved over and offered us seats up front.

On the stage, two young Panthers stood at attention, clothed all in black, wearing leather jackets and berets. Fred Hampton was introduced. I was surprised that he was so young; I think only nineteen at the time. He was tall and eloquent, delivering a flawlessly rousing speech. He mentioned that as a child he had stuttered very badly but that watching and listening to Panther party members had inspired him to work on improving his speech so that, now, he could speak like the best of them. It was a moving revelation. The Chicago chapter of the Black Panther party provided free school meals and health facilities for inner-city blacks and other poor. For me, Hampton represented the promise of a better future—through pride and confident action.

After the speech I was invited to join with Hampton and members of the all-black radical student alliance for a reception. When I was introduced to Hampton as being from Cornell, Fred said to me, "Hello, sister. You guys saw some action at Cornell. Yeah . . . I guess you know how to use your piece. Glad to meet you." His handshake was warm and firm, his smile infectious. I felt proud that he had recognized me in front of the others. At that moment, I felt genuinely close to him. I knew, however, that I had *just* learned how to use a "piece" very recently when Mack had taught me how to shoot a rifle just after the Straight stand-off. I also knew that I did not look forward *ever* to having to demonstrate that particular ability. In fact, I now recognized that I was scared to death of guns, preferring peace much more than a piece.

Shortly after Rand, Rob, and I arrived in California, we had another fortunate meeting. We were looking for a friend of theirs who lived somewhere on Mt. Tamalpais. As we climbed the mountain roads on foot, a rain began to fall, gently at first and then more freely. At one house, we saw a petite young woman, red-haired and freckle-faced, doing something or other on a raised deck. We asked if she knew the person, and rather surprisingly, she said she didn't know anyone at all in the area or anything about the place itself. Noting the weather, she told us that if we didn't find him, we should feel free to return and come in from the rain. We had no luck locating the friend, so shortly afterward, we took her up on her offer.

She met us at the door with a large plate of sliced oranges and several marijuana cigarettes rolled in brown wrappers. We settled in to a pleasant and, as always, political conversation. Her own story left me spellbound. She'd been offered this house as a refuge and respite before she had to begin serving a three-and-a-half-year prison sentence in Washington State for encouraging draft resisters. The house, she said, belonged to an artist famous for his anti-American political posters. We knew his name and one of his posters in particular: a graphic portrayal of several police officers gang-raping the Statue of Liberty.

It turned out that this diminutive woman also personally knew the Black Panther party contact person I was supposed to meet in Oakland. She said there had been recent rumblings about his abusive tactics with female Panther party members. Just as had been the case at Cornell, black women were to keep in the background; they were to be the black man's natural complement, but they were not to take any leadership positions. Yet at Cornell, in spite of being a black female, I had tasted power. The leadership had consisted of eight seniors, seven men and myself. There I had been in charge of women's safety. Though I admired the Panthers' cause, I did not want to have to be a doormat in the background. In a certain sense the power dynamics that operated in society separating blacks and whites were being duplicated here all over again between black men and women. All this information added to my confusion about the decision I faced.

Every place we went in California, we saw newspaper photos of Huey Newton and other Black Panthers brandishing shotguns on the steps of the Sacramento State Capitol. Everywhere I looked, this brazenly militant movement seemed my only alternative. The images and rhetoric of the Black Panthers pervaded all conversations. Many a morning I woke up in a cold sweat.

Unrelenting questions pummeled my mind: Was I ready to be shot and killed by Alameda County police? Was I ready to serve a prison term like the one that freckled-faced girl at Mt. Tamalpais was awaiting? Would any of my activities really help to turn things around in this country? No matter, wasn't it time to stand up? Wasn't it time to stop pleading for justice and to take up a gun and demand it? A piece or peace? The questions literally shook my mind. I walked around with a constant fever and a buzzing in my head. The closer we got to Oakland, the more the questions tormented me.

My choices could not have been farther apart, and no assurances of success were offered by either. I had always been a good girl, eager to please. I had always shunned the limelight, knowing since early childhood that conspicuousness brings with it danger. It was not in my nature to desire to fight back; the day the Klan showed up, I had wanted to talk. I sought the more peaceful path. Though I thought it seemed awfully cowardly on my part, I could not see myself standing defiantly on the statehouse steps brandishing a shotgun. I talked to myself a lot. The real truth was that I was scared, scared down to my bones.

Right then in California there was a factional war within the Panther party. Though the Northern wing, headed by Huey Newton and Bobby Seal, got all the notoriety, a Southern branch out of L.A. was busy trying to disseminate information in written form. Huey had dubbed them the "Paper Panthers." I didn't know how to contact the folk in the South. If I had, perhaps I might have decided differently. But it seemed to me that my only choice was between this Northern faction of the Panthers and Nepal.

I was, and am, a Pisces, always deliberating between choices. I knew that either of these choices would freak out my family. I did not want to worry them, but I had to do something. Amid the revolutionary timbre of the times, I was tossed and pushed along, it seemed inevitably, toward guns and violence. But then, just before taking that fateful step, I bolted. My whole being—mind, body, and soul—bolted. And even though doing so made me feel like a coward and chickenshit deserter, I had to turn away from it.

True, I had learned to shoot a piece. I had even helped deliver guns to the Straight when I had to. But I had also marched, nonviolently amid violence, in Birmingham with King. And I had wanted to talk with those Klan folk who'd burned a cross in front of our house. "To thine own self be true," the saying goes, and my sister, San, had always said, "Trust your *first mind*." I decided not to meet with the Panthers.

I didn't know where the path of Buddhism would ultimately take me, but it seemed to offer at least the possibility of peaceful transformation. I told myself that it offered the best opportunity for clarity—about personal as well as political strategies. Now that I had made that westward journey, turning eastward seemed the best and most viable alternative. I took a deep breath. I felt calmer than I had in months. I picked up the phone to call that professor at Cornell. I would go back to Nepal.

Only a few months passed before I saw the article about Hampton's death. My heart was saddened to think of him, cut down in his shining prime. But I had made the right decision.

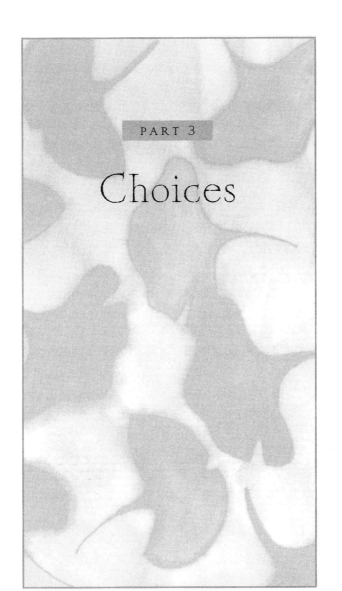

PART 3

Choices

DREAMING ME, III

❦

It was the dead of night and pitch black. San and I found ourselves standing outside the doors of a massive, wooden-slatted barn just at the edge of Docena. I pulled back one of the giant creaky doors, and amid a sudden flood of light from inside, the two of us slipped in. Throngs of people from all of Docena—blacks and whites together—had assembled here and were standing shoulder to shoulder in silence, their faces peering toward the far end of the barn. I pushed in a little farther in order to see. There, upon a raised platform, sat a hefty-bodied but sweetly smiling Tibetan lama. He seemed to be enveloped in soft light. Apparently, the entire town had gathered to hear this man speak. The thought occurred to me, "I didn't know these people knew anything about Buddhism, or Tibetans."

The gentle-eyed Tibetan spotted me. Something made me think he had been awaiting my arrival. Without a word, he beckoned me forward. In response, I pointed to my chest as if to ask, "Me?" He bowed his head and I stepped forward. As I began my approach, the crowd parted, creating a pathway that seemed to be made of a stream of light.

When I approached, I noticed that on the floor next to the lama was a

133

weathered wooden bucket filled with water. From some place the lama took what appeared to be three fresh, green, pine-needled twigs. After briefly swishing these through the water, he released them and, wordlessly, invited me to step closer and have a look. Doing as he had bidden, I moved closer and peered into the bucket. For a moment, the small green twigs seemed to stand on their own atop the water and to do a sort of dance. Their swirling created a soft white frothiness on the water's surface. Entranced, I watched more closely. As the twig-churned water began to settle, the face of a lion slowly emerged. The floating vision touched something deep and mysteriously powerful inside of me.

AN ACCIDENT IN
SOUTHERN FRANCE

☙

F*rance?!!"* I heard Randy scream out in amazement. A few seconds passed. Another frantic question screamed, *"India?!!"* She did not know where we were going. Then I lost consciousness.

Randy, Rob, and I were on our way to India en route to Nepal, traveling to the East together for the first time. They'd been listening to me rave about India and Nepal, and now we all had the time to go. We had determined that on the way, we'd see a bit of Europe. We had flown in to Luxembourg, and now we were hitchhiking around western Europe. It was fall of 1969. The three of us had toured some in Brussels, spent a week in Amsterdam, tried twice unsuccessfully to get up to Stonehenge, been carried home by a student protester in Paris and welcomed warmly by his mother, and now, finally, we were headed south and west, overland to India.

Hitchhiking, or "auto-stopping," in Europe had so far been an efficient way of traveling, and we'd met warm and wonderfully kind-hearted people. On the outskirts of Paris, a young Arab man, Abdur-aman, pulled over his old Peugeot station wagon, and we piled in, our three steel-framed backpacks, sleeping bags, and all. Abduraman was Algerian. He told us, in his broken English, about how happy he was to be on his way home to his country and to his wife, Fatima. His time working in France had been more like slavery, he said, and the racist condescension of the French had been almost unbearable.

We liked Abduraman immensely. Though clearly tired, we could see that he was strong and vibrant. Under his thick dark moustache, an infectious smile was often visible. The farther away from Paris we got, the wider his grin became. Then, just before we neared Lyon, Abduraman became a little fidgety. He said an old friend lived somewhere in the environs and that he would like to see him before leaving the country. He began driving slower in order to look more closely at the highway signposts. On this stretch of road, the highway was four-laned, each direction divided by a grassy median. Though we were in the right-most lane, sometimes the Peugeot veered uneasily toward the left, as Abduraman paused to make out the names on signposts. At one of these pauses, we heard the deafening blare of the horn of a big semi-truck.

Randy's desperate scream woke me up. When I came to again, she was gently rubbing my forehead. "Don't worry, babes," she was saying. "They'll have you out of here soon." My left leg was pinned under the front seat. French emergency people were cutting away sections of the car. I was not in pain. My eyes closed again.

I found scenes of my life racing at top speed before my eyes. I was standing on a high green cliff, the wind blowing my hair, though it was tied in a bun on top of my head. I wore a full-length dress and an apron. I was older, perhaps sixty-five, my hair was white, and I felt satisfied, as though my life had been fruitful. I stood above the cliffs, the cool wind lifting my dress. Below me, the deep blue ocean pounded against the rocks. The day was brilliant. I was convinced that the place was Ireland. A deep smile of contentment crossed my lips.

Then suddenly I was snatched back. There was another great spiraling. Confused scenes whirled by. I felt myself being born. I saw Dot holding the snake that made me drop my bottle, the white school superintendent, Sandy, my mom and dad, the dogs and hoses, the Klan. Suddenly I woke up and realized that I was in this body again. I struggled to say, "Oh, no . . . !" Then I heard Randy's voice.

"Everything will be all right."

I thought, "But it won't. I shouldn't be . . . I don't want to be back here!" I was lying on the green grass of the median. I had never thought much of the doctrine of reincarnation. In my philosopher's heart of hearts, I reasoned that the idea of successive rebirths was thoroughly untenable in a system of thought, like the Buddhist one, that advocated the doctrine of *sunyata,* the absence of independent, inherent existence. If one's identity were truly insubstantial and without permanence, how could one advocate the notion of reincarnation, which suggested that one could traverse several lifetimes with one's identity intact? I was sure I had never died before, but my experiences during that accident told me quite a different truth. I knew I liked Irish music and had always thought that rather odd. An Irish folksong sings to me; a jig causes my feet to move of their own accord. I told myself, whenever I gave it any thought at all, that perhaps my affinity for the Irish had to do with their history of suffering oppression and with their longtime political struggles. Yet it was their music that captivated me, something in the plaintive sounds themselves that struck a deep chord. In my bones, I felt kinship. I determined to journey to Ireland someday to see.

The crash had happened in an instant. Apparently, Abduraman had swerved the car too far to the left as the big semi behind us was attempting to pass. The Peugeot had been smashed in the back, spun completely around, and smashed again in the front before being pushed yards off into the median. Our backpacks had cushioned us.

Robbie and Abduraman had remained conscious throughout. Randy had lost consciousness for a while and, we learned later, suffered a pretty serious concussion. I had lost consciousness too, but except for having to be cut out of the car and some gashes along my ankle, I was okay. Randy and I were put in an ambulance and taken to a little hospital in the town of Chalon. Poor Robbie, shaken and no doubt worried, especially after Rand's amnesiac cries, followed us to the hospital. From that moment on, Abduraman was gone—perhaps to his friend's place, perhaps just into hiding. He knew the French had no love for "L'Arab," and he was desperate to see his beloved Fatima.

Rand and I were kept in the hospital in Chalon for two days. We were put in a tiny room together. The French nurses were sweet to us, and Robbie was allowed to stay with us most of the time. To this day, I don't know where he went or how he fared during those two nights. Luckily, Randy did remember Robbie and me, though she could not remember Abduraman or what we were doing on a highway in France. The police began to visit us. It was clear from their tone that what Abduraman had said was true. They scowled at us for riding with an Arab; they clearly wanted to find him at fault and to have him imprisoned for it. Each day Rob and I coached Rand: "Abduraman is an okay guy. We shouldn't say anything that leads them to accuse him." She went along. The arrogant, condescending French policemen finally tired of our unified story and left us, in disgust, pronouncing us "Arab-lovers"!

When we saw a photograph of the crashed car in the local newspaper, even we couldn't believe it. The caption read, "Four make it out of this, alive." After being released from the hospital, we decided to give up on auto-stopping. So, in Chalon, we boarded a train headed for Milan.

We went through a number of other adventures during that overland trip to India. In Istanbul, the accident some days behind us, we hooked up with a small London-based Land Rover tour. The group was headed for New Delhi, and they allowed us to squeeze in. Traveling in a Land Rover tightly packed with cranky British teenagers was certainly no picnic. But after days of doing so, we finally made it. That familiar odor of pee wafting through the air of central Delhi brought a broad smile to my lips. India, at last!

At the time, neither Robbie nor I could have imagined what the accident had actually done to Rand. Though she'd say to us fairly often how strange things seemed to her, we had no idea that her bump on the head would turn out to be so serious. She was experiencing a genuine disjuncture with reality, one that would dramatically catch our attention only when we had returned to the States and her illness turned into a full-blown crisis requiring serious help and treatment. But for the time being, we simply carried on, together, as we always had.

We were so close that some people mistakenly perceived our relationship to be some kind of a threesome arrangement, though those who knew us well understood the depth of our friendship. Randy and Rob had a strong relationship, but I had not yet become interested in ordinary love. Whenever I thought about relationships, I saw how easily they became mired in possessiveness. If a friend were late for a date, one worried; if it were one's special friend, however, one was more likely to become angry. Most times attachment and possessiveness ruled. The idea was unattractive. I would be thirty years old before I even considered any love interest of my own.

For Randy and Rob, traveling and living in India and Nepal were dreams being realized. For me, doing so carried more urgency. I had made a conscious decision to turn away from violence and to seek a way of bringing healing and peace into my life. Although I didn't yet know exactly how this would be accomplished, I hoped that on our journey I would find the answers I sought. The three of us traveled on. We had a great year, briefly traveling in India and living, for months, in Nepal. Best of all, we met there a Tibetan teacher, Lama Thubten Yeshe, a wise and gentle man who would change my life forever.

BODHA

༄༅

After hovering over the snow-draped Himalayas, our plane lightly touched down on a green, grassy runway in Kathmandu Valley. Rand, Rob, and I took a cab into the city and checked into a small hotel. For a couple of days we toured the town. Then, leaving the two of them at the hotel, I went out alone to the monastery in Bodha where, the year before, I'd been invited to stay and study. Now, on Cornell's fellowship, I was able to do so.

A ruddy-faced boy in monk's robes ran up to me as I entered the monastery's central compound. Grinning, he grabbed my hands and began screaming at the top of his lungs, "Sonam! Hey, Sonam!" Out of a small, dark, and smoke-filled room where gigantic vats were bubbling, a tiny monk appeared.

"Hello. I am looking for Lobsang Chonjor. Is he here?" I asked the monk, who stood before me, perhaps four and a half feet tall. Along with his faded burgundy robes he sported a broad smile and a huge bunch of keys that was tied around his waist.

"Lobsang Chonjor." He nodded. "Lobsang Chonjor, *India!*"

"*Oh, no!*" I exclaimed in a voice that must have made my disappointment clearly evident. I had come twelve thousand miles because of Chonjor's invitation to stay and study with the monks of this Gelukpa Monastery in Bodhanath, Nepal. Now that I had at last arrived, he was not there, and he was the only contact I knew. I tried to continue.

"I am Jan Willis. Last year he invited me here." Sonam's smile became a broad and welcoming grin. "*Yes! Jan Vee-lis, Jan Vee-lis!*" He was pulling the pieces together in his mind. "Jan Vee-lis, Lobsang Chonjor room, Lobsang Chonjor room!" With childish glee, he took hold of my arm and began pulling me farther into the monastery's compound. When we stopped, I found myself facing a small doorway along a short row of rooms running the length of the main temple. Sonam pointed. "Lobsang Chonjor room!" I tried to smile.

"Yes, his *room*," I said, "but when will he *return*?" Sonam continued to smile. Finally, he said, "Yes. Lobsang Chonjor room, Jan Veelis room!" He raised an outer entrance cloth and stepped into the room, beckoning me to follow. Bowing, I ducked my head and stepped in.

The room's interior was dark and windowless. Its ceiling slanted away from the door, being perhaps six feet high at the entrance and sloping downward to about five feet at the far side. A small bed of perhaps four and a half feet ran flush against the opposite wall, draped by a wine-colored Tibetan woolen carpet. The floor plan was roughly six feet by six feet. There was a tiny bit of linoleum on the concrete floor that was partially covered with another Tibetan carpet. I could only stand erect just inside the door, but Sonam had no problem at all. At the head of Chonjor's bed was his altar, arranged with offering bowls placed before photographs of the Dalai Lama, the Panchen Lama, and a number of other teachers I did not recognize. On the wall above the altar were pasted pictures of Shakyamuni Buddha; Chenresig, the Buddha of Compassion; Manjusri, the Buddha of Wisdom; Vajrapani, the Buddha of Power; and Green Tara, the Goddess of Long Life and

Wise Activity. In the near corner, a kerosene-burning stove sat on the floor. Against the left wall just at the room's entrance stood a small cupboard covered by a green cloth with floral print.

Patting the air, Sonam made welcoming gestures again. "*This,* Jan Veelis room!"

"Thank you . . . but I can't accept." I knew he meant well, but at the time, I was disappointed to the point of despair. Besides, I couldn't imagine how I, or anyone, could live in such small quarters.

"Yes. *This* Jan Veelis room. *Okay? . . . Okay!*" he reiterated.

All this time, the two of us had been attempting to speak to each other in English. Now, as if more at ease, Sonam asked, in Nepali, if I'd care for a cup of tea.

"Chai?" he asked.

For the first time, I smiled, and responded in Hindi, "Yes, uh . . . *Hahn-ji! Dhanyawad.*" We walked back to the kitchen.

News of my arrival had already spread throughout the monastery. As Sonam stood smiling while I drank my specially prepared English tea, other monks began to filter into the tiny soot-filled kitchen. One of these monks, named Lobsang Tashi, spoke a few words of English. I told him a bit of my story. Afterward, he told me that Lobsang Chonjor was studying in Bodhgaya. They didn't know exactly when he would return, but he had told them about me, and they had been expecting me. I was to stay in Chonjor's room. There was no problem with that. They wanted me to go back into Kathmandu and bring my things.

The monks were extremely gracious and generous, but this was certainly not what I had anticipated. Other than the oft-repeated greeting *Tashi delek,* I didn't know a word of Tibetan. I had counted on Chonjor's help in getting my studies under way. Still, I felt I couldn't just go back to the airport. I had come a long way to be here, and I had agonized a great deal about the decision to do so. I had to give it a try. I went back into Kathmandu, told Randy and Rob about the news, and after gathering up my things, left them to continue their touring fun while I returned to the monastery.

The Gelukpa Monastery's full name was Samteling (pronounced Some-day-ling), the "Place of Blissful Thought." In Tibet, it had been founded by Yeshe Gyeltsen, an eighteenth-century Gelukpa scholar who'd been the chief tutor, or *yong-dzin,* of the eighth Dalai Lama. When I arrived there in 1969, it was the largest functioning monastery at Bodhanath, housing some fifty Tibetan and ten Mongolian monk refugees. Of these sixty, at least a quarter were junior monks, little boys between the ages of six and fourteen; so this particular monastery was thriving and had a group of younger monks to ensure its continuance.

No one ever questioned my being a foreigner—let alone a woman—amid these sixty monks. They, as well as the abbot, accepted me warmly and without hesitation. In fact, from the beginning, I was treated as a very special guest. In those first mornings, separate groups of monks would visit me, bringing sweet breadsticks, called *kupsay,* and thermoses of piping hot Tibetan tea. Like most Westerners, it took some time before I could finish a cup of this thick brew, made with incredibly strong black tea, salt, and churned butter. While I tried to be gracious and talk, though feebly, with my guests, my tea often cooled in my hand, leaving a thick layer of fatty butter floating on top. Thankfully, one morning Sonam told me that I didn't have to finish the tea once it had cooled. "When cold, just throw out!" he said.

I was gradually initiated into the routine of the *gompa*. Like the others, I awoke at the sound of the conch shells and gong—about 4:30 A.M.—when it was still dark. I dressed quickly and ran out back to pee and brush my teeth before the other monks arrived at the single water faucet that stood in the center of a two-by-three-foot concrete slab on the ground. Then I ran back to report to my class. Because I was just beginning to learn Tibetan, this meant that I stood at the end of a line of six or seven little "lama-las," as they were called, junior monks ranging in age from six to ten. Standing against the outside wall of the main *gompa,* just feet from Chonjor's tiny cell, we sang, at the top of our voices, two short prayers. The first was a beginning prayer that included the Buddhist Refuge; the second, a brief veneration of Tsongkhapa, the fourteenth-century founder of the Gelukpa school of Tibetan Buddhism and, hence, the founder of this particular branch of Buddhism.

For the others, this beginning stage included only rote memorization. But I was also learning to read the prayers at the same time. I tried as best I could to imitate the singsong of the chant. I had brought along a grammar of the Tibetan language and Chandra Das's *Tibetan Dictionary,* but I didn't know how to spell or even sound out the language— to say nothing of speaking it. Most times, I got along by speaking Hindi to the monks, who replied to me in either Hindi or Nepali, a near equivalent.

After the morning chanting class, I was free to receive guests in my room or to sit inside the main chapel while the monks as a group did their lengthier daily prayers. A special Tibetan carpet was always laid out for me near the chapel's entrance, and when the monks were served their tea, a cup was always provided and poured for me. Other times I simply roamed around the monastery. I watched the little monks playing and the older monks studying or making ritual preparations. Sometimes I popped into the kitchen to see Sonam. I asked questions about everything, and most times I found smiling monks eager to attempt answers in whatever language was the most freely flowing that day. In these ways, the daytime hours seemed to fly by.

But nights were a different story completely. At the end of each day,

I retreated alone into Chonjor's room for another attempt at sleep. I was in a tiny monastic cell thousands of miles away from home and most creature comforts. There were many strange, mysterious, and frightening aspects to this new environment. Even during the day, I had begun seeing things that cried out for explanations though I was unable to ask for them. For example, when a group of monks was visiting me one morning, I was looking among Chonjor's things for another glass when I put my hand on an actual skull cup. Trembling, I quickly put it right back. I had read about bizarre rituals in which Tibetans were said to drink human blood from such skull cups, and I didn't want to think that such a tale might actually be true. Of all my many visitors, I was frightened by two of the older Mongolian monks whose stares made me quite uncomfortable. I wondered whether they made use of such implements, but I didn't have the language to ask Sonam about it.

Then, too, during the first week of my stay, a nightly phenomenon began that almost scared me to death. After a couple of hours curled up on my side on Chonjor's tiny bed, a thumping would begin on the tin roof of the room. Next came a series of blood-curdling screeches. The thumping became banging that went faster and louder. I would lie there frozen in fear, sweating, eyes opened wide, waiting for the community to awake and stir. Each night, after some minutes, the screams and bumping would finally subside. I couldn't wait for the sound of the morning gong. But each morning when I pointed to my roof and tried to ask Sonam to help me by explaining the strange sounds, I found that I could not describe to him the source of my great fear. Every day I tried not to think of the coming night and of what dark witchcraft might be afoot in the monastery. I kept telling myself that these monks certainly meant me no harm, that they had taken me in without question. Even so, it took much longer before I felt this way about those two Mongolian monks.

Somehow I managed to survive the nightly ordeal—for almost three weeks—before I finally discovered the source of the frightening noises. Feeling restless and, no doubt, edgy from lack of sleep, I decided to leave the compound and take an afternoon walk outside of Bodhanath's environs. I followed a dusty trail up some small hills. The sun was bearing down, and I started to look for some trees and shade. Not seeing any near, I sat down on a small boulder just off the path. Suddenly I heard that familiar sound. Frozen in place, I jerked my head around to see, just out of the corner of my eye, a group of light brown monkeys with bright red anuses rushing up from below the hill and scampering across the path just in front of me. They were jumping on each others' backs, grabbing on to each others' tails, screeching and screaming the whole while. *A sudden swarm of monkeys.* I almost fell off the rock, first in fright and then in utter relief. *This* was what tormented my life each night: a band of screeching monkeys. No secret devil worship, no bloody tantric rituals, no evil midnight journeys on brooms by those Mongolian fellows. Just monkeys. At last, I would be able to sleep. Praise the Lord!

My learning liturgical Tibetan had to do, pretty directly, with my relief at this discovery. For I was so relaxed that the very next morning after seeing the monkeys, I overslept. I never heard the morning gong at all. When I lifted my head, I heard my class chanting away at our prayers. Too late to join them, I lay there in the pre-dawn light and listened.

Tibetan is a monosyllabic language, and each syllable has its own unique meaning. The secret to mastering the language is to know how many syllables ought to be connected in order to form meaningful units. Learning and reading liturgical texts, as we were doing, is even harder since they are mostly written in verse form and lengthier meaning-units are often abbreviated. One has to know, or devise a system in order to know, how to properly connect the many syllables.

Some chants are written in 2–2–3 form, others in 3–3–3 form, and so forth. But no Tibetan grammar book ever mentions this most essential fact. Without knowing it, one can waste thousands of hours, spinning hundreds of individual meanings from the separate syllables.

The secret was in the chant! Too late to make my morning class, I lay on Chonjor's bed and listened as the tiny lama-las loudly intoned: *da-da da-da, da-da-da, da-da da-da, da-da-da.* In a flash, I saw it: 2–2–3, 2–2–3! I grabbed my wood-block-printed edition of the prayer. It was true! If the syllables were connected in this way, the meaning became clear: first, the qualities and attributes of a given religious figure were mentioned; then, in the last three syllables, that figure's name was given. It was as though, suddenly, a bright light had clicked on inside my head.

From that moment on I started to feel comfortable at the monastery. I began to learn and absorb things at an astounding rate. And Bodhanath began to feel like home.

I bought burgundy and saffron Tibetan shirts to go with my jeans and corduroys. I began having weekly conversations with the abbot. I became a regular in the kitchen and learned more and more about the duties of a monastery's manager. Sonam was the current manager. After six months, Lobsang Tashi would assume those duties. I traveled into town with the monks and went on various escapades with them. I became known in the area as the American student at Samteling.

All this settling in occurred before I met Lama Yeshe.

MEETING LAMA YESHE

𝕰

I should have told him the truth when he'd first asked; should have blurted out that I suffered; that I was often frustrated and angry; that slavery and its legacy of racism had taken their tolls on me; that I had come seeking help in coping with feelings of inadequacy, unworthiness, and shame. I should have told him that I felt a certain kinship with the Tibetans because they, too, had suffered a great historical trauma and yet seemed able to cope very well and, indeed, even to be quite joyful. And I should have told him that I also felt a special and unique kinship with him in particular, though we had only just met, because from the very first moment I had heard his name, I had somehow known that he was to be my teacher. But at our first meeting, I said none of this. When Lama Yeshe asked us why we had come, I had responded with a textbook answer, saying with superficial glibness, "Because *samsara* is suffering."

As Randy, Rob, and I made our way down the switchbacks from Kopan that evening after our first meeting with Lama Yeshe, these were the thoughts that troubled me. I felt like a complete jackass; and

I could only hope that I hadn't forever missed a most important opportunity, perhaps *the* most important opportunity of my life.

Everything before our meeting had gone just as those two strange fellows who'd come to visit in Banaras had predicted. With half my attention focused on the ruts in the makeshift road from Kopan back to Bodhanath, the other half vividly replayed that evening in Banaras.

Cletus, Randy, and Rob had gone out to a nearby cinema to see an Indian movie. I stayed in. About an hour after they left, I heard a knock on Cletus's door. When I opened it, there stood two quite odd-looking Americans. One was a long-haired man dressed in pants and a Western-style shirt with an Indian *jola,* or bag, draped over his shoulder. The other was a giant of a man dressed completely in Indian-style clothing with long matted hair and facial makeup like that of a Hindu *sadhu,* or holy man. Both men also appeared to be quite stoned, a fact that was no accident in a place where state-run shops sold marijuana and hashish by the gram. I tried not to appear too nervous, but my expression must have given me away. The shorter man explained, "Hi. We're friends of Cletus. Is he around?" I told them about the movie and then invited them in for tea.

During our ensuing conversation, I learned that both these men had been on the India circuit for quite some time. The tall one—who stood more than six feet five inches, caused a stir wherever he went, not only because he dwarfed most Indians in size but because he dressed like a Siva devotee, right down to wearing a *dothi* and a sacred thread across his chest. He was actually a Sanskrit language student at the Sanskrit University in Varanasi. The shorter of the two men spent his time mainly studying with Tibetans in Sarnath and Dharamsala. They asked what I and my two friends were planning for our subsequent travels. When I explained that we were headed for Nepal, that I had an invitation to stay at the Gelukpa Monastery in Bodhanath, and that the three of us had hopes of somehow hooking up with a Tibetan

Buddhist teacher there, the smaller, soft-spoken man became quite deliberate in his speech, and I craned closer to listen.

"Well, there are two really good teachers who live just a few miles outside of Kathmandu," he said. "Actually, they live in small *gompas* just outside of Bodhanath. There's a road that winds behind the main *stupa* there; anyone can point it out. The road travels up past a place called Kopan. At that place, there is a lama called Thubten Yeshe." As he continued to talk, I began to experience a strange, though pleasant, sensation. It was unlike any sensation I had ever experienced before: a sort of warm tingling feeling that began at the nape of my neck and then radiated downward and outward to encircle my whole body. Then, as though I had suddenly stepped into an invisible field of static electricity, I noticed that the hairs on my skin stood up erect. As the warm tingling continued, I tuned back in to the stranger's advice. ". . . I don't know this Yeshe fellow, but I hear he's guarded by a woman named Zina who is famous for discouraging visitors." At that remark, the two men looked at each other and shared a wink. Presumably, this woman was the brunt of some joke. But again, at the sound of "Yeshe," all the hairs on my skin gently stood erect. He went on to describe a second teacher, but I only vaguely heard his words. Something had subtly happened to me, and I was by then thoroughly intrigued by the thought of meeting the first lama he'd mentioned, this Lama Yeshe. I thanked the man, and the two visitors left before Cletus and Rand and Rob returned.

During the next few weeks, leaving Cletus to study for his exams, my two buddies and I made our circuit around India, traveling by train. Yet during all of our travels, I couldn't get the thought of that lama out of my mind. We returned to Banaras, said our good-byes to Cletus, and caught a flight on Royal Nepalese Airlines to Kathmandu. We were heading for the sacred valley rimmed by the wondrous snow-clad Himalayas, the green valley where we might actually make contact with our teacher.

By the time we had been in Kathmandu for a week, I was installed in Lobsang Chonjor's room at the monastery in Bodhanath, and Rand and Rob were still enjoying the pleasures of hippie life in Kathmandu. When I'd asked my new monk-friend Sonam about the high lamas in the area, he'd taken me out back of the *stupa* and, pointing to a distant hill, said, "Up there is Kopan. Lama Yeshe lives there. He is a very good, a very high lama." I felt the tingling sensation again. So I hurried into town, picked up Rand and Rob from their hotel, and returned in a taxi with them. Then the three of us set out walking up to Kopan to meet Lama Yeshe.

The walk began fairly pleasantly. It felt nice to be away from the bustling of crowds. But the sandy and mica-sprinkled road gradually became ever more steep. By the time we hit the base of Kopan hill, we were all pretty winded, and the steeper switchbacks were yet to come. When at last we reached the top of the hill and turned into the compound of the Nepalese Mahayana Gompa, we were relieved. We walked down a grassy path to a gate and opened it. On our left was a small building containing perhaps two rooms. Farther in and up some stone steps to our right was a fairly large brick house. All was quiet. We saw no one. Then, from the larger house, preceded by the tiny yelps of two Lhasa apsos, a tall Western woman in robes appeared. She greeted us and introduced herself as Zina. When we explained that we'd come in hopes of meeting Lama Yeshe, her smiling countenance immediately changed and, while waving her hands for emphasis, she said, "Oh, no! That will be quite impossible! The lamas—both Lama Yeshe and Lama Zopa, are very tired, you see. They are resting now and cannot be disturbed. You cannot meet them today. Sorry, but you simply cannot."

We were crestfallen. Then, with pity in her eyes, Zina added: "Well, you've walked a long way. You must at least stay for lunch before going down. Go there and sit in the shade." Tired, hot, and dejected, in silence we did as she bade us. Seeing our compliance, Zina turned away from us with a regal flourish, clapped her hands, and called, "Machela!" A small, skinny Tibetan man in dark pants and a white shirt appeared. She gave him some directions. The man disappeared in a flash and just as quickly returned with a large straw mat. It became a picnic tablecloth, and before too long, Zina and the three of us were dining in the shade and cool breezes of Kopan. We had seen no one else; no lamas were visible.

Zina became animated. She was in her element, entertaining guests and happily narrating the story of how she came to be living here with Lama Yeshe and his chief disciple, Lama Zopa. After breaking up with her former husband, Conrad Rooks—the director of the movie *Siddhartha* and others—she had met the two lamas in Darjeeling. She had pleaded with them to become her teachers, took ordination at their suggestion, purchased this compound (a former Astrologer's House), and brought the lamas here to be her private tutors. They had some plans to turn the place into a monastery for teaching Westerners, but those were plans for the future and there were, at present, no other people in residence. It was clear that she enjoyed her status as the "mommy" of this fledgling monastery.

Zina talked while we ate and listened. A couple of hours went by. Then, rather abruptly, she announced that it was probably time that we started back down to Bodhanath; we would want to make the walk while there was still daylight. When we inquired about a future date to meet the lamas, she told us she had no idea. She would ask them, but she couldn't give us a time to return. We thanked her for her hospitality and gathered ourselves for the trek back. Zina turned away and quickly mounted the steps to the large house. With no further fanfare, she disappeared back into its darkened hallway.

Slowly, the three of us headed for the gate. But then, just as we reached the farthest corner of the smaller house, now to our right side, its door creaked open and a hand both shushed us and beckoned us inside. The hand was attached to a broadly smiling, shaven-headed Tibetan man in robes with large dimples and a gap between his teeth. Quickly we glanced around. The coast was clear. We silently slipped inside. In makeshift English he said, "Hello! I am Lama Yeshe and I am so glad that you have come." We could hardly believe what was happening. Zina was somewhere in her house, hardly twenty feet away, and here we were, actually meeting Lama Yeshe in spite of her efforts to dissuade us. Speechless, we simply grinned and bubbled in our good fortune. "Was your meal well?" he asked. "Yes, very well, ah, very good, thank you!" we finally managed, still awestruck. There was a radiant youthfulness about Lama Yeshe. He seemed both calm and playful, alert, present, and genuinely happy to see us. We engaged in brief introductions, and then our conversation just began to flow. At a certain point, he asked, "Now, please tell me, why have you come?" It was then that I gave that dumb textbook response. Lama Yeshe only smiled and said, "Yes. That is true. Hm-hum." He told us a bit more about how he and Lama Zopa had come to be there with Zina, and about the few other Westerners whom he had met since coming to Kopan. He added, "Zina . . . Mommy . . . is sometimes . . . how you say? . . . too much protective, but she is becoming a good nun. Well, I hope you will come again." Grinning from ear to ear, we stood and prepared to sneak out. Then, Lama Yeshe said something that completely bowled us over. In the course of our conversation, none of us had made any mention of our accident in France. Yet standing in his tiny little room, our mouths dropped open in unison when, leaning over and looking deeply into our eyes, he said, "Lama is so happy that you three have come, especially after . . . you know . . . that bad thing in France." When our dumbfoundedness subsided, we told him that we would, most certainly, return.

THIS, TOO, IS
BUDDHA'S MIND

֎

Randy and Robbie, with Zina's help, had managed to secure lodging with a Nepalese family—the Bahadurs—right on the other side of the hill where Lama's fledgling Kopan monastery was housed. I was living in Bodhanath, in the Gelukpa Monastery there. Though my own situation was an exceptionally generous arrangement, made possible by Lobsang Chonjor and the other monks at the monastery, I had to admit that I was pretty envious of Rand and Rob's arrangement so near to our main teacher. I had to walk over an hour up the rugged sandy road to Kopan to spend time with Lama Yeshe, whereas for them only a quick jaunt separated them from Lama Yeshe's establishment.

The Bahadur family had welcomed Rand and Rob with open arms in spite of the fact that, being Hindus themselves, they were pretty suspicious of the Buddhists living on top of the hill. In fact, once the deal to house Rand and Rob was reached, the Bahadurs had actually divided their own tiny mud-brick house into two equal parts. With lightning speed, they installed new walls on both stories and reshuffled all eleven members of their family—Laxman and his brother, their parents, wives, and five children—into one side, giving the other side over to Rand and Rob. Randy's outgoingness aided in the Bahadurs' ready acceptance of them. The extra rupees, curiosity, and sincere openness of the Bahadurs to this new friendship helped as well. Rob, too, was happy to be at long last living in Nepal.

But the trek from Bodhanath up to Kopan often took its toll on me. So sometimes, after a long and usually very fruitful day of teachings and meals with Lama Yeshe, I'd spend the night at Rand and Rob's place. This required an adjustment from my more private space at Bodhanath. Life at the Bahadurs' was fully communal. Everything happened in the tiny mud-caked courtyard out in front of their house. The family's big water buffalo lived in its own hut just at the corner of the yard, and Laxman's two sons brought in freshly cut grass to feed it. The brother's wives were usually carrying cut grass, or spreading corn to dry, or pounding the family's wash on the rocks nearby. The three of us sat on the one-step porch watching these various activities and trying to speak Nepali. Often Laxman brought puffed rice or popped corn to us, and with all the family peering and laughing, we sat together. Several times during those early months, the family tried to get me to eat and drink the flimsy yogurt substance known as *bigotie* they'd painstakingly produced. "Just try a little," they'd urge. Rand and Rob had no problem with the thin sour stuff, but I didn't like yogurt of the more substantial variety even in the States, and I found this form even more repugnant. I was uneasy in this public environment.

One morning after spending the night there, I woke up a little late. Rand and Rob had already gone downstairs, probably, I thought, to do their morning bathroom ritual out in the field behind the Bahadurs' house. I was determined to do the new sitting meditation Lama Yeshe had recently given us. Rolling out of my sleeping bag onto the smooth mud-caked floor, I quickly reshuffled the bag to form a cushion and began my meditation. Only a minute or two went by before great plumes of heavy smoke began filling up the whole of the second floor. Feeling that I was about to suffocate to death, I ran down and out of the house into the tiny courtyard out front, coughing and gagging. I stumbled right past Randy, who was fanning the hearth in an attempt to start a fire for breakfast. I was furious. From the courtyard, I shouted back inside to her, "What the hell are you doing? Didn't you know I was trying to meditate?" With a nervous chuckle, Rand began to make some reply. I didn't hear her because I was racing up the slick footpath away from the two of them, away from the Bahadurs, who'd come running out at all the commotion, and away from my remarkably insensitive and inconsiderate so-called friends.

At the crest, just where the footpath broke out onto the sunny side of the hill, stood Lama Yeshe. With my head down and in my fury, I almost knocked him over. "Good morning!" he said cheerfully. "How is your meditation going?" This was Lama's typical greeting to each of us. Usually whenever he asked it, always gently smiling, we melted into smiles ourselves.

But this time, nothing doing. "I cannot work with these people, Lama! I will not work with them! Randy just built a fire under my meditation. She knew I was meditating. I don't want to be friends with them anymore!"

With a broad smile, he asked, "But aren't the three of you going into town later today?" The question stopped me. Hadn't he heard what I was just saying? I asked him, "Lama, you are very kind and compassionate, but didn't you just hear me? I don't think the three of us can be friends anymore."

"You *are* friends," he said, "and friends for life. More important, you three are *Chos-ru,* Dharma sisters and brothers. You will feel differently later." My body bristled. Then, stepping forward and looking deep into my eyes, he whispered, "Sometimes, when anger rises up so forcefully, it's good to say to yourself, 'Buddha's mind is angry today.' " Because of the way he told me this, as though it were a secret teaching just between the two of us, I listened. The suggestion that *my* mind, even filled with anger, was also the Buddha's mind brought a big smile to my face. My body began to release its tension. Then, almost abruptly, Lama turned away and continued his morning stroll down the sunny side of the footpath. Over his shoulder, he said softly, "Don't forget your town trip." I was never able to look at myself the same way again. And of course, I went to town with my two best friends.

I had come to Lama Yeshe loaded down with guilt, shame, anger, and a feeling of utter helplessness. I couldn't think or see past the rage I felt from the untold indignities I'd experienced in life prior to meeting him. Such anger had crippled me in countless ways and had almost sent me down the path of violence. Yet wounds like mine had a flip side too, a false and prideful view of entitlement: Look at all that I've endured. I'm great. In time, Lama Yeshe would find a way to pull the rug out from under this pride.

THE TEST

ᘒ

Why remember the pain?
Why try so hard to speak
Unspeakable black people grief?
Because such great psychological
And spiritual
Harm
Cannot be undone,
Cannot be begun
To be healed,
Unless we remember
That it was done.

One morning after spending the night at Rand and Rob's, I sat perched upon the grassy knoll just above the little house that served as Lama Yeshe and Lama Zopa's abode. Lama Yeshe pushed open his door, toothbrush in hand and towel draped across his arm, heading for the bathroom on the other side of the house. For a brief moment he paused, looked up at me piercingly, and before continuing his journey, said, "Living with pride and humility in equal proportion is very difficult, isn't it? Very difficult!"

In that moment, it seemed to me, he had put his finger on one of the deepest issues confronting not only me but all African Americans. There is a great existential difficulty in attempting to count oneself a human being equal with all others after having suffered through the experience of centuries of slavery. Our very humanity was challenged and degraded at every turn and yet, through it all, we have maintained the desire to stand tall, with dignity and love of self. Only two decades before Lama Yeshe's remark, throughout the civil-rights marches in the southern United States, African Americans had carried signs that poignantly proclaimed, "I am a man!" and "I am somebody."

It is the trauma of slavery that haunts African Americans in the deepest recesses of our souls. This is the chief issue for us, the issue that must be dealt with head-on—not denied, not forgotten, not suppressed. Indeed, its suppression and denial only hurt us more deeply by causing us to accept a limiting, disparaging, and at times even repugnant view of ourselves. We as a people cannot move forward until we have grappled in a serious way with all the negative effects of this trauma. With just a glance that morning, Lama Yeshe had captured my heart's dilemma: How to stand dignified, yet humbly, in the world?

I was soon to discover that Tibetan tantric Buddhism offers tools to help with this dilemma, for it provides methods that show both how to get at those deep inner wounds and how to heal them. One method, for example, employs the meditative notion of divine pride. According to this theory, we are all inherently pure, or divine, at our cores. Our task is but to realize this truth. There is, of course, a very fine line between confidence and arrogance. Belief in one's own innate purity and power can easily be confused with an all-too-human pridefulness. The consequence of misunderstanding this crucial distinction, and of thereby going astray, is the creation of more suffering rather than the elimination of it. Hence the great need for a true and authentic guide on this most important journey of discovery. This fact was brought home to me personally and powerfully in the ensuing weeks.

For Randy and Robbie, Lama Yeshe was everything they could have imagined in a teacher: his face glowed, his eyes twinkled, his smile radiated loving compassion and gentleness. He was well educated and seemed genuinely happy to teach us. In my heart of hearts, I was greatly attracted to Lama Yeshe as well and had strangely felt drawn to him even before we actually met. Now that I had had my own experiences with his warmth and wise counsel, I felt all the more fortunate.

But I was still cautious and tentative. I held back, wishing not to seem so easily won-over. I saw humility as a virtue and I wanted to be humble—like Lama Yeshe. Yet I also wanted to be strong and not to feel as helpless, weak, and vulnerable as I had so often in the past. These two opposing forces seemed to be doing constant battle inside of me. Given all the disappointments, demeaning instances, and frustrations I had suffered since early childhood, it was, quite simply, difficult for me to trust anyone. I said to the two of them, "Yes, he is compassionate, but so are lots of Tibetans. I want to learn something about wisdom." Lama Yeshe, for his part, was patient and loving toward me, even when I was not so nice to him.

One day as we were finishing up a session with him, Lama Yeshe surprised me by saying, "I think you should go and study with my teacher, Geshe Rabten. He is a great teacher and is especially skilled in teaching about Buddhist wisdom. He is living in India, in Dharamsala, but since you know Hindi, traveling there will be no problem for you." I felt both proud, that he recognized my academic intellectual side, and a bit rejected, since he made it clear that Randy and Rob were to stay there with him at Kopan. I told myself that this arrangement would be better. I would finally get to be with the wisdom-being, the master teacher I wanted and deserved. Surely, pride goeth before the fall.

On the way to Dharamsala, I stopped off in Banaras to visit Cletus. I stayed there for two or three days, going to movies, relaxing, and just playing around before I headed up to the former British hill-station of Dharamsala. Finally arriving there, I found my way to Geshe Rabten's place. He was actually in retreat, living in an old mud-caked hut out in the woods. Serving him there were only a monk-cook and a young incarnate lama-charge of his, named Gonsar Rinpoche, who stood in as his translator.

I waited a moment outside the hut while Gonsar introduced me. When he motioned me inside, I touched my hands together in *anjali* and began to bow to Geshe Rabten. These were the normal forms of greeting. But suddenly, Geshe Rabten abruptly cut me off, delivering a long and seemingly angry tirade in Tibetan. He pointed his finger at me and went on and on in a raised voice. Clearly I had done something wrong. After a while, Gonsar Rinpoche translated: "Geshe-la wants to know why you have arrived late," he said.

"I beg your pardon?" I began, but a longer outburst from Geshe Rabten followed. I couldn't understand how he *knew* that I could have arrived any sooner. Lama Yeshe had given me a letter of introduction, and since I was myself carrying that letter, how could Geshe Rabten know that I had stopped off in Banaras? Still, his lengthy and animated declaration left little doubt that he did know and that he was chewing me out for my tardiness.

He didn't want to hear any excuses. He asked nothing about my background or personal history and didn't care who I was or where I had come from. He was a teacher, I had been sent by one of his disciples, and he would teach me. That was all. I was told to take a seat. He began right away, that very day. After getting over the shock of that first meeting, I felt like I was in paradise.

I lived in Dharamsala for six weeks, taking lessons each day from Geshe Rabten. They were lessons about how creating and then clinging to false images of ourselves only serve to create more suffering for us, about the impermanence of such self-projections and the need to lessen our attachments to them, about the pitfalls and burdens of swapping one pretense for another, and about how, ultimately, since we create our own suffering, only we can put an end to it by living life authentically. Eventually the time came when I had to return to Nepal. Six weeks was the arrangement I had made with Lama Yeshe, and my Indian visa was up. Geshe Rabten had been inordinately kind to me. I gave little thought to the fact that he was trying to do a meditative retreat of his own. I told myself I was learning a lot from this master teacher about lessening self-grasping, but in fact I was self-centered, elated at my good fortune, and completely oblivious to anyone else's needs. I was also proud and more than a little arrogant. I thought I deserved to study with a teacher of Geshe Rabten's stature because *I* was such an intelligent student.

As I returned to the compound at Kopan near dusk late one evening, I glimpsed Lama Yeshe in the distance coming down the stairs on his way to his room. He seemed to see me, too. But rather than that warm smile he always gave, he turned his head sharply away and continued his steps. He seemed to make a point of ignoring me. Returning after so long, I felt immediately rejected again. After all, I was coming back from studying with his guru. I walked toward Lama's room and noticed Randy and Rob's shoes outside his door. Apparently, he had begun giving them extra lessons. Again, I was the outsider.

I tapped gently on the door and slowly entered. Lama Yeshe was quietly talking with them. Then, suddenly, he looked up at me with what seemed a completely different look in his eyes, almost like anger. Before any of us knew what was happening, Lama Yeshe pointed his finger at me and began yelling in Tibetan. The string of words that issued from his mouth sounded *exactly* like those Geshe Rabten had used at our first meeting. Lama Yeshe had never spoken to any of us like this before. Rand and Rob, like me, were completely stunned.

Then, in a flash of insight, I knew what Lama was doing. It was a teaching directed solely at me, and it was perfect. Lama Yeshe knew a great deal about me. He knew that I had been judging between him and some other type of teacher. He knew that I prized wisdom over compassion, not seeing that both qualities were essential requisites in any true teacher. He knew that my seeming arrogance was only the flip side of my low self-esteem, and that low self-esteem was my deepest and oldest wound. He also knew that I was intelligent and determined. He had sent me on that journey to Geshe Rabten's so that I would come to see all these things about myself; and so that once they were clearly recognized and claimed, he and I could begin to work on the delicate balancing act needed to heal them. I realized then how difficult it must have been for this kind teacher to feign anger toward me, or toward any living creature for that matter.

I fell forward on the tiny floor, bowing to Lama Yeshe, and sobbing full-force. I asked for his forgiveness. He had seen into my heart and soul. It struck me that such wisdom and compassion are truly inconceivable. And I knew—from that moment—that I could trust Lama Yeshe to be my teacher and my guide.

Such testing is a time-honored tradition between teachers and students within Buddhism, and the teacher-student relationship is the subject of much of Buddhist literature. For many years I have treasured one Buddhist narrative above all others, *The Life of Milarepa.* Some books are great because they tell a good story, and some are great because of the way they are written, but rare is the book that accomplishes both. For me, *The Life of Milarepa* is such a book. It is one of Tibet's greatest literary and religious classics. I have loved it since I first read it decades ago. And on page after page of this poignant narrative, I see myself reflected as well as my source of hope.

Milarepa is revered as the man who, in a single lifetime, managed to transform himself from being a person who had committed horrible deeds early in his life to one who attained complete enlightenment. His story is unique because Mila, as I affectionately refer to him, narrates his *own* story.

Mila was born into a modestly comfortable family of loving parents. When he was a child of seven his father died. On his deathbed, he entrusted the family's wealth to Mila's uncle until the child reached maturity. But when that time actually arrived, the uncle reneged on the promise. As a consequence, Mila, his mother, and his sister were forced to live in abject poverty. Mila's mother threatened to kill herself before his eyes unless he swore an oath to get revenge on the uncle and his family by learning black magic and causing their deaths. He did so and caused the deaths of some thirty-five people. Afterward, he suffered incomprehensible remorse and felt completely helpless to reverse his evil deeds. In a hopeless and desperate state of mind, he sought out a Buddhist teacher who could help.

That teacher was a rather raucous, boisterous character named Marpa. After diagnosing Mila's main problem as being feelings of helplessness and unworthiness, Marpa made him agree to build, single-handedly, a series of stone towers. When each was completed, Marpa had him tear it down and completely rebuild it in a different spot or in a different style. Marpa later explained that he was helping his young disciple both to have the results of his former evil karmic deeds ripen sooner, in this life, so that he could move on to positive fruits and that he was preparing Mila's fragile psyche so that he would actually be able to receive the teachings.

Many see Marpa's tactics as being quite abusive. But consider what the ordeal of the towers does *for Mila* himself. As he builds each tower he's building up confidence in his own abilities. Once he comes to believe in his own abilities to create as well as to destroy, then and only then does Marpa give him the teachings; and meditating one-pointedly in the snow mountains of Tibet, Mila attains full enlightenment. Thereafter, in poetic verses numbering more than 100,000 and in the life story he narrated, Milarepa goes on to teach others how to do likewise. When Mila found his teacher, Marpa, he arrived carrying an inordinate amount of self-pity. Because he had actually killed people, he was inconsolable. Even though he had done so at the urging of his mother and, in fact, in order to prevent her from killing herself, he felt the hordes of retribution for his actions hounding him at every turn. In a moving passage of the account, Mila describes the constant dissatisfaction and fear he felt prior to meeting Marpa:

"I was filled with remorse for the evil I had done by magic and by hailstorms. My longing for the teaching so obsessed me that I forgot to eat. If I went out, I wanted to stay in. If I stayed in, I wanted to go out. At night sleep escaped me. I dared not confess my sadness to the lama or my longing for liberation. . . . I asked myself unceasingly and passionately by what means I might practice the true teaching."

What Mila needed was a good dose of self-confidence. Building the towers helped him to gain it and to begin to feel that he actually *deserved* to receive the teachings Marpa held. Because Mila's life story shows the transformation of sinner into saint in such moving and dramatic fashion, all Tibetan Buddhists revere it. But like any truly great story, its themes of dejection, struggle, and triumph over insurmountable hardships have universal appeal.

When I first met Lama Yeshe, I arrived carrying a lifetime's worth of self-pity and low self-esteem. I knew that I worked hard and was determined; I kept plugging away, in spite of often feeling beaten down. I also knew some of the causes for my particular state of being. But I usually saw these as having to do with external conditions or persons. Lord knows, I had my reasons, and many of these were true. But peace was what I was after, some way to still the constant frustrations I experienced and to feel comfortable living in my own skin. Whether our suffering takes the guise of self-pity or self-absorption, its source is the same: holding too tightly to our projected images of ourselves. We know, for example, that when we are depressed, our minds turn about one point: me. Poor me. Why me? How could this have happened to me? The nub is always me, me, me. Though it may be more difficult to see how self-absorption causes pain, here, too, attachment to self-image wreaks havoc with any contentment. Always there is the desire for more. More attention, more applause. More recognition of *me*.

Lama Yeshe saw my wounds, correctly diagnosed my chief illness, and like a skilled doctor, over the course of the next fifteen years, worked with me to help me heal.

Of course, my own story is far less dramatic than Mila's. I had not actually killed anyone—despite, at times, wishing to have done so—nor had family members cheated each other out of their possessions. Nor, thank goodness, did I have to endure the same harsh treatment as Mila did from Marpa. Apart from the one instance when Lama Yeshe yelled at me to teach me a lesson about my own judging mind, he used gentleness, encouragement, and respect for my intelligence to help me build up my confidence and regain self-worth. Still, I see myself as having initially arrived before him feeling just as Mila had when he found Marpa: bearing the burdens of guilt and self-pity. I understand Mila's torment and I rejoice at his finding peace. And I rejoice because I know that as Marpa diagnosed and treated his pupil with precisely the right medicine to help him to heal his particular illness, just so did Lama Yeshe understand and help me to treat my own.

JOY OF THE DHARMA

ᄋᎧᎧ

I had been taking myself pretty seriously up to this point. It was only by facing my self-esteem issues and getting out from under the self-pity I'd been carrying around for so long that I could begin to develop a healthy sense of who I was—and a healthy sense of humor. In Buddhism, as in most of the world's religious traditions, gaining a new name is part and parcel of the ritual one undergoes when one *commits* oneself to the faith or to a particular path of practice. Though I very seldom use my Tibetan name, it is quite special to me.

The truest marker of any Buddhist is that she or he takes refuge, or places full trust in, the "Three Jewels," namely: the Buddha, the Dharma, and the Sangha, or, again, in the founder of the Buddhist tradition, in his teachings, and in the community of his followers. But there is also, for each Buddhist, a ceremony that is performed—usually early in life but at least at the beginning of a specific path of practice—that marks her or his official entrance into the community. This is how I came to earn my Tibetan name.

Lama Yeshe had already given me a new name shortly after I began studies with him. He had dubbed me "Lobsang," a name that echoed the monastic name of Tsongkhapa who had founded the specific order in which Lama practiced. "Lobsang" means "of keen intelligence." I liked it. But when Lama Yeshe sent Randy, Robbie, and me together to study with his teacher, Geshe Rabten, he had advised us to ask *him* to perform the ritual initiation for making us official lay Buddhist practitioners. In Dharamsala, we made our request.

Geshe Rabten graciously agreed to perform the initiation just for the three of us. We were so proud. We entered his tiny retreat hut carrying flowers and incense offerings. Gonsar Rinpoche translated as Geshe Rabten explained the ceremony to us in detail. He told us that the ritual required that we plead for the vows of an *upasaka,* or lay follower. This meant that we should make our requests with folded hands, down on our right knees. "Of course, you don't have to stay like that because the ceremony goes on for some time. You should start out in that position, as a symbol of requesting the vows, but when it becomes uncomfortable, please sit down comfortably." I heard those words, but being stubborn, I determined that I would do the ceremony from beginning to end on my right knee.

So the three of us got down on our right knees and the ceremony began. After some time, I saw Rand and Rob sit back. I thought, "Hah! Not me! I will see the initiation through till its end like this." Well, two and a half-hours later, I was still on one knee on the cold and damp mud floor of Geshe Rabten's hut when the ceremony ended and we each had new names. Rand was now "Light of the Dharma," Robbie "Dharma's Accomplishment," and I "Joy of the Dharma." My friends stood up, beaming. But I, of course, could not move. I was completely frozen in place. My right leg had been numb for more than an hour and a half. So, Rand and Rob had to help me up. Each had me under the arms as I stood—on my left leg—trembling, between them.

Suddenly, Geshe Rabten began calling to his monk-cook to come and see the spectacle. When the cook arrived, he told him what had just transpired, and the cook doubled over with laughter. Gonsar translated for us, "Geshe Rabten is delighted. He says, 'What a perfectly great name you have been given, Joy of the Dharma. Just look at all the joy you are causing!' "

In my youth, I had been dragged—kicking and screaming—to be baptized. In spite of all my protests then, I had found the immediate aftermath of that experience to be quite wonderful, for it was as though, for the first time, I was lovingly enveloped in the arms of a community. Now, as an adult, I had entered into this Buddhist naming ceremony freely and of my own choice. Even so, my old stubbornness—about following the rules, about being a good Buddhist—was still there. If anyone could use a little lightheartedness in her life, I figured it was me. The monks' laughter was spontaneous, joyous, and nonjudgmental. I could see that, though painful, my stern antics had actually been quite comical. I liked this warm and welcoming community; and I looked forward to the time when my new name might actually be an accurate description of my inner being. Here, in the midst of these Buddhists, I felt the hard shell of my rigid self beginning to soften. And, joining in with them, I burst out laughing.

A SPOT OF BLONDE

ᏆᎧ

$\mathbf{M}$y appearance at birth, which caused so much trouble, would come back to haunt me with the Tibetans in a totally unexpected way. Everywhere I turned with them, my confidence and self-image couldn't help but improve. When I was born, my head was covered with curly blonde hair. As I grew older, the overall color became darker as the blonde hair contracted inward, leaving a blonde spot of hair about two inches in circumference at the center and top of my head just slightly to the back. This spot of blonde has remained to this day; it adorns my Afro, almost like a tiny, flat crown.

Just before I was to leave the country on my very first journey to India, my blonde spot came to the attention of a black woman who frightened me no end when she literally began to dance with joy upon seeing it.

Miss Dolly Green ran a beauty shop in Urbana, Illinois. I was there doing summer studies in preparation for the Wisconsin program trip. Just days before our departure, I decided I would go to get my hair done. This was a pretty futile effort, as I was going away for at least nine months. Since I didn't have a perm, my hair, once straightened with hot combs, would not last very long without turning back to its natural state. But neither did I, as yet, wear an Afro. So one day during our last week in Urbana I asked someone about beauty salons and was directed to Dolly Green's place.

A small bell above the door jingled as I entered her shop. Miss Green, motioning me over to a chair, told me she'd be with me soon. She was a dark-skinned woman, short in stature but sturdy. She wore a flowered print cotton dress over which she'd tied a clear plastic apron that was stained with smudges of hair tints and dyes. I hated going to beauty shops. It was as much a big social thing as a service for making women feel better, that is, prettier. I always felt ill at ease in such places: "A college student with nappy hair!" "Oughtta have more respect for oneself!" I told myself to calm down. After all, I didn't know anyone here.

One might be able to imagine then how thoroughly surprised I was when Miss Green suddenly grabbed my arm, spun me around in the chair, and started dancing as she shouted: "Praise the Lord! Chile, now I know why the Lord put me here in Urbana! I's seen eleven of you now. Blessed saints. Praise be to God!"

"Ma'am? What, ma'am? I beg your pardon?"

Miss Green was doing her dance. I'd seen it before. It was the dance holy rollers did, a kind of praise-step where one dances without lifting the feet completely off the ground. If either foot actually left the floor, the dance became secular, and the work of the devil. I knew then that Miss Green was sanctified. I, on the other hand, was simply scared to death.

I had been reading Dick Farina's latest novel that summer. In the novel, when things got scary, Dick's main character intoned the phrase, "Monkey-demon week." That phrase now reverberated in my frightened mind. What had I done to cause this woman's outburst? And was it, I hoped, only temporary?

I wanted to race to the door and get away from there. Forget the hairdo! But Miss Green blocked the door. She was happy and she wanted to tell me, and the two other ladies who sat there waiting their turns, exactly why.

"Yes, Lord. Now I know why He sent me here. Praise the Lord! Jesus done showed me eleven of you. The Bible says he anointed fifty in heaven 'fore sending them here. You sho' are one, chile! Now I can rest easy. I done seen eleven of you."

"Monkey-demon week" echoed louder in my mind.

I don't remember whether Dolly Green ever calmed down enough to do my hair that day. I don't remember if I ever calmed down enough to have her do it. Anointed? Me? In the midst of my brewing anger at the rest of the world, I found it highly unlikely.

Over the years, many of my students at Wesleyan have asked me how, or why, I came to be so involved with Tibetan Buddhism. Given my background and appearance, the question strikes me as a fair one. But honestly *I don't have a clue.* Of course, I know the general contours of how my interest unfolded, but as to why a black American woman in the late sixties came to be so enamored of and so readily accepted by Tibetan Buddhist refugees living in India and Nepal, that question is deep and perhaps ultimately unfathomable. Now, what is interesting and also true is that Tibetans seem to have no problem with the question at all. Without ever asking them, they have eagerly, and often reverentially, explained to me that in a former life, I was a Tibetan. And more than that, I was instrumental in helping to establish Buddhism in Tibet.

The first time I heard this explanation was in 1970. That year in Nepal, I had become friends with a teenaged Tibetan girl named Tenzin. She had continually pleaded for me to visit her and her mother at their home. One day, I left my quarters—Lobsang Chonjor's room at the monastery—and went into town with her to do so.

Her family—she, her mother, and other siblings—all lived together in two tiny rooms in a larger house owned by a Sherpa. I remember being struck by how old her mother looked. Too old, I thought at the time, to be Tenzin's mother. Her brow had numerous deep grooves, and though she still maintained a head of long, well-greased dark hair, her body seemed leathery and weather-worn. She smiled and I saw that her mouth was almost completely toothless. She did sewing of various kinds, making and embroidering pillowcases and other things that she hoped would be bought by tourists.

I bowed to her respectfully and then noticed that she became very animated. After she'd told Tenzin to make tea for us, she put her sewing tools to the side and launched into an excited narrative. My spoken Tibetan was not very good then. Consequently, I was relieved when Tenzin set three cups down before us so that she could interpret.

As it turned out, Tenzin's mother's excited tale was all about me. Not exactly about the "me" of this present life, rather, it was about who I once had been, and who I now simply reincarnated. It seems that when the first Buddhist monastery had been built in Tibet, back in the late eighth century A.D., whoever I was back then had helped to build it. The mother called me one of the earliest Buddhists of Tibet. I was flattered but I didn't pay much attention. We sat in silence, had our tea, and smiled at each other.

I would probably not have remembered this particular story were it not for the fact that some days after that visit, back up at Kopan, Lama Yeshe had suddenly summoned me to the second-floor balcony of the monastery. He was standing next to a Western woman who had arrived at Kopan earlier in the day. "Arrived" is not the most appropriate word, since her coming had been heralded long before we actually saw her. Great plumes of dust were raised up the winding hillside, and the grunts and spurts of the rickety taxi—of all things!—she had somehow bribed and cajoled into driving her up had preceded her appearance. This woman was clearly a foreigner and unlike any of us who normally lived at Kopan. We knew that cars never attempted to drive up to Kopan owing to the simple fact that there was no road leading there. Everyone—Tibetans, Western hippies, and the Nepalese whose hill it was—walked; and walked fairly slowly at that!

The woman with Lama Yeshe had come for the day only. She was quite a sight, in her sequined high heels and heavy makeup. After lunch and a conversation with Lama, she wanted to meet with Tulsig Rinpoche, a renowned lama of the Nyingmapa lineage who was residing in Bodhanath. Lama Yeshe told me to take the woman to meet him. I wasn't thrilled to serve as the woman's chaperon, but I was delighted by the prospect of actually meeting Tulsig Rinpoche. This renowned teacher rarely came down from his mountain monastery. The chance to see him was a real opportunity, a gift, worthy of even the bumpiest and scariest taxi ride.

At the house in Bodhanath where Tulsig Rinpoche was staying, Tibetans moved in and out of rooms silently as if floating just above the floors. Messages were being passed in hushed tones. A line of guests were waiting their turn to visit this grand teacher. I spoke to the monk who seemed to be in charge, and taking his hand gesture to mean that we should wait there, I stood feeling a bit awkward next to the woman in her white suit and sequined shoes. After a few minutes, we were both called in.

I motioned for the lady to go in ahead of me. When I reached just inside the door, I glanced at Tulsig Rinpoche and began to perform my prostrations to this most holy lama. Suddenly, he stopped me and beckoned me forward. I moved trembling toward him, head bowed. He cut a lovely figure in monk's robes, large in size, powerful though gentle.

His smile was captivating. With his right hand, he tenderly raised my head. Then everything took on an air of magic.

As his fingers lightly held my chin, he began a discussion with the other monks flanking him. When I gave a puzzled look, one of the monks began to interpret.

"Rinpoche says that you should not bow to him. He says that he should make prostrations to you, since you are one of the people who built the first Buddhist monastery in Tibet." I forgot completely the woman I was supposed to be accompanying. The monk continued.

"Rinpoche asks if you know the name of that first monastery."

"Yes. Its name was Samyas Monastery," I replied, still trembling. "The name means 'Inconceivable.' Legend has it that the monastery was constructed by ordinary beings during the day, and during the night by the gods." The other monks approved of my response.

"Rinpoche says that when the great Samyas Monastery was completed, the king of Tibet, King Trisong Detsen, had all those workers, all those who built the monastery, line up and pass before him. When they did, King Trisong Detsen sprinkled *tsampa* (barley flour) in their hair. Rinpoche says that the light spot of hair on your head comes from this sprinkling. He says *he* is fortunate to meet *you!*" Tulsig Rinpoche, still gently holding my head, then beamed a broad smile right into my eyes.

After that, I was motioned over to a cushion, given tea, and the conversation turned to the business of the woman I had brought.

It was only a spot of color I happened to have in my hair. Yet Tulsig Rinpoche's explanation of it made me feel really special. Like a proud father, his appreciation gave me the sense of being a worthy human being. A part of me was deeply touched because it was one of the first times anyone had actually looked up to me, let alone anyone of Tulsig Rinpoche's stature. Part of me felt those old wounds begin to resurface from all the times I had been told, or made to feel, just the opposite. Part of me smiled in disbelief since I had never accepted the notion of reincarnation. And part of me just wanted to put the whole idea far away because I couldn't imagine that I might have anything positive to contribute to this world—whether now or in the past. I wanted to believe him, wanted desperately to believe Rinpoche and Dolly Green and Tenzin's mother. It was only right. It had to be true. All people were special, each and every one of us. But truly feeling this would take some time. Finally, I managed to let go of all these conflicting emotions. And I sat there, basking in the warmth of Rinpoche's presence.

FLESH-AND-BONES
BUDDHA

⤫

After we had been given our new names by Geshe Rabten, Randy, Rob, and I stayed in Dharamsala for another six weeks. The weather was cold and rainy. We had arrived totally unprepared for it, or the harsh conditions, but being hippies we made the best of it. The floor of our little room in what was called "Naro-jee Villa" was concrete. At the one street market of Dharamsala, we bought straw mats upon which to lay our woefully inadequate sleeping bags. So when we were not having a session with Geshe Rabten, or clambering up and down the steep trail to the market, or preparing a meal on our borrowed kerosene stove, we each sat in meditative posture, facing a wall of our room, trying to bring to mind a sharp, crisp image of a Buddha, our teeth chattering. Life was challenging but good.

Being in Dharamsala meant that we were in the place where His Holiness the Dalai Lama actually lived. In subsequent years, it became much more difficult to arrange for a private audience with the Dalai Lama, but in those days, it was a simple and quite informal matter. His Holiness's private secretary, though soft-spoken and refined, counted himself a simple monk. In the late afternoons he often strolled the one street of Dharamsala's marketplace. As our time of training with Geshe Rabten drew near a close, one evening we approached Tenzin and told him of our desire to meet with His Holiness. He reached into his robes and took out a small datebook. Looking it over, he raised his head and asked, "Would tomorrow at three o'clock be all right with you?"

"Why, yes! Yes, it would. We will be there. Thank you so much." That was all it took.

The next day we prepared by taking good though frigid baths, dressing in our cleanest clothes, and getting our best *kattas,* or greeting scarves, folded neatly and ready to offer to His Holiness. When we arrived at the residence just behind the Namgyal Monastery, we were ushered into a simple but eloquent foyer. Tenzin inconspicuously ducked into a room and then came out to tell us that His Holiness would see us.

The thing I remember most about that first meeting, for there have been many since then, was that His Holiness seemed much taller than I had thought him to be. His voice, too, was quite incredible, deep and rippling and, at times, seeming to come from other parts of the room. Like the student-hippies we were, just after entering the room we had begun doing prostrations. His Holiness quickly put an end to this formal ritual by coming over to us and saying as he gestured with his hand, "All right, stop that. None of that is necessary. Please, come and sit down." We found ourselves completely at ease.

He was charming and energetic. His very being exemplified the ideals of Mahayana, that form of Buddhism in which all spiritual practice aims at, and is perfected through, compassion and service to others. He was the true *bodhisattva,* a being whose sole intention is to make himself into a proper tool to serve and fulfill the needs of all beings; who compassionately strives to do whatever is necessary so that others can be helped and not harmed.

After graciously commending us for studying with Geshe Rabten and for being students of Lama Yeshe, he wasted no time in engaging us in a discussion about student protest in the United States. His Holiness wanted to know everything about recent demonstrations and unrest. We talked for some time about the shootings at Kent State. He made it clear that he wanted to know how we, as students, saw what was happening and why. He listened with eyes set firmly upon us and with a kindness and compassionate understanding that made our own words flow smoothly.

I was supposed to be following the same path that helped the Dalai Lama become as kind and great as he is, so I asked, "Given that we have taken *bodhisattva* vows, Your Holiness, what are we to do if, once back in the States, we find ourselves in a position where we too are facing policemen or National Guardsmen who want to shoot us?" Talking with the Dalai Lama brought up again for me my old dilemma about violence versus peace. Back at Cornell and on my subsequent trip to California, perhaps to join the Black Panthers, I had had my own near brushes with violence, and I had thought a lot about the possible consequences of armed confrontation. Though I had chosen to turn away from violence, I was still concerned about becoming too passive. I knew that the Dalai Lama himself had had to face similar issues when his own country was violently invaded by the Chinese. His Holiness became intensely reflective. Then with deliberate and attentive clarity, he advised us as follows:

"You have now entered upon the Mahayana path. That is very good. Very good, indeed. The Mahayanist, the *bodhisattva*, as you know, works for the benefit of beings. He or she wishes to aid beings wherever they are in need. You should know that your first duty, now that you are on this path, is to practice *patience*. You are meditating to gain clarity. You must have clarity in order to act appropriately. With patience and clarity, you know with certainty whether you can or cannot help a given situation. If, after looking at the situation with clarity, you determine that you cannot help, then it is better not to worry. Worry accomplishes nothing. But if you are clear and you can help, then you will know what to do and how to do it. So, patience and clarity are essential."

"Yes, Your Holiness," my impatience made me push, "but what if you think you have looked at all the alternatives—with clarity—and you find that your only course of action is to be on that line along with others, facing those policemen or those guardsmen, then what?"

"Again," he said, "patience is most important. But if you are certain that there is no other alternative, if you are clear and certain about this, then what you must do is this: First, you must think lovingly and with compassion about the policeman. If you think or call him a pig, then you must let him shoot you! But if you can wish him well, and pray for his future happy rebirth, then of course, you stop him from harming the others. You stop him by any means necessary." We were relieved and amazed.

He continued, "When I came out of Tibet, many Khampas with guns accompanied me. They were concerned about me. They wanted my safety. I could not say to them, 'You are wrong to have guns.' Many monks too in Tibet took up guns to fight the Chinese. But when they came here, I made them monks again. You should not believe that the Mahayana asks you to think of beings' welfare only in some future time. You should try as much as possible to help in the here and now. Still, patience and clarity are most important, most important."

Lama Yeshe had made a similar point several weeks before we came to Dharamsala. He had been talking with another student and was telling him that one should actually do whatever is necessary to help

beings and not cause them harm, even if that sometimes meant breaking one's vows. He had said, "Sometimes, compassionately helping
someone requires what a purist might view as breaking one's vows. For
example, suppose a woman runs by you screaming that a man is after
her and wants to kill her. In a few moments, you see a man brandishing a big knife who asks you, 'Where did that woman go?' Now, your
vows tell you that you should not tell a lie. But if you tell the truth,
the man will probably kill the woman. So you choose to tell a lie here
in order to protect the woman from harm. Doing so also protects the
man from creating negative actions. The vows are not so much pro-
scriptions as they are guidelines. You must use your intelligence, your
wisdom and clarity, as well as your compassion to be of service to
others."

Talking with the Dalai Lama brought this truth home again.
Buddhism was a process; one did not need to delude oneself or to pre-
tend to be other than oneself, and one did not have to become completely passive in order to embrace the notion of peace. Choosing
peace did not mean rolling over and becoming a doormat. Pacifism did
not mean passivism. Still, patience and clarity were essential. My heart
basked in the glow of his words.

Before we knew it, almost two hours had gone by. His Holiness had
been so open and so frank with us that he seemed to me to be like an
old friend and wise counselor rolled into one, a true flesh-and-bones
Buddha.

PART 4

Becoming

DECIDING TO BECOME
A TEACHER

∞

Although I don't remember exactly when I first formed the intention to become a teacher, the precise moment when I articulated my desire stands out vividly in my mind. It was during a conversation with Randy in 1970, just after the three of us had returned to the States from Nepal. Since the accident in France, she had been saying that things seemed strange. As an immediate result of the accident, she had suffered amnesia, but the serious psychological problems that would follow neither Rob nor I could fathom.

I had entered graduate school at Columbia to undertake Buddhist studies in earnest, and since Rand and Rob lived in Brooklyn, she and I met pretty regularly on the weekends. I would try to talk with her, asking, "How does it feel, Rand? How do things seem to you now?" She would again repeat, "Things are so strange, Jan. So strange." This was exactly what she'd been saying in France in the hospital recovering from the accident; it was what she'd said throughout our time in Nepal and, now, throughout the first year we were back.

One day Rand and I together carried a blanket and some sandwiches to Prospect Park in Brooklyn. We put our blanket down along-side one of the small ponds where kids sail their tiny boats. It was a bright, sunny day. We were both lying on the blanket looking up into the blue sky. She asked me, "What is it that you want to do?" In Randy's mind, she told me afterward, such a question had only a very short-term answer, like what we'd eat for dinner or what we'd do to-morrow. But I said right away, "Me? I want to be a *teacher!* I've always wanted to be a teacher."

Without warning, Randy jumped up from the blanket and began screaming at the top of her lungs, *"What?! How can* you make plans for the future?" At the sound of the terror in her voice, my whole body went into spasms. I mean, this was my best buddy and she was out there, way out there, alone, and hanging by a thread. Then looking down at me, she said in a slow, deathly calm voice, "I can't think past dinner. Making meals, Jan, is what orders my time. This is how strange it is for me." She sat down again and we embraced.

When Randy told me her problem in these terms it was the first time I had ever heard anyone, especially anyone whom I knew and loved, articulate it like this. She repeated, "All I can get, all I can think, extends only up through today's dinner. I can only get as far as dinner, that I have to make dinner tonight. And when I hear you say you want to be a teacher, I just can't imagine that far ahead." In Prospect Park, the two of us sat, peering into the little pond, mute.

Randy's question to me had evoked my response, but in our shared silence, I tried to think back on when the idea to become a teacher had first crystallized for me. In my childhood days I had determined to be any number of things: a symphony conductor, a mathematician, an as-tronaut, a theoretical physicist. I had always loved languages. I was drawn to any form of universal communication, whether mathemat-ical equations or musical notation. And though my schools were seg-regated and poorly equipped, my teachers had gone out of their way to help me, a young black girl in the Jim-Crow South, to learn as much as possible. But when had the idea of becoming a teacher formed itself?

Ideas grabbed me with force and wrestled with me, sometimes against my wishes. I was in turmoil for weeks from the questions my father posed to me, like Zen *koans,* when I had yet to begin first grade. I saw the universe as a great mystery inviting deep, thoughtful engagement. When, at last, I was allowed to enter school, I was overjoyed. Often my quickness brought negative consequences, as when solving my sister's math problem got me promoted early but embarrassed her. My mother's response to my smart mouth often enough brought on unintentioned wounds, as well. But it was as though I couldn't stop myself; I loved learning too much.

I recalled that I had never minded sharing what I knew. I helped out other classmates who were having difficulties. In high school, my physical education teacher, Mrs. Calloway, had forced me to become a cheerleader, a role that I thought little of at the time, so ensconced in academic pursuits was I. But that experience had actually turned out to be most satisfying. In many respects, it was the salvation of my senior year of high school.

Thinking of Mrs. Calloway made me smile. She was a feisty woman, tall, skinny, fair-skinned, and gangly, with a high, hoarse voice. Other kids made fun of her, as she strode back and forth along the sidelines of Westfield's meager basketball court shouting, "Now! Punch it in!" At the end of gym class one day, she'd called me over and surprised me by saying, "We know you're going to win all the scholastic awards. I want you to win the 'all–around' award, too. That means I want you to be a cheerleader next semester." I was completely taken aback. "Me? A cheerleader?" I said. The idea just didn't compute. "Yes, a cheerleader! I need someone to lead the cheers who's a fast learner and can lead the others. I need *you* to do it."

I had thought the whole idea preposterous at first, not really because I thought it was below me, an advanced academic student about to become class valedictorian, but because, quite simply, no one at the school frightened me more than those dark, tough, and fast girls who made up the current cheerleading squad. Surely she didn't think they would agree to be led by me! If anything, they'd have a field day verbally abusing me, if not literally beating me up, every chance they got. I told Mrs. Calloway that I'd think about it, but I didn't tell her the truth, which was that I was just too chicken.

My folks thought it was a good idea. They were concerned about my moodiness and low spirits going into my senior year. Perhaps Mrs. Calloway, too, was concerned with this more than about increasing my cache of senior awards. Baptists say that angels are everywhere; and Buddhists that compassionate *bodhisattvas* manifest in many different forms in order to aid beings. After some mental wrangling, I agreed to take the challenge. In retrospect, it could not have been a wiser decision. I found that I liked being able to get out of classes in order to work on school cheers with this group of seven rough-and-tumble girls I would not have met otherwise.

At our first meeting, they liked that I remembered all of their names. I have always been good at this; it still serves me well in large classes at Wesleyan. Anyone appreciates being recognized as an individual. And when the girls of the squad didn't, I remembered all the cheers. I encouraged them, showing them easy ways to get the cheers, while letting them show me the moves. We bonded as a team. I liked them and they liked me. In fact, rather than bully me, they became like my own private bodyguards. "Did that guy say anything about you, Dean? We'll get him!" And, "Did she say anything to you? Just let us know and we'll take care of it!" Against all odds, I had won them over. And my method had been simple and uncalculated: respect and kindness. I decided that I liked teaching.

Perhaps, I reflected, sitting there with Randy, I had always liked teaching. I could not imagine a more worthy profession. From the time I had wanted to teach those angry, misguided Klan folk who had attacked my family and me, I had considered teaching to be the single most valuable means of communicating and of sharing peace on earth. In our shared silence, I continued to muse.

I realized that at first I had thought communication was the main issue. I thought, if I could just explain my family's situation, the Klan folk would understand and change their menacing ways. Then I realized that communication alone was not enough. First, people had to realize that they had minds of their own that they could use. It was not simply a matter of pumping knowledge into their brains. People had to know that they had the ability to use their minds to bring about change. If they were made to feel confident in their own abilities to think for themselves, that could change their lives. At key points in my own life, various people had given me the gift of believing in myself. This gift helped me to heal many of my inner scars and insecurities. I wanted to become a teacher to pass the gift along.

TEACHING IN PARADISE

∾

The term Buddha *is not a proper name. Rather, it is a title, a badge of recognition, that is given to anyone who has "awakened to" and "understood" (the term's literal meaning) the true nature of reality. And what flows out of such understanding is selfless compassion, offered fully, universally, and spontaneously for all beings still bound in suffering. Therefore, while we most often associate this term with the sixth-century* B.C.E. *historical figure Siddhartha Gautama, the great Indian teacher who founded the tradition, there are, have been, and will continue to be countless Buddhas wherever and whenever beings awaken to the truth.*

Siddhartha had been born a prince of the Shakya clan. But when he was twenty-nine, he abandoned his royal estate, his wife, and his newborn son to seek answers to the age-old question of beings' suffering. At the age of thirty-five, after six years of arduous meditation, he woke up, attaining a state of knowledge and insight that has been known since that time as enlightenment, and earning for himself the title Buddha. *The Buddha Shakyamuni spent the next forty-five years teaching primarily two things: understanding suffering and its cessation. His emphasis upon the suffering inherent in our continual, unsatisfactory circling through the unhappy states of birth, sickness, old age, death, and rebirth has caused many over the centuries to view the tradition as being pessimistic. In reality, however, the Buddha preached a doctrine that asks us to perform an in-depth analysis of suffering and its causes in order to bring about the end of suffering and, therefore, to usher in a new state of tranquillity and insightfulness.*

The most succinct formulation of the Buddha's doctrine was provided in the very first sermon he delivered. That First Sermon set forth the Four Noble Truths of Buddhism, namely:

1. There is suffering.
2. There is a cause of suffering.
3. There is the cessation of suffering.
4. There is a path leading to the cessation of suffering.

As footnotes to each of these Truths, we are enjoined to understand fully the first, find and eliminate the second, realize directly the third, and practice the fourth. Far from being a pessimistic tradition, Buddhism offers the promise of freeing ourselves and others from suffering. In the end, it sounds quite hopeful. For almost 2,600 years, and for hundreds of millions of people, following the Buddhist path has led to genuine and lasting happiness. So, please don't forget: the Buddha was a human being just like you and me. He realized the Four Noble Truths and taught them to humankind. As a result, the very next Buddha in the world just might be you."

At the end of my talk, students jumped to their feet in applause. Some even cheered. I smiled, feeling warm and appreciated, and then, with unfeigned modesty, opened the floor for a question-and-answer period. The very first question brought an end to my euphoria. It came from a slim black student who sat on the front row holding a sort of stick cane in his arms.

"Okay," he began, "so just who was this guy you called 'the Buddha'?"

Had I not made my remarks clearly enough? Should I have been more historical in my presentation? The question seemed to be some kind of challenge, but I could not quite figure out what the student was really asking. A good deal of lecturing is performance, but one also needs to be able to recognize where the students are coming from and so be better able to pitch one's remarks appropriately. To that student I began again, offering a brief sketch of the Buddha's life and his historical context in India. It seemed to satisfy him. When I finished, he said, "Okay, thanks."

"Oh, Dr. Jan. You're a perfectionist!" Josie King, a counselor in Student Supportive Services, later said to me following that very first lecture at UCSC, the University of California at Santa Cruz. Josie meant it both as a comfort and as a diagnosis of my chief problem. She suggested that I worried too much about nothing, adding that that student had simply wanted to relate to me, and so he had asked a question. *I* was the one giving it too much weight. She proposed that I try to be kinder and gentler to myself.

Her remarks made me think back to the day I first arrived at UCSC. I had flown in to San Jose, the airport closest to Santa Cruz. Since my new boss, Herman Blake, could not pick me up there, he had sent one of his best students, a most impressive young black man named Sabre Slaughter. Sabre was a fifth-year student. He had been working under the mentorship of Herman for most of his time at UCSC and was just about to complete his major in Herman's area of expertise, sociology. On the way from the airport to my temporary residence, Sabre and I stopped off for a light dinner at Denny's (of the now-infamous restaurant chain), just inside downtown Santa Cruz.

A few other students happened to come into the restaurant, and after friendly introductions, we gathered around the same table. At some point our wide-ranging conversation turned to zodiacal signs. A couple of the students declared their signs and then looked at me. "I'm Pisces," I said. "Water sign, peacemaker, and often worried about making decisions." As the round-the-table discussion was going, it fell to me to put the question to Sabre. I turned to him and asked, "Well, Sabre, what are you?"

He looked at me with a penetrating stare. After what seemed an awfully long pause, he said, slowly and with careful enunciation of each syllable,

"O-ppress-ed."

A slight shiver ran through me. Things tended to get pretty heavy here, pretty fast. It was certainly going to be an interesting and challenging experience teaching in this environment.

A few years before, when Herman had first begun recruiting me to come to UCSC, I had had hesitations. "You know that I will be teaching *Sanskrit* and *Buddhist* studies?" I had responded to him.

"I know that. But what's the problem?" he'd said. "You can teach those students how to *think!*"

I doubted myself a lot in those days. I felt like I had let my people down by not becoming a Black Panther party member. I had abandoned the confrontational route and chosen the Buddhist path of peace. Now, I was unsure about what kind of reception I would get from my own people because of this.

Herman was actively engaged with the Panther party. Though his early work had focused on the role of women in Latin American revolutions, most recently he had helped Huey Newton to write his autobiography, *Revolutionary Suicide.* And at our very first meeting, Herman had just flown in from the trial of the brother of George Jackson, the cause celebre black man who, at Soledad Prison, had spent the longest time ever in solitary confinement. Herman was a very powerfully built, bespectacled, dark black man who sported a wispy goatee. He spoke with commanding authority and was full of the restrained fire of revolution. But he was sensitive to my insecurities and uncertainties. Whenever he was visiting New York while I was still in graduate school at Columbia, he made it a point to call me or to arrange a dinner. That constant encouragement had paid off; and now here I was at UCSC, about to begin doing what I had always wanted most to do: teach.

The next morning following Sabre's unsettling remark, Herman picked me up and gave me a tour of the magnificent campus before taking me to my office. It was from him that I first heard the oft-touted claim about the Santa Cruz campus, that not a single tree was cut down to build the school. I loved the way the buildings were nestled in. However, I had difficulty with not being able to readily locate the university library. I was used to Cornell and Columbia, where the library was the focal point of the campus. My early comments about UCSC's library being almost hidden within the trees later earned me the reputation of being an "East-coaster" and, I suspected, "overly serious" went along with this description.

When we arrived at my office, Herman took me over to its broad window and pointed out that I could actually see the tip of Monterey, some forty-five minutes' drive away, at the other end of the bay. The grand vista of rolling wheat-colored land and frothy blue sea was breathtaking. The office itself was unfinished, bare and of rough cinder block construction. I had told Herman about the conversation with Sabre, and he already knew my history of being jittery. Like the wise sage that he was, he also had a prescription to help me settle into the newness of my first real job. He said, quite matter-of-factly, "The building's new. This gives all our faculty the chance to decorate their offices exactly as they'd like them. Go downstairs to the secretary and choose a color. She'll make sure the paint's delivered tomorrow. This weekend would be a fine time to paint."

It was the perfect anti-jitters medicine. And so, I spent the first full weekend of my time in Santa Cruz dressed in sneakers and sweats, listening to the soul music that rolled from a little radio the secretary had loaned me, and painting my office a soft, creamy, rich, light yellow. Alone but happily busy; preparing to teach in paradise.

The University of California at Santa Cruz was designed to be the state's experimental, interdisciplinary campus. Its entire structure echoed this new notion about higher education. Unlike other campuses in the UC system, there were no departments. The faculty was comprised solely of individual specialists, the idea being that people would therefore be encouraged to talk across disciplinary lines. The campus itself was organized into separate thematic colleges wherein faculty and students with primary interest in a particular theme were clustered together. For example, there was Merrill College, which focused on international political issues, and Kresge College, where diversity was taught by complete immersion in an international environment. UCSC had been slated originally to house thirty colleges, but when I arrived there in January of 1974, there were only seven. An eighth came into existence while I was there, and I believe the number of colleges has remained eight. Herman headed the seventh college, later to be named Oakes College. Its focus was domestic, that is, U.S. social and political concerns.

Rather than the two-semester system I was used to, the academic year at UCSC was divided into quarters of ten weeks each. There were no grades given throughout four years of study. Instead, each student received a detailed written evaluation of his or her performance in each class and a transcript that reported only "pass" or "fail." As can be imagined, this meant a lot more work for faculty members, but it was thought to be a better system for students.

Faculty and students were not only clustered around thematic issues; individual college faculty and student bodies reflected those themes. I was especially proud to be associated with Oakes. We had a total of twenty-six faculty, thirteen men and thirteen women. Among these twenty-six, there were African American men and women, Chicanos and Chicanas, Asians, Native Americans, and others. We embodied a true "Diversity University."

Oakes enrolled a relatively high percentage of so-called non-traditional students as well, namely, those who were older—many of them much older than I—and who had come from educationally de-prived or depressed backgrounds. Herman, and Josie, who became my closest friend, were especially good at recruiting bright but under-educated students from as far away as the Sea Islands of the Gullah and as close by as Oakland and Bishop, California. Looking around at the group of us gathered together—at a convocation, for example—one saw a sea of diversity, which meant that, for the first time, we saw our-selves. I loved it.

Apart from our resident faculty members, Oakes invited an ever-widening series of guests to the college. In this way we all got to meet such luminaries as Septima Clark, Dee Brown, Angela Davis, and Alex Haley.

Alex Haley and Herman were good friends. Haley and I, too, formed a special bond. He was a gentle and generous human being; a quiet, modest, and self-reflective soul. His blockbuster book, *Roots,* had not yet been published, but everyone was excited about its immi-nent appearance. In the meantime, Alex was already into his next big project: a comparative study of the keepers of sacred history and tra-ditions around the world, folks who were akin to the African *griots* who had given him back his family lineage. I talked with him about the *dharas* of India, individuals who retained in their memories such mammoth works as the Vedas and the entirety of the Buddhist Canon before these works were committed to written form. He asked me to write up my thoughts on the Indian *dharas* and send them to him. I did. A few months later—after the publication of *Roots*—as I walked into Oakes, the secretaries' office was all abuzz. I had received a telegram from Haley saying how "great, first-rate, and helpful" he thought my report was. Owing to that telegram, which the secretaries copied and posted around the college, I became somewhat of a local celebrity myself! I regret that several years later, Haley died before I could tell him about my own family history work, research that he directly inspired.

While Oakes had a high number of African American students, others were scattered throughout the other six colleges. But within my first few weeks there, I had met almost all of the hundred and thirty or so blacks on the campus because they came to my office to meet me, singly or in small groups.

I soon settled into teaching and discovered, to my great pleasure, that I not only loved the profession but that I was pretty good at it, too. I offered large lecture courses on Buddhism to overflow crowds, and smaller seminars on Sanskrit. I taught "Ancient Indian Religious and Philosophical Systems" and the "Philosophy of Theistic Arguments." Together with other Oakes faculty, I co-taught courses on the "Religions of the Oppressed" and "Religion and National Liberation Struggles." I developed a popular course called "Three Generals in the Lord's Army" that focused on the slaves' religion as a revolutionary tool during the antebellum period of U.S. history. And I began to feel at home.

However, California itself represented an entirely different culture for me. I must have carried East-coast dust particles with me wherever

I went, for something about me—my conversation? my seriousness?—always gave me away. My age was consistently guessed to be at least *ten years older* than I actually was. Old, heavy, East-coaster. That was a blow to my ego since, when I first began to teach at Oakes, I was only twenty-four.

Moreover, while I was used to four seasons, here there were basically only two: *dry,* marked by its wheat-colored grasses (in other words, dead), and *wet,* which ushered in and was responsible for the wonderfully rich greens. Santa Cruz and the surrounding communities of Capitola, Aptos, and Soquel, were each idyllic places in their own right, filled with upscale boutiques, natural health food stores, great bookstores, and fine restaurants. The area was bounded by the great churning ocean, sandy beaches, salt spray, sea gulls, seals, and cold-water surfers. I enjoyed the newness of this place; loved its open spaces and broad vistas, loved its great variety and abundance of fresh flowers throughout the year, loved the ocean. But in the end I remained an East-coaster, a tourist, an outsider.

UCSC and my job were home for me. I lived on campus in one of the student townhouses during my first two years, and served as a faculty preceptor for Oakes. On weekends I was always in my office working on my dissertation, a translation and analysis of a fourth-century Buddhist philosophical treatise. I remember once my parents phoning and my mom saying how she hoped one day *not* to reach me there! I did finish the dissertation, and returning to defend it at Columbia, I was treated more as a colleague than as the timid student who'd left there, prematurely, to accept a job. After that I moved off campus, to a nice place not far from the ocean. Still, teaching at Oakes was all that kept me in California. The students were great. Intelligent, eager, and interesting, every one of them. I recall with delight the first batch of Sanskrit students I had. One always chipper, bright-red-haired young man rode several miles each day back and forth to campus on his bike. He was something of a sports star and, at the same time, an excellent cook who supplied us periodically with mouth-watering fresh baked bread. He gobbled up the difficulties of Sanskrit grammar with a gleefulness unknown in my graduate classes back at Columbia and went on to become an Asian librarian in the UC system.

Andrew Schelling, now co-director of the writing program at the Naropa Institute of Buddhist Studies in Boulder, was also a member of my earliest classes. Sanskrit caught fire in Andrew; he continued his studies of the language in grad school and went on to become a fine translator of Sanskrit poetry. It never ceases to amaze me how the vocation of teaching works. Like parenting, I imagine, one cannot fathom what the consequences will be. One can only try one's hardest, with genuineness and kindness, and hope for the best.

I count myself fortunate to have encountered and advised another remarkable student during those days. His name was Jim Willis, and he was a full-blooded Apache Indian. I took pride in the fact that we shared the same surname. A tall, long-haired, and strikingly handsome young man, Jim also possessed incisive intelligence. Indeed, he graduated first in Oakes's senior class. He had graduate school offers from a number of prestigious universities, and we communed all year about what choice might be best for him. His choices were complicated because he felt torn between accepting what he called "the white man's offers to co-opt him" and his desire to return to his people and work for their welfare more immediately. It was a dilemma I was quite familiar with myself. In the end, I advised Jim to accept the fellowship from Berkeley. I reasoned that not only would a graduate degree help his work in the future, but given the school's location, he could also remain close to the issues and concerns affecting his people, who were located just outside of Fresno, California. Ultimately, however, Jim decided to refuse the fellowship offers. After his graduation, he returned home to work against the Bureau of Indian Affairs.

To my surprise, black students flocked to my Buddhism courses. And I came to find their challenges stimulating to my own thinking. They were keen to know, for example, why attention was so focused on suffering. Hadn't they seen enough of that in their lives? They wanted to know more about getting rid of it. That desire made them listen with a purpose.

Sometimes I gained new understanding from them of Buddhist technical terminology. There was a black woman who was a single mother living on campus with her two children who almost never got to class on time. One day, she came in late again and stood at the very back of the large classroom. I was lecturing on the Indian notion of *karma,* the law of cause and effect. All of a sudden, from the back of the room came her booming voice, declaring her insight: "Oh. You mean, what goes around comes around!" Never having heard that particular slang expression before, I had to think about it for a moment, but she was right.

A main problem area for a great many of our students was that they had been educated in California public schools that shunted them into vocational fields like food preparation and management rather than into academic tracks. As a result, these students were, at a very basic level, ill prepared for college work. Our job as faculty was not only to teach them our particular area of expertise but also how to read critically and how to write. Additionally, Oakes hired a black director of mathematical studies, a former high-level mathematician in the corporate sector, named Al Stewart. A brilliant, gentle, and compassionate person, Al ran a twenty-four-hour math tutorial program.

I found myself spending a number of extra hours in the office helping students with their writing, whether or not they were taking my courses. Two young black men showed up at my office like clockwork for help with written assignments. They were best pals and always came together, Joe Grant and Jim Brown. We worked through two quarters; then they enrolled in my introductory Buddhism course. One day they appeared at my office door. "Hi, guys. Any problems?" I asked. They seemed suddenly shy. They began their sentences together, then fell into a sort of staccato declaration in which one continued the phrase of the other.

"No writing problems today, Professor Willis. But some of that stuff you're teaching . . . well, our *sensei* talks about that, too . . . and, well, it seems a lot alike. So, we were wondering. We'd like to invite you to our *dojo* to meet him." Joe and Jim were *tae kwon do* martial artists. I'd heard from other students that they were pretty good at it, too. It was one of the sweetest invitations I had ever received. As it turned out, I joined that *dojo* and became a student of *tae kwon do* myself. I was thrilled to see the two of them in their element, confident and strong; and I realized how important it is to find and to appreciate that special arena wherein each of us is at our best. I never much liked to spar, so I was still a white-belt beginner when I finally left the Korean system. By the time Joe and Jim graduated from Oakes, however, they were both black belts, qualified to teach. Jim later opened his own *dojo.*

Still, nothing had quite prepared me for the day when several black students, perhaps six or seven in number, came to my office hours together. A young woman, who is now a professor of anthropology, was selected to be their spokesperson. She asked me straight out:

"Do you know about Buddhist meditation?"

"Yes," I responded. "I know a bit about it. I've practiced some."

"Would you teach it to us?"

"Well, yes. I could teach you some of what I know."

"What we mean is will you teach it to *just us; in a group all our own.*" I almost fell off my chair, so taken aback was I with surprise, and then delight. One among the group in particular had immediately caught my eye: he was none other than Sabre Slaughter, Mr. "O-ppress-ed" himself. I agreed to lead the group in a private session of meditation once each week.

As I look back on my first real teaching job, I cannot imagine a more exciting and more supportive environment in which to have begun to practice my vocation. Back in the days when Herman was recruiting me to come to UCSC, he had promised to have me tenured by the time I was thirty. And he kept his word, undertaking a grueling amount of bureaucratic work to make it a reality. In the meantime, however, I had been offered and had accepted a one-year visiting appointment at Wesleyan University in Connecticut. After three and a half years of teaching, counseling, and offering extra writing support to students, I was suffering from burnout. Moreover, I realized that in fact, I missed the intellectual stimulation offered by departmental structures. Herman loved introducing me to people as Oakes's Sanskritist, but I rarely got the chance to communicate with others about how that felt and what it meant to me.

Life at Oakes revolved around two distinct passions: radical politics and education, and partner-swappings. To the first, I was fully committed; but the second held little interest for me. At the conclusion of my visiting year at Wesleyan, the letter offering me tenure at UCSC arrived. Within one week, Wesleyan convened its own bureaucratic constituencies and matched the offer. At a time when most of my other colleagues were worrying about the dread tenure decision that would determine whether they kept their jobs or lost them, I was fortunate enough to have *two* offers. Ultimately, I chose Wesleyan. It broke my heart to face Herman when next I visited Oakes; and for his part, he was so disappointed that he couldn't speak to me for almost two years. I'm happy that, with distance, we are once again good friends.

I BELIEVE I CAN FLY

෨

One of the essential practices at all levels of tantra is to dissolve our ordinary conceptions of ourselves and then, from the empty space into which these concepts have disappeared, arise in the glorious light body of a deity: a manifestation of the essential clarity of our deepest being. The more we train to see ourselves as such a meditational deity, the less bound we feel by life's ordinary disappointments and frustrations. This divine self-visualization empowers us to take control of our life and create for ourselves a pure environment in which our deepest nature can be expressed. . . . It is a simple truth that if we identify ourselves as being fundamentally pure, strong and capable we will actually develop these qualities, but if we continue to think of ourselves as dull and foolish, that is what we will become. . . . The health of body and mind is primarily a question of our self-image. Those people who think badly of themselves, for whatever reasons, become and then remain miserable, while those who can recognize and draw on their inner resources can overcome even the most difficult situations. Deity-yoga is one of the most profound ways of lifting our self-image, and that is why tantra is such a quick and powerful method for achieving the fulfillment of our tremendous potential.

—*Introduction to Tantra*, Lama Yeshe

A few years ago a movie called *Space Jam* swept the country by storm. It was a family movie, aimed at providing inspiration primarily to kids. So, what better person to feature in such a film than basketball's all-time greatest player, Michael Jordan? Millions of kids around the world already proclaimed the wish "I want to be like Mike!" The film's other stars came from the cartoon world, and with the aid of high-tech computers these animated characters were blended seamlessly into a story about a high-stakes basketball game in which Michael was the protagonist. *Space Jam* had all the ingedients. Not least among these was a catchy and rich musical score.

The signature song of the movie was composed and sung by R. Kelly, previously known for his less-than-inspirational hard rap. Entitled "I Believe I Can Fly," it caught fire. It has aired almost continually since the movie, especially within the black community, and has been adapted into the musical repertoires of other noted black performers like Patti LaBelle. It is a song about hope, faith, triumph, and especially about confidence. In the video of Kelly singing the song, he stands on a basketball court flanked by a full gospel choir. At its conclusion, the choir booms forth a happy hum. The song not only gives confidence, it describes a method for achieving it—the power of visualization. It seems to me that this particular song offers an important bridge for explaining what tantric Buddhism is all about.

Though *Space Jam* focuses on the sport of basketball, most athletes have always known about, and employed, the method of visualization. Prior to a competition, they usually visualize themselves performing a certain move, or series of moves. Whether for Olympic skaters, track and field athletes, or football players, the technique of visualization plays an integral part in their preparation. At the conclusion of the 1998 Super Bowl, Denver Broncos' running back Terrell Davis, who was voted the game's Most Valuable Player, said that all week prior to the game he had visualized himself running in the game, making his particular moves and plays. He had never visualized anything except the Broncos winning the game, and it paid off. Michael Jordan knows about the payoffs of visualization, too. Former Chicago Bulls' head coach Phil Jackson learned meditation from Zen Buddhists and taught specific visualization techniques to the members of his team.

According to Mahayana Buddhism, we have the ability, right now, to transform ourselves into fully enlightened beings, that is, into fully awake and conscious beings of unlimited compassion and wisdom. Our problems and our suffering stem from not knowing this fact. We don't know it because our core—which Buddhists believe is peaceful, clear, and spacious, like the sky—is obscured by quickness to anger, jealousy, and all-consuming desire. We want to know whether or not we have as much as we can have. These habitual negative patterns are like clouds covering the clear sky of our Buddha-nature. Clouds are transient, but the sky's pristine nature remains unblemished. Hence, becoming enlightened is definitely possible. We only have to let our Buddha-selves shine through. It is often said in Buddhism that none of us could ever become enlightened beings were it not the case that we already possess—within each of us at this very moment—the potential to become so. In Buddhist terminology, this potential is usually referred to as our inherent Buddha-nature. The historical Buddha was an ordinary human being just like us. All he did was manifest the potential of all sentient beings.

The heart of tantric Buddhism is transformation, the idea that we can change our ordinary negative patterns of seeing and feeling into positive ones. And the method employed to bring about such a transformation is nothing other than visualization, in this case, deity-yoga. Buddhism's great pantheon of deities, however, is often misunderstood. It appears to some that the Buddhist tradition is advocating the worship of numerous external gods. This is not the case. The deities of tantric Buddhism are none other than projections of our own innermost selves. Each represents an aspect, or specific quality, of our own enlightened mind—whether compassion, wisdom, tireless beneficial activity, fierce service to others, or universal love.

The method of visualization is already quite natural to us since we think in images all the time. Usually, however, we spend most of our time visualizing ourselves in negative ways. If we see ourselves as shameful, limited, and unworthy human beings, that is what we'll project and become. The practice of deity-yoga simply involves our changing this nonbeneficial view of ourselves into one that brings benefit, both to ourselves and to others. Hence, in tantric Buddhism, we begin to visualize ourselves as being infinitely compassionate, wise, and fearless persons. The goal of the practice is to have us touch, and then bring forth, these positive qualities that are already within us.

Most of Buddhism's vast pantheon of deities are depicted as having peaceful appearances. However, some forms appear in wrathful guises, having bared fangs and sporting numerous arms all brandishing weapons. Yet far from being menacing, these deities actually represent our innate power and capability bursting forth.

When considering the meditative visualization of benign deities, it also would be incorrect to cling to outward appearances. For example, the goal of doing the practice of White Tara, the Buddha of Compassion and Longevity, is not that we develop a white body with seven eyes—as White Tara appears in her iconographic form—but that we get in touch with our own infinitely compassionate and healthy selves. Likewise, visualizing Green Tara isn't aimed at having us develop green bodies, but rather wisdom, compassion, and the ability to accomplish beneficial activity. By perceiving ourselves as having these positive qualities, we become more and more able to let them shine through and to replace our former negative perceptions of ourselves.

Tantric Buddhism is called "the speedy path to enlightenment" because it uses our ordinary abilities to visualize as a method for rapid transformation; a method that encourages us to exercise our minds in ways not dissimilar to the ways athletes train and exercise their bodies and their minds. I do not mean to suggest that tantric visualizations are a piece of cake; many deity-yoga practices are quite complex, requiring both mental and physical internal yogas that are conjoined with very detailed visualizations. Still, it is true that we have the capacity to bring about a most marvelous transformation within ourselves *if* we are willing to undertake the disciplined exercises prescribed.

Of course, much commitment and hard work are necessary for the journey. But then, no one could ever accuse Michael Jordan, or Terrell Davis, or Jerry Rice of being lazy. And in the end, what could possibly be more important? In this case, the prize is becoming a Buddha: happy, loving, generous, reliable, patient, disciplined, focused, and wise. Sounds like a good gig to me. Black folks have a saying: "Keep your eyes on the *prize!*" The two traditions are not so far apart here.

Even so, tantric meditation is not something to be undertaken lightly. Some pretty weird things can happen on meditation retreats and along the spiritual path. I'm speaking from experience, and I've certainly had my share of bumps along the way. In other words, don't try this at home without adult (read: lama) supervision.

MY GREAT SEAL
RETREAT

ᘒ

He did not mean the sea mammal of that name. Lama Yeshe was offering me the chance to try out the advanced system of tantric meditation perfected by Tibetan yogic masters who had quickly attained enlightenment by using it. It was the early summer of 1981. I had been living in Nepal for a year and a half. I had gone there on a National Endowment for the Humanities fellowship to work primarily on collecting the oral histories of certain living Tibetans. But first Lama Yeshe had asked me to translate the lives of some of the early Gelukpa saints who had gained full enlightenment very quickly. These particular practitioners had followed the meditative instructions developed by Tsongkhapa, the founder of the Gelukpa school. His system was known either as the Ganden Oral Tradition or the Gelukpa Mahamudra, though the great yogi Milarepa had first brought prominence to the method. *Mahamudra* means "Great Seal" or "Great Gesture," referring both to the subtle shift, or gesture, of the mind, which ushers in enlightenment, and to the badge or "seal" of this attainment. For more than a year I had worked on the translations Lama wanted, which became the basis of my book *Enlightened Beings*. Now, I planned to get on with my oral history work.

Though the translation work had been challenging, as well as inspiring, it had never crossed my mind to try out the grueling methods of the Great Seal tradition. For example, one of its practitioners, a sage named Jampel Gyatso, had chosen to sustain himself while he meditated for almost three years by eating only tiny pills fashioned from crushed juniper berries mixed with mud. Another, Gyelwa Ensapa, had continued his strenuous practices even while his body was being ravished by smallpox. Even though by 1981 I had been doing some meditations for about twelve years, the commitment required to tackle Great Seal practices seemed to me almost superhuman.

Lama Yeshe was preparing to leave Nepal for a tour abroad that would begin in Australia and keep him away from Nepal for the remainder of my stay there. One day he asked me, in quite a serious tone, "Don't you want to know what the system these people practiced was like? I mean, don't you want to *try it yourself?*"

One part of me was flattered. The other part of me was scared. Immediately I thought, "Right. Does he really think that *I* could actually sample anything so lofty as the practices that had ensured these men enlightenment?" I had meditated a bit during the years I'd known Lama—had even had some pretty good results—but this was serious stuff and a big commitment. I didn't think I was ready or brave enough to undertake it. My response to Lama Yeshe's offer came out of my mouth with far too little reflection. It was a cowardly and knee-jerk response. I said, "No. Thank you, Lama, but *no way!*" He looked a bit stunned.

"Why, daughter, wouldn't you want to try something so wonderful?" I said, with emphasis, "Thank you, Lama. I am happy you'd consider introducing me to such mysteries, but I don't think I'm ready." Probably sensing my fear, his response then was compassionate and gentle: "Well, think about it, dear. Think about it." When he turned toward other activities, I left the monastery and literally ran down the hill away from Kopan.

All the way home, his offer stayed with me. I had been translating the lives of these saints for a year. I had studied other *nam-thar,* or "liberation life stories," for many years before. These were exceptional practitioners. Devout from the beginning, committed to the Dharma until the end. I didn't think I could practice like they had. I didn't have the will, the determination. I was chicken, right down to my toes.

Moreover, those Great Seal practitioners had felt the great Mahayana wish to liberate all beings from suffering from the time they had issued from their mothers' wombs. I wasn't sure I wanted to save all sentient beings. I surprised myself with that thought. In a flood of emotions, all the hesitations and doubts I had previously only thought about regarding Buddhist renunciation, about giving up everything in order to help others, came rising up. One thing seemed certain: I did not possess it. Could it actually be that I liked suffering too much? And then, I didn't know what to expect from the practice. I was afraid I might end up in some strange place, like Castaneda's Itxalan, catatonic and alone. I was afraid that I might actually *succeed,* and thereby *lose* myself. These fears surfaced all together and at once. I was a wreck by the time I reached home.

I tried, with no success, to have a restful afternoon. In spite of my fears, there was something so tantalizing about Lama Yeshe's offer. I knew it would be stupid to let it slip away. "Be brave," a stray thought encouraged me. "Be a Buddhist, girl! Here's a chance to really practice. Put your actions where all your study and thinking has been. Answer Lama with your heart."

Almost without full awareness, I called Lakshman, my young, ever-smiling yardman, and gave him a scribbled note to carry back up to

Lama Yeshe. The note said simply, "I would be happy to try the practice. Thank you so much. Your Daughter."

Lakshman had recently purchased a new bicycle with the ample rupees I was paying him and he liked nothing better than a mission such as this. I had asked him to please hurry back, but several hours passed before his return. When he did enter the front gate, ringing the bell loudly, I raced out to the porch to meet him. I could see that he was grinning from ear to ear. In fact, his face was luminous, as though Lama Yeshe had performed some special magic just for him. Which, of course, he had.

"Ma'am *sahib!* Ma'am *sahib!*" Lakshman blurted out through gleaming white teeth. "Your Lama has sent you a special present!" From his *jola* bag Lakshman pulled out an object wrapped in layers of rice paper. Cook Kanchi joined us in the living room as Lakshman excitedly narrated the details of his splendid adventure. After reading my note, Lama Yeshe had been very pleased. He had ordered a very fine meal for Lakshman, with tea and dessert. Lakshman had eaten on the top patio of the monastery while Lama Yeshe rushed back and forth preparing the statue that was contained in the rice paper.

"That statue, ma'am *sahib,* is very precious. Your guru, Lama Yeshe, told me so. And he has *filled* it, ma'am *sahib,* with many precious things!"

In their presence, I carefully unwrapped the gift Lama had sent me. It was a Nepalese terra-cotta Buddha about eight inches in height. My first impression was that the little image was rather gaudy, painted in thick and overly bright colors. I had seen lots of statues much more subtly executed. Perhaps, I thought, Lama Yeshe's student Lama Zopa had painted this one; he loved doing such work. But perhaps Lama Yeshe had done this one himself. I was not taken by the statue's attractiveness. It was clear, however, as Lakshman had reported, that the statue had been very recently sealed up at the bottom; rice paper was freshly glued around its lotus base. The idea of Lama Yeshe's having stuffed the statue with many precious things made me smile. I knew that lamas did this when statues were ritually consecrated, stuffing every available nook and cranny with everything from soil from sacred Buddhist sites to hairs from famed teachers to gemstones and minutely written mantras. Lama Yeshe had consecrated this Buddha image just for me and my practice. It was a gift from him. And it seemed to carry along with it his joy that I was willing to undertake the practice. I touched it to my head in reverence and I treasured it.

The next day I walked up to the monastery at Kopan to meet with Lama and discuss the details of my upcoming retreat. He met me with a broad smile and said, "I am happy, dear, that you will do this practice. And I am sure—one-hundred-percent sure—that you will be able to taste the great Mahamudra bliss. Don't worry, dear. You will."

I apologized for having at first turned down his offer, to which he responded, "All right, dear. Now you will do it. That is very good." He then reminded me that I was extremely fortunate at this time to possess all the external necessities for doing such a retreat, namely, a nice, sturdy, and quiet house; a cook to prepare my meals; a yardman to handle any needed shopping; and a fireplace in which to conduct nightly fire-offerings. The external conditions, in fact, could not have been better. The retreat would last six weeks. It would be a *silent* retreat. I could walk inside my house's compound but could not go farther than the yard. I could not read or enjoy any form of entertainment. Nor could I receive visitors. I balked a bit at the silence part but, upon reflection, thought that it might be a relief. So far so good. I was still willing to give it a try.

Next, Lama told me that we would discuss the specific details of the practice at a later time but that for the time being there were certain requisites that I needed to begin assembling. First, I would need to have another statue made, one of Dorje Sampa, whose Sanskrit name is Vajrasattva. The Buddhist deity used primarily for purification, his meditative practice is a necessary requisite to all advanced tantric meditation. I had been doing a practice that focused on this deity since 1969. The statue required now would need to be a special one, one that I had myself commissioned, made to certain specified standards. *And* it would need to be specially consecrated by a group of monks. Lama suggested that I request someone at Samteling Monastery, my earliest monastic home, to handle the consecration for me. I should also begin collecting the necessary grains and various other offering materials to be used in the fire rituals I would have to perform each evening during the retreat.

The preparations for my retreat took a full two weeks. As it turned out, I was fortunate to get everything done by then because Lama Yeshe was leaving on his trip just a day or two later. I had Lakshman shop for most of the grains I needed. He had to purchase big bags of rice and black sesame seeds, enough to last for six weeks. Some of the offering materials, like *kusha* grass, I had to shop for myself.

To have a statue made just for me required several trips out to Patan, the little town that had once served as a capital of Nepal. Many artisan families lived in Patan, descendants of people who had been supplying monasteries in Tibet with their statuaries for centuries. Visiting a number of stores that sold such statues, I finally found my way to a respected and trustworthy clan of artisans. Before a deal was actually struck, I was guided through numerous back alleys and up and around several darkened stairways. Finally, I stood in a room, lit only by the light from a tiny window. The chief bronzecaster offered me a wooden stool and then reached under a low thatched Nepali bed. Pulling out a tray, there suddenly appeared twenty or so bronze molds of statues, lying on their backs. They were each about ten inches tall, half-bodied and still rough, but somehow wondrously lifelike.

The bronzecaster asked me to choose the statue I liked most. Surveying them, one in particular caught my eye. Even in this early stage of production, its limbs were graceful and its face sublime. Watching me, the bronzecaster gently lifted out that particular form and, holding it up, said to me, "This is your Dorje Sampa." I smiled.

I saw my Dorje Sampa statue twice more in differing stages of completion. I decided at the next meeting that the statue should have its exposed limbs gilded and, on the subsequent viewing, that its face should be delicately painted with gold. When, after ten days, the statue was finally presented to me, it was magnificent. In fact, it was the most beautiful Dorje Sampa I had ever seen.

Still, I had to have the statue filled and consecrated. Lama Yeshe's suggestion proved right about who would be best to handle this part. I took the statue to my friend Lama Thubten Palden, a respected monk at Samteling who was also the monastery's ritual specialist. Lama Palden listened attentively as I explained that I needed the statue in order to do a six-week Mahamudra retreat under Lama Yeshe's guidance. Moreover, he seemed unruffled when I added that I needed the consecration done in just a few days. I learned later that Lama Palden had begun work on the statue as soon as I left him. He himself had made trips around Kathmandu Valley gathering various materials with which to fill the image. He had traveled up to Swayambhunath to get certain substances from teachers living there: dust from Bodhgaya, diamond chips and rubies from other lamas, hairs from revered lamas of the past. Back at Samteling, he had filled the statue with these items, dressed it, and then recruited three other lamas to help him perform the consecration rituals. The four monks conducted special ceremonies that lasted two complete days and nights. When next I saw my statue, it was as if it had become alive. It was draped in a tiny brocade robe and wore a necklace of coral and turquoise, and it evinced a living spiritual presence. As the traditional Buddhist saying goes, "Its eyes had been opened." I thanked the lamas and Lama Palden and made them a small offering. The preparations for my Great Seal retreat were done.

During that week, Lama Yeshe had sent me a note asking me to come to Kopan to receive final instructions for the retreat. When I arrived, I found the *gompa* in a buzz. Lama was leaving the next day. He motioned me over to his own small room.

A huge suitcase was flopped open on his bed. Various articles were scattered all over the tiny room. Lama searched through his stack of *pejas,* Tibetan woodblock-printed texts, wrapped in various colors, until he found the one he wanted. He turned to me, licking his fingers and flipping through the long pages, as he said, "As you know, dear, you are about to undertake the great Mahamudra retreat, the retreat taken by so many precious Gelukpa saints, and that brought them to the experience of actually *tasting* the Dharma's power and richness. This great meditation involves both deity-yoga and voidness-yoga, both generation-stage and completion-stage practice. Its central deity during the deity-yoga stage is Dorje Sampa."

Suddenly he paused, as if having an afterthought, and asked me, "How many Dorje Sampa mantras have you already completed, dear?"

"Well, now. Let's see. . . . I did the practice for two hours each night while I lived in Ithaca," I said as I began trying frantically to tally the specific number of sessions I'd completed, then counting 100 mantras for each session and multiplying. Fortunately, at that point a nun came in holding up for Lama's inspection a sleeveless yellow shirt worn by Geluk monks under their robes.

"This one, Lama?" she asked. Lama Yeshe gave his quick assent, "Yes, all right, dear. That one will be okay." The interruption gave me a chance to complete my tally.

"I'd say roughly thirty-five thousand Dorje Sampa mantras, Lama."

He looked at me with a startled expression on his face. *"That's all?"* he asked in disbelief.

"Well, yes. I think so. Maybe a few more, but not many more than that." No need to lie to your guru at this point, I thought. He began flipping through the *peja* again, perhaps, I thought, to find a watered-down version of the practice, one more suitable for a lazy practitioner like me.

Another nun entered the room carrying a monk's shawl. "This *dzen,* Lama?"

"No, dear, I have enough *dzens* already. Thank you."

I was thinking, "What a way to get such a powerful initiation!" Yet amid all the busyness of Lama Yeshe's packing and all the things he'd no doubt have to attend to later in the evening, he kept instructing me. Things began to calm down. Lama Yeshe was now reading aloud from instructions on the retreat. He began to speak slowly, intently, and directly.

"This retreat requires some strict, that is, some rigid meditation, and some relaxation meditation. It is important that you do the relaxation part fully as well." I took out the small notebook I'd brought up and began to scribble notes.

"You are to practice in six sessions for a total of eight hours each day," he said, "and to perform a two-hour fire-offering *puja* every evening. The schedule should be like this: Wake at five-thirty A.M. Take tea. Begin your first session at six, six to seven. From seven to seven-thirty, attend to your altar. From seven-thirty to eight-thirty, second session. Break nine to ten, third session. Ten A.M.–one P.M., break and lunch. One to two, fourth session. Two to four, break. Four to five, fifth session. Five to six, break. Six to eight, Fire-*puja*. Eight to nine-thirty, dinner. Nine-thirty to ten-thirty, sixth session. Then, sleep!"

I asked Lama questions about the overall practice, and he cleared them up quickly and easily. He checked that I knew how to correctly perform the fire-*puja*. I did. He stressed to me again that *relaxation* was very important to the success of this retreat. No visitors. No talking.

No reading, even. It was to be a completely silent, completely relaxed retreat experience.

Satisfied that I'd grasped the details of the retreat, Lama Yeshe closed the *peja,* hurriedly rewrapped it, and sat it back upon his stack. Looking kindly at me and almost shyly, he then said, "Now, I have to do this little thing, and tell you this." He made a quick gesture of pointing up to the sky, while he leaned forward and said to me, "Mind is like the sky."

I felt something quite simple and quite extraordinary at the same time; something akin to grace. A vast, blissful calmness. A stillness that was, in its immensity, all of a piece and all peace-filled. I had glimpsed such peacefulness only once in my life, as I emerged from the baptismal waters outside our little church in Docena. Then, the touch of hands reaching down for me had kept my mind from completely spacing out. Lama Yeshe never actually touched me, but, I am absolutely convinced, his blessings allowed me to touch, and to taste the richness of, that vast infinity of peace. Years later, I would read Buddhist texts that described that special moment of instruction as the "deep pointing out."

"Okay, dear," Lama was saying. "That's all. Have a good retreat. Lama will be praying for you."

I don't know how long I sat there. When I came back to myself, a nun was walking out of the room carrying some other item of clothing. I thanked Lama Yeshe. He told me again that he would pray for me and that I should remember to relax!

Of course, relaxation was the farthest thing from my mind. I was, after all, a Pisces, determined to *do* anything that I could. Now, with this jewel of a practice, I wanted nothing more than to throw myself completely and wholeheartedly into it. Lama Yeshe flew out of Kathmandu the next day.

At my cozy house in Maharaj-ganj, everything for my Great Seal retreat was in order. Kanchi understood that I could speak to her only sparingly, to give assent or not to meals. She agreed to keep Lakshman busy, making sure that fire-*puja* materials were sufficient and that a fire was prepared at the appropriate time each evening. Under ideal conditions, my retreat began.

Each evening, my retreat practice required that I perform a two-hour fire-offering. To my amazement, Lakshman proved totally inadequate as a firemaker. Perhaps it was the modern fireplace. The first couple of days I demonstrated for him, in silence. Still, it took him a few days to catch on. The practice itself was simple but powerful: I sat on a raised seat before the fire. Within the flames of the fire, I envisioned a squatting, dwarflike deity called Dorje Khandro, with an upturned face and gaping mouth. I made mental offerings to this deity, who is viewed as the great destroyer of negativities.

Next, I thought about all the suffering beings throughout the realms of existence. Thereafter, I visualized taking into myself all those beings' various sufferings in the form of smoky streams that I inhaled, letting them come to rest at my heart-center. After some minutes of such inhalations, I breathed out several times into the mixture of grains and butter that had been prepared beforehand. It was this mixture that I then offered, in ladlefuls, to the gaping mouth of Dorje Khandro, visualized inside the fire. The crackling sounds of the mixture's being consumed by the fire brought the day of meditation to its completion and assured me that countless negativities and situations—whether of harmful emotions or physical ailments, mine as well as those of all other sentient beings—were being purified. It was a very satisfying way to end each day.

Keeping silent has an uncanny way of sharpening one's other senses. During the early days of my meditations, especially during break times, I found my sense of vision in particular to be greatly enhanced. I began to take special notice of the birds that came each day to rest on the wall of my house's compound. Indeed, the wall seemed to be a favorite spot of these tiny blackbirds with bright yellow beaks. One particular morning, early on in my retreat, I noticed that each bird, though of the same species, had its own distinctive face, body, and idiosyncracies. I noticed. I took notice. I was astounded: each was different. I began to take special delight in watching the birds, *seeing* whole families, *seeing* individuals and mates, *seeing* what they talked about. Lama Yeshe had continually reminded me to relax. I found that relaxing with the birds was a joy beyond measure. Wasn't this the same bliss the Christian mystics had spoken of? For the first time, I felt I had some understanding of the great joy and peace that St. Francis enjoyed with God's creatures. This kind of peacefulness was not limited to Buddhism.

Then one day during one of my breaks, after I'd been practicing hard for about two weeks, quite unexpectedly a most tantalizingly blissful awareness occurred. I was sitting on my bed, looking out of the window. Thinking about nothing in particular, I noticed that I could see myself standing on the roof of a house some distance away. I had the strange sensation that I was not only standing there but that I could also look back toward the house I was actually in and see myself sitting there. My mind and body felt completely free and unhindered. My normal seeing orientation just suddenly, and subtly, shifted. It was no longer anchored to my physical eyes. I could see myself anywhere I chose, and I could see anywhere. It felt as though my mind suddenly became immeasurably vast. It encompassed everything, the very universe, itself. There was no longer any separation between me and everything else in the universe. The duality of "subject" and "object" simply dropped away and disappeared. The birds and I were of one essence. I was completely convinced that I had tasted that ineffable knowledge about which only the saints can speak. I felt happy, light, ecstatic, completely blissful.

My meditation sessions thereafter became seamless with the rest of the day. There was no distinction between my meditation periods and my nonmeditation periods. My awareness was consistently lucid, vast, and fully attuned to life. Nothing was a distraction any longer because everything was part and parcel of the great encompassment I had directly experienced. This new way of seeing, and the state of utter bliss it engendered, lasted for several days. Kanchi must have thought I was nuts. I moved around, silently, with a permanent grin on my face.

Then the bottom dropped out. It was not that the luminous state of mind departed. Rather, it was that my physical body began to fail me. I began to notice a sort of dizziness. Later this state turned to one of slight nausea. My head started to droop and fall forward. I could not look down or to the side without almost falling over. Things began to spin. Because this was a tantric retreat, it followed the guidelines of earlier Indian practices wherein tantric practitioners, in reversal of traditional religious norms, imbibed forbidden substances: alcohol, meat, fish, and some others. Consequently, for the practice, I was required to sip a tablespoon of *rakshi,* Nepali liquor, at the beginning of each session. Always watchful, Kanchi began to worry. She suggested that perhaps the *rakshi* that I was taking was bad. *"Rakshi karaab, ma'am sahib!"* She strongly encouraged me to discontinue taking it. But I was as stubborn as ever. Taking a sip of *rakshi* was part of the requirements of this retreat, and even though I suspected she might be right, I didn't want to leave off following any of the directions I had been given. Why it didn't occur to me to have Lakshman search out another brand of *rakshi* I don't know. The sickness got progressively worse.

I began to do my meditations propped against the wall. During break times, I literally had to hold my head up with my hands. Kanchi was beside herself with worry. "Please, ma'am *sahib.* Stop this meditating. Your Lama would not want you to suffer so!" But I tried to keep at it.

Sometime, after I'd been suffering like this for a few days, two Tibetans came to the door. I was on break and had decided to sit in a chair downstairs in my living room. Visitors were off-limits, but no one had told these Tibetans that. I recognized one of the men. I had met him in California some years before. He had come to Nepal to visit friends while on his way to Tibet. Not knowing about my retreat but knowing where I lived, he and the other monk had decided to visit me. Kanchi gladly let them in; she wanted me to get help.

I, too, decided that, given my physical condition, I needed to talk to someone, and these teachers were certainly capable of offering me advice. After listening to me and seeing the shape I was in, the two monks counseled with each other. Then one gently spoke: "It seems that you are experiencing what we call *"tsok-loong,"* a type of inner-wind disorder. Because of your strenuous efforts with this Mahamudra practice, your winds have become crossed and entangled. It is a condition that often happens when performing such retreats. Even in Tibet, monks used to make several attempts at this practice before succeeding with it. Also, it can be life-threatening. We suggest that you consult with your guru right away and that, for the time being, you take things very slowly."

I felt like crying. I did cry. Lama Yeshe was far away. I didn't know if I could reach him. But I thought until I could reach him, and until he advised me, I shouldn't break off doing the meditations. Lama had said over and over again that I should relax. I blamed myself. Because of my ambition, my overzealousness, I was suffering. I told myself to just try and take things easier.

Wisely, and weakly, I did manage to scribble a note to Lama Yeshe and asked Lakshman to send it as a telegram to the center in Australia where I hoped Lama would be. I described my symptoms and told him what the two lamas had said. I ended the message with the straightforward, and urgent, question: "What should I do?"

A couple of days after the lamas left, I could not get out of bed. Everything was spinning all the time. I could no longer walk on my own. Even Lakshman had become concerned. When Kanchi arrived, I called her upstairs. "Have Lakshman go for the American doctor, Kanchi. Ask him to come right away." I could see the relief in Kanchi's face as she ran from the room screaming, "Lakshman! Ho, Lakshman!"

Hours went by. Miserable, I lay helpless on my bed. I heard the ring of Lakshman's bicycle bell. Then Kanchi's angry rejoinders. Lakshman had not found the doctor in. He had waited, but he'd never returned. But Lakshman had not left a note or message for the doctor. Kanchi was furious. When she came up to report Lakshman's incompetence, I found myself trying to soothe her: "Tomorrow," I told her, "I'll send Lakshman with a note and forbid him to return without the doctor. If he's not at his office, Lakshman should go to his house." The American doctor lived somewhere in Maharaj-ganj; it could not be too far from my house. I made it through one more night.

The next day around noon, Chad, the doctor taking care of American AID people and other American officials in Nepal, came to my house. When he observed my condition and listened to my symptoms, he made two recommendations. The first was to stop doing the retreat. I told him I didn't think so. The second was to begin taking that most dreadful stuff, Flagil, for amoebic dysentery.

"But I don't have dysentery!" I whined. "I just can't hold my head up."

"Nevertheless," he said, it was still indicated.

I took the Flagil, and for the next day and a half literally crawled into my bathroom and threw up globs of red stuff that looked like stewed tomatoes. The dizziness and weakness continued.

I stopped trying to sit. Chad began dropping by in the evenings on his way home. In spite of the Flagil misprescription, we became friends. He didn't have a clue about what was happening to me, but I enjoyed his company.

I was a little more than halfway through my Great Seal retreat. I had had incredible experiences and had gained actual insights in a really short time. Perhaps if my desire for success had not been so all-consuming, I might have done better.

One day, feeling slightly better when I woke up, I determined to move from my bedroom into the adjoining room where I'd set up my altar and where I meditated. I would stay here permanently. I would meditate when I could. A part of me resigned myself to the idea that I might very well die here, as well. This Joy of the Dharma, I mused, was anything but joyous now. A little while later, Kanchi came running upstairs with a telegram. It was from Lama Yeshe. Trembling and weak, I took out the typed note from its envelope. Its message read: "Health most important. Stop retreat!"

Seeing those words, I finally really broke down. Perhaps the retreat had been too much of a strain. At any rate, my sickness certainly pushed it over the edge. Stopping the sessions altogether, slowly, slowly I regained some steadiness. I still could not walk well on my own. And I found Chad's advice not to move very fast—"No bicycles or taxi rides!"—to be, in fact, very helpful.

Years after my Great Seal retreat, I discovered that I am allergic to the sulfates in liquor. Taking a tablespoon of *rakshi* six times a day had been slowly but surely poisoning me. Yet I believe the diagnosis offered by my two Tibetan visitors was more on the mark. Tibetan Buddhist medical theory says that the root of all sickness, whether of body or mind, is holding too rigidly to the self. The mental poisons that arise from this grasping are the harmful emotions of ignorance, hatred, and desire. The physical ones are closely related and are, therefore, also classified into three main divisions: a disharmony of bile is said to be caused by hatred; of phlegm, by ignorance; and a disharmony of wind energy is caused by desire. During that retreat, desire was clearly my problem. Though Lama Yeshe had constantly encouraged me to take it easy, I had gone after the goal of the practice with greediness and with a vengeance. Telling myself it was a tantric and, therefore, speedy practice, I went for overnight results. It was like getting my Buddhist name—stubbornly, on one knee—all over again. How many times had I heard Lama say, "Be gentle with yourself, with your mind and your body. If you are gentle with yourself, then you can be truly gentle with others"? How many times, as we meditated together, had he counseled, "Let go, dear. Just let go"? The point was to let the drives and the worries go, to let the ambitions go.

Tantric Buddhism offers methods for transformation, but change doesn't happen overnight. It is a gradual process. When I look back at myself, at the timid and insecure self that first arrived before Lama Yeshe, I can clearly see how I have changed, how I have become less fearful and more confident and capable. These changes occurred in small increments and over some time. The point is to allow them to happen, without grasping and attachment; to have faith that positive change will come and, in the meantime, to try to be gentle with yourself. It was like this for all the Buddhas throughout the ages. They were each, at the beginning of their journeys, beings just like us: tossed and pummeled by ordinary fears, worries, and insecurities. And yet, with steady and patient practice, they each became Awakened Ones. They have given us a model of moderation to follow. If we practice as they did, who knows? We might just become the next Buddhas.

PART 5

Return

DREAMING ME, IV

⚬

The lionesses are everywhere. They roam, hungry and bloody-mouthed, heads bowed, all over our backyard in Docena. Only my mother, sister, and I are there, all of us in the backyard, all outside, with them.

I hold a tiny branch in my hand. With it, I smack the wild cats on their rumps, trying to keep them away from my mom and sister, who are trying to get to the fence and climb over it. We are in the thick of it.

Then I am up in a tree that stands at the far end of the yard. I am trying to divert the cats; to get them to follow me, and so give my mom and sister a chance to escape. Several lionesses follow. The tree is not tall enough. They begin to snarl and claw at it. They lunge for my feet. I see their bloody faces. Their mouths snap at me. They swipe at my feet. I wave the twig, ineffectively, at their upturned faces.

HAVING CROSSED
THE LINE

൭

As long as I could remember, I had dreamed of leaving the South. I had wanted to escape the daily threats—not so much to life and limb, though those had been everywhere apparent, but the intangible threats to a tender soul and psyche, the subtle yet constant assaults on one's very identity and dignity. I could have been no older than four or five when I formed the strong determination that I would not be raised up to adult life in Alabama; I was not going to live in a place that asked me to squash my dreams and ambitions.

But when, years later, I found myself free from those Southern threats, when I reached college in the North and discovered a whole new world, I paid a heavy price. As former escaped slaves had discovered once they'd reached safety, there being no friends and family to greet and welcome them there, they were strangers in a strange land. I had gained freedom, but my family was left behind. They were still in the South. And my own freedom meant less because they were still there.

So, as every black child must who has ever left the rural South for the Ivy-covered halls of Northern educational institutions, I felt guilty from the beginning. Guilty that I had made it out; guilty that I had succeeded. And in spite of the fact that my family tells me they're proud of me, in all subsequent years that I have lived in the North and enjoyed the comforts that come with a good job and a position of respect, this burden of guilt has remained with me.

On early visits home, this guilt manifested itself as false modesty and as shame. I always had to watch my newly gained speech, both in terms of highfalutin language and pronunciation. For "dicty" language was the surest sign that one had gone over to the other side and chosen white values over black. Everyone was on the lookout for any signs that I might have contracted this dread disease.

Even today, whenever I phone home, my language immediately changes. I speak with my family in our familiar dialect—not the slow drawl of white Southern speech, but the laughter-filled dialect of black speech. My colleagues and students might not be able to understand me. And after lengthy trips home, I've joked with my closest friends about worries that I might not be able to shed this dialect before classes resumed.

My guilt at having reached freedom also manifested itself in the strong desire to share as much of the good life as I had discovered in this strange new land of the North: books, music, plane trips, vacations, money. Gifts offered freely, but always cautiously lest I be seen as "flaunting," or "Miss moneybags," "know-it-all," or "white gal."

On the extended family side, pride easily slips into jealousy and derision, and then my own guilt erupts into shame. Once, after returning home from my junior year of college in India, I learned of two different stories that had been troubling my parents terribly. At their church one Sunday, after being introduced during services, a long line of my mother's friends stood in the receiving line to tell me how badly I had treated my family by not writing to them more often.

"Chile, you sho worried your poor mother. Don't you *ever* do that again, you hear?" There was simply no way of convincing these women that I had in fact written home on a weekly basis but that the mail service from India was completely unreliable. Yet having seen my mother's worries, they were rallying around her. I could understand that. I had to bite my tongue and take the lashing.

The other story was much more vicious, though neither I nor my parents could do anything about it. I learned that one of my aunts and some cousins had been spreading the rumor that I had *not* been out of the country at all. Instead, I'd been off having a baby! "See what all that education got her? Nothing but a baby out of wedlock! Now, I guess she's not so high and mighty!" My parents had to suffer through that lie for months, and years would go by before that particular rumor died down completely.

I often thought that my parents would have been much happier had I not gone off to college in the North. What good was an education if one couldn't brag about it without incurring jealousy and even wrath? They'd probably have enjoyed life more if I'd gone to a Southern school and gotten a job in Birmingham. Why did I have to travel so far? All those feelings and suspicions might have been avoided. I carry the guilt of not giving them that less complicated life as well.

I sometimes wondered, as a child, why I had been born into this particular body, this family, this place. The whole thing of it never seemed quite right. I was born with black skin when having that attribute meant coming to know rejection for no good reason whatsoever. I was smart and quick-tongued, which seemed to place me at odds almost immediately with those around me. I tended to be dreamy and melancholy at far too young an age. I thought in ways that seemed older than my years.

But then sometimes it seemed that in spite of all the troubles I had brought on them, my mother thought too well of me. Having yelled at me unmercifully as a child for thinking too highly of myself, one day on a visit home from college, she privately announced an unbelievable assessment. She sat reading a copy of *The Autobiography of Malcolm X* I'd given her. I had come in from outside and was walking across the living room. She looked up from the pages of the book and said to me, "This is exactly how I think of you. And sometimes it worries me."

"What do you mean, Mama? What part are you reading now?"

"Right here," she said, pointing to a passage. "It says Malcolm was so straightforward and righteous. That he was dignified, godly, and powerful."

After her frequent outbursts earlier in my life when she seemed not to think of me in such glowing terms at all, I wanted to scream back at her, "Why say such things, Mama? Why tell me that now? Don't you know what you've done to me? Don't you know how hard it's been out there?" But I knew it was not all her fault. And I couldn't find the words to say, "Mama, I just want you to love me." In the end, I was too surprised, and too moved, to respond.

Even so, as a result of having crossed the line, I still find myself doing battle with the burden of guilt.

LITTLE THINGS

৩৩

A woman in Jasper, Texas—a baby-boomer, modern, "with it" liberal—said on "Racism in America," a TV documentary in the 1990s, that she hadn't known how badly divided her community had become or that the division between whites and blacks had widened rather than narrowed. She hadn't known that day in and day out, blacks in her own community still suffered so from racism's soul-crushing hatefulness. She told the documentary's interviewer, "It's the little things, like not putting their change actually back into their hands, just laying it on the counter." She recounted, as if in amazement, the simple question raised by a local black man, "Why can't you put the change back in my hands? Am I so low, so disgusting to you, that you can't touch me?" The liberal-minded baby-boomer hadn't known it was so bad, went so deep, and was reflected in such little things.

Not long after I arrived in Middletown, Connecticut, and assumed my new position as a tenured professor of religion at Wesleyan in the late 1970s, I ventured down the three blocks from campus to Main Street. It was almost Christmas. I had a smoking friend, and I had decided to get her a nice cigarette lighter. Off I went, happily. There were already several lines of shoppers in the first jewelry store I entered. It was Christmas, I thought to myself. I waited, patiently, with all the rest of the shoppers. When finally my turn came at the counter, I said to the slim, gray-haired, bespeckled saleswoman facing me, "Hello, I'd like to see some lighters, please."

"We only have *expensive* lighters here!" she said, dismissing me abruptly. For a moment, I was completely stunned. I wasn't sure I had heard her right. I stood there in silence.

Before her remark could register and draw forth an outburst from my innermost core, a young white man in the line next to me said aloud, "Ah, lady! Show the woman the lighters!" He had recognized the woman's dart as being intended to wound me. He had seen what I had just suffered, and it embarrassed and angered him. But I was too angry and too hurt to speak. My inability to respond to her made me even angrier. I turned away from the counter and thanked the man as I exited the store.

More than a foot of snow had blanketed all of Middletown, and I fumed as I plodded through it back to my office, my breath issuing forth like steam from an engine cranking and churning but getting nowhere. My now-too-late rejoinder boiled: "You racist white piece of shit! Don't you know that I could buy you if I wanted to? That I could pay your measly salary three times over on only half of my own? I came to the store to buy a nice lighter; expense was not an issue. But seeing a black person, you assume, you presume, you poor, distorted excuse for a human being, you racist mother—!" Curses silently fumed at the snow.

There are no visible traces left of these encounters. No news media coverage or legal proceedings to keep the specter of racism before the eyes and minds of others, even well-meaning others. Such little things as these happen, day in and day out, to most blacks, while the world continues along. Why raise a stink about them? They are so frequent for a black person on any given day that they begin to seem natural.

It took years of gentle cajoling before my sister, San, agreed to open a bank account in Birmingham. She preferred to pay her monthly bills by standing in lines at separate stores. "Checks would be a lot easier," I told her. But she didn't want to have her money held for her by whites who refused to call her by anything but her first name. "Okay, Sandra," they would say. "That's it," in that slow, patronizing drawl. Never a "Thank you, Mrs. Williams." Never the money in her hands. She knew all too well the little things, the little slights. How often had she responded to a patient's call—a patient for whom she was the primary difference between their life or death—only to be rudely told, "I called for the *head* nurse" when she was the head nurse?

It does not take the blatantly hostile taunt "Hey, boy!" shouted by some toothless, menacing white trash in Southern dialect to signal the continued well-being of racism in these as yet un-United States. The countless other silent, invisible, or seemingly innocent indignities thrust daily and hourly upon blacks here—and browns and yellows—accomplish this quite well enough. There is an immensity of pain and harmfulness in the little things.

Matters of money draw the lines even more starkly. Everyone knows, for example, that rich people (read: whites) know how to hold on to their money, while poor folk (read: blacks and other minorities) never seem to be able to get ahead. At the same time, minority folk are often charged more for the meager commodities they do manage to purchase, while the dominant class gets unseen perks solely by virtue of their skin color, neighborhoods, and higher economic status. This truth was brought home to me personally one summer in Marietta, Georgia.

As was typical during my two weeks home in the second half of June, I was taking my family on a little vacation. That year, in 1980, we'd decided to make a short trip over to Atlanta, to visit the Underground, Six Flags, and the Martin Luther King Memorial. My dad, not being particularly interested in Atlanta, decided to stay home. As was also typical, I did all the pre-planning, relying on my trusty AAA tour books for listings of motels and discounts. For my family, the hotel was as important as the attractions. My nephews were young and liked a place with a pool; my sister, San, enjoyed room service; my mom, like me, simply liked traveling. Before leaving Birmingham, I'd chosen a Ramada Inn not too far from downtown Atlanta and made reservations. The fact that the inn was located in Marietta didn't really make an impression on me. The five of us happily set off for a few fun-filled days away.

Upon entering the Ramada in Marietta, we were met with some surprised and cold-hearted stares. My mom and sister noticed this right away, but after trying to soothe them a bit, I marched up to the reception desk and gave the young woman there our confirmation number. A few other white people passed us in the lobby. All gave unfriendly looks. After some uncomfortable moments, we were shown to a nice room, Sandy began reading the room-service menu, and the boys ran off to scope out the heated indoor pool that they would try the next day. My mom was still grumbling about our less-than-warm reception. She'd also noticed that we had seen no other black guests there. I told her to try and relax; we hadn't seen *all* of the guests here and, besides, we were here, and we were staying at least for the night. We settled in, selected a pay-per-view movie, and ordered dinner.

The next morning, after breakfast in the room, as we were about to head out for downtown, a rather gruff woman from housekeeping knocked on the door. "Are you about to check out?" she asked. "No, we're not," I responded, "but if you return in about half an hour, you can do our room then." Without a verbal response, she grumpily turned away. My mom had just about had it then. She turned to me and said, "Dean, we should get out of this place! Can't you see they don't want us here?" The "they" meant white people. I tried as best I could to calm her fears. "Look, Mama, maybe that woman was just having a bad day. Anyway, there are laws now. Nobody can make us move out. Our money's as good as anybody else's. So let's try to enjoy ourselves today. Okay?"

We went off to Atlanta's Underground, where we did a little souvenir shopping, walked along Peachtree Avenue, and then found our way to the King Memorial. On the way there, we noted the run-down condition of this section of Atlanta and the long rows of black people waiting for buses to various places. Even the memorial was less well tended to, we thought, than it should have been. All in all, after our long day of touring, we were ready to head back to our motel. I secretly hoped that the experience would be better this time.

It wasn't, but nothing overt happened. The boys wanted to try out the pool. So, while San and my mom relaxed, they changed into their swimming trunks and grabbed two towels. I accompanied them. The pool was quite large; the room containing it was steamy and was covered by a high, vaulted glass dome. When we arrived, there were four or five white kids in the pool and a couple of white women lying on lounge chairs. I walked the boys around the pool, pointing out its different depths. As we did so, one by one the white children were summoned out of the pool. By the time we'd completed our circuit, the indoor pool area had completely emptied. Only the three of us remained. Not wanting the boys to feel badly or to forego their fun, I announced loudly, "Well, guys, it seems as though we have the place to ourselves. Nice! So, get in there and have fun!" I pulled out my camera and took a few pictures of them as they doggy-paddled and tried to look like real swimmers. They seemed happy enough not to have any real swimmers watching their fledgling attempts. Then I sat down in one of the lounge chairs and lit a cigarette. I smiled at the boys, cheered their efforts, and waited there with them until they were ready to come out.

When we got back to our suite, San said she didn't know about our ordering room service here again. The food hadn't been so great. She thought that she and I should go out and find a local supermarket and buy some stuff to bring back—if I wasn't afraid to drive here. I told her it sounded like an okay plan, and I was sure we could find a store not too far away. In the car, I told her what had happened at the pool and we agreed to head back to Birmingham the next day. We'd seen what we'd come to see, anyway. "Bump these racist folk!" she declared.

I spotted a supermarket and we turned in and parked. The store was a massive Bruno's, bigger than anything we'd seen, at the time, in Birmingham; so big, in fact, it could have been a tourist attraction. But again, there were no black people in sight, not even behind the counters. We wandered down aisles and aisles of well-stocked shelves and rows of imported delicacies. There was a full deli and a large counter of hot meals, in addition to a wonderful flower shop, barrels of imported fine wines, and large refrigerated bins of cheeses from around the world. In many ways, it was a wondrous store. But it was simply a supermarket for the white folk who lived in Marietta, Georgia. Then our hearts almost stopped. Looking for something we could easily make in our rooms, we found the aisle with canned goods and scanned its shelves for tuna fish. We found a host of brands, but what surprised us were the prices. Every item in that store was cheaper than we'd ever seen. What we normally paid $1.59 for back in Birmingham was $.79 here! We began turning over other cans throughout the long aisle. Everything here was a lot cheaper. Saying to each other almost in unison, "Okay, let's try the imported sections," we set out like a team of investigators. Our quick survey confirmed our first impressions: it was as if this store were simply a front, a vehicle for providing gifts to its white consumers, a perk for living in this particular neighborhood.

If you could eat fine foods for almost nothing, no wonder you could save your money and live well! San and I exclaimed to each other, "So, it *is true*! The rich get richer, and the poor get poorer." We saw it with our own eyes. We bought a big bag full of hot and cold goodies and left the store. The next morning, leaving our grumpy maid a tip that was less than we would have normally left, we drove away from that Ramada Inn, from the surreal world of Marietta, Georgia, and headed home.

The commandments entrusted to Moses tell us that we should love our neighbors as ourselves; and in the Gospel of Matthew, Jesus is quoted as having said that second only to the great commandment "to love the Lord thy God with all thy heart" is the commandment that is "like unto it, thou shalt love thy neighbor as thyself." One of the earliest scriptures of Buddhism, the *Dhammapada,* also speaks of the baseness and unworthiness of hatred and ultimately declares: "Hatred is never appeased by hatred in this world; it is appeased by love. This is an eternal law." Its verses go on to add that "Not to do any evil, but to cultivate good and to purify one's mind, this is the teaching of the Buddhas." And again, "Happy, indeed, are those who can live without hate among the hateful; who live free from hatred amidst hateful men." At the dawn of the new millennium, these are difficult injunctions to follow. They are difficult to practice for any human being; but they are especially challenging for blacks and other people of color who have been historically demeaned in a world where racism still rules. I have learned the hard way that one cannot simply decide to love one's neighbor. To do so takes commitment, prayer, and practice. It also requires that one know how to love oneself. I draw strength from the examples of loving beings I have personally encountered in this life since they show that it is possible to live a life of peace, without hatred in one's heart. When oppressive situations arise, I silently intone, "All beings wish happiness and all seek to be free from suffering. As we are all exactly the same in this respect, I will try to return love." I believe this sentiment motivated Martin Luther King, Jr., and that it continues to motivate Nelson Mandela and the Dalai Lama. Now, thanks to Lama Yeshe, it also empowers me.

MY SEARCH FOR KIN

ୡ

"W-h-e-r-e'-re you f-r-o-m?" That question, with all its lilting, accusatory, white Southern drawl, was invariably the very first thing that greeted me whenever I entered a county probate office and asked to be directed to the record's room. In at least twenty different Southern counties—throughout rural Alabama, Georgia, and South Carolina—there was not a single variance of that one question. I often wondered, was it my Northern accent? Or the fact that I looked them directly in the eyes? I had little doubt, however, about the meaning of their response. The different clerks were all saying the same thing; each was asking where I'd gone to lose the sense of my "place."

Sometime in the late 1980s, I had formed the intention of turning the research skills I had honed so well in distant lands—in the Himalayas with Tibetan Buddhists—toward home. I wanted to work on my own family history and genealogy. I can still see the joy that came over my mother's face when I first proposed the project. "Oh, yeah! *Do* it, Dean! Write a book about *us*!" Grinning from ear to ear, she'd gone on to add, "Yeah, a book about us. No need to wade through Sanskrit or those other languages." She was relieved. Studying Buddhist philosophy and practices had been paying my salary for years, but those things, she clearly thought, had occupied my time long enough. A good storyteller herself, she was ready and eager to help.

Without skipping a beat, my mom launched into a long and rambling narration about her grandmother Mama Dinah. She talked about visiting Dinah down in the country, about having to ride in an old, mule-drawn buggy to get there from the train depot, about Mama Dinah's special cook house that stood detached from her wood-framed home. From time to time I nudged the conversation along. Then, after seeing my mother become a little girl again, gleeful and smiling, her animated account abruptly ended. "Well, that's about it. You'll have to fill in the rest," she said. "Now, now, I can't just fill it in, Mama! We'll have to talk more." Then she said something that touched me deeply: "Well, really, I've always thought I was just plopped here, without much family to speak of. But I'd love to have you write a book about us."

My grandmother had died when my mom was only nine years old. She'd told us that she often felt alone in the world, trying to make her way. I knew *exactly* what she meant. Even as a small child I had wondered how I had come to be a member of this particular family. Though, for the most part, I felt cared for, I often puzzled over why I had been born into a black family in a place where racism was a palpable feature of the environment. What was I supposed to learn from the experience? What was I supposed to pass on about it later?

My mother's mournful declaration moved me to tears. Still, I felt exhilarated and full of promise. At last I could do something that would be accessible and meaningful for my family, as well as for me.

Though I had published my first book at the age of twenty-four, which, of course, made everyone in the family proud, still there was some embarrassment whenever anyone asked, "Oh, really? What's it *about*?" I had sometimes witnessed their nervous replies: "Ah, it's about Buddhism." My parents had seen me go off to a school in the North, an Ivy League school at that, to study physics, philosophy, and finally Buddhist philosophy. They'd seen me go off to India during my junior year and had said, "We can't imagine why you would want to be in a country so poor that dead people lie in the streets!" "What do those Buddhist monks have that our own Baptist churches can't provide? And what will you possibly be able to *do* anyway after all that studying with them?"

In the late 1980s I was approaching forty. Perhaps it was as simple as that: having reached what I assumed was half my life, my thoughts turned homeward. I made at least two trips south every year: one around Sandy's birthday in June (which also allowed time for us to celebrate Father's Day together) and one at Christmas break. Each of these visits was for a couple of weeks. I phoned home every weekend at a pre-set time without fail whenever I was in this country. But this family history project, I hoped, would give me a way to make amends; to show my family that I loved and valued them—valued us—as a family. My waking and dreaming thoughts began to turn solely around this aim.

Whenever I was home on school breaks from Wesleyan, I talked with my mom and dad about their memories of their parents and grandparents. My dad took me to see the houses where his grandparents had lived and where he'd played with his brothers as a young boy. I met and talked with aging extended family members who told me wonderful stories but often jumbled genealogical histories. A year's sabbatical in 1990–91 gave me my first real chance for hands-on work in state archives and county probate offices. Slowly, I formed our family's charts.

Over the next few years, I became a seasoned ancestor detective. I experienced tremendous highs and abysmal lows. For I was not just doing any family history; it was my own. And being black in America, that history involved slavery. It was a topic the family did not want to talk about.

Throughout the family, word soon passed that I had a special camera and would reproduce family photos for everyone. In fact, I had only purchased a cheap set of close-up lenses and attached them to my aging Pentax. The close-up lenses enabled me to take photos of photos, then to have them developed, printed, and often enlarged without ever having to take them away from those who owned them. It also gave me a fresh set of negatives. Photos poured in from relatives. A wonderfully rich cache of them was produced from my deceased grandmother Jennie's album, now in the possession of my aunt Nate.

Jennie's album preserved much bounty, indeed. These were images of my kin that captured moments special to them, spots of time that, though frozen by an earlier camera's eye, reached into the present as a lifeline. One photo in particular became central to my earliest family history work. It showed six people—three seated adults and three boys, in their teens, standing behind them. The boy who stood in the middle was Belton, my grandfather. Jennie had somehow acquired this picture of her husband as a young man. I was overjoyed to see him so.

In the photo, Belton looked to be about fifteen or sixteen years old. Knowing his birthdate to have been January 26, 1894, I deduced that the photo must have been taken around 1910. The picture showed Belton flanked on either side by his identical twin brothers, one year younger than he, whose names were Fred and Freddie! When I was a young child, I remember my grandmother telling us kids stories about "Fred and Freddie." I had always thought she was just making up these tales, for who would name twin brothers the same name? Who came when one was called? And weren't black people more creative than that, especially when it came to names? But when my father and I visited the old cemetery in Inverness, Alabama, in 1986, I had seen the twins' tombstones, side by side, bearing these names. When I had queried my father on this seemingly odd naming practice, he'd responded rather sternly, "There's never been any problem resulting from it." Now here stood those three sons of the family—Belton, Fred, and Freddie—in suits and ties, staring straight ahead, proud and unsmiling.

Seated in the foreground of the photograph were three adults, the boys' father and mother, Rolan and Mary, and an older woman. Both my father and my uncle Lamar pointed out Rolan and Mary. They each remembered spending time in their early childhoods in the country with these grandparents. Rolan (whose name, I was to learn, was spelled variously on the census records—sometimes as "Rolin" or "Roland," sometimes as "Rolan," and even as "Rolling") was a big man, dark and stout. His jacket seemed tight over his sturdy frame and he wore no tie. His gaze looked taut and tired. Mary was the petite lighter-skinned woman who sat on Rolan's left. Her dress was white. She held flowers in her hand, and there were some in her hair; but her face, too, seemed tense. The woman who sat on Rolan's right was older. She was dark and heavy-set. She wore a print dress with a lacy white collar and sat against a chair that was draped in white. With hands resting across her lap, she seemed to me to be the most relaxed of the group; and though her face appeared tired and drawn, there was a faint hint of a smile. Atop her broad nose sat tiny wire-rimmed glasses. The photo had been taken outside. Trees and foliage framed the group.

But neither my father nor Uncle Lamar could tell me who the older woman in the photo was. My father had no clue as to who she might be. Uncle Lamar, who was seventy-five when I presented him with a copy of the photograph, thought she might have been their great-grandmother, but since he had been very young when she had died, he could not remember what her name had been. Neither of them remembered ever seeing or hearing anything about their great-grandfather.

Verifying this woman's identity and finding out her name became the fuel for my first visit to the Alabama State Archives in Montgomery. What the photo had given me was a picture of my grandfather as a handsome young man, of his identical twin brothers, Fred and Freddie, and of my great-grandparents, Rolan and Mary Willis. Perhaps, I thought, it was also giving me the rare and special treasure of an image of my great-great-grandmother. I was anxious to know more. And now both my father and uncle were also engaged in the quest. I wanted to be able to tell them the name of their great-grandmother; to be able to give them this gift, in addition to the newly printed frozen spot of time.

In retrospect, it seems remarkably easy how this early treasure hunt proceeded. Yet I can still remember how nervous and awkward those first few days in Montgomery had felt. The basis of all genealogical work is to begin with what's known. I had guessed that the photo was taken around 1910. So, when I'd learned the intricacies of using the archives' machines and of locating specific reels of microfilm, I pulled out the roll for the Alabama "1910 Census Index—Family" and began. Before too long, the household that I was seeking came up on the screen. The little index card read: "W420—Head of Family: Willis, Rolan." On the next two lines, it noted: "Color: B" (for "Black") and "Age: 40." Under the heading "Other Members of Family," it listed the names of individual members, together with a notation describing that member's relationship to the head of the family and his or her age. Under Rolan's name were enumerated the following persons:

Mary	W(ife)	40
Caroline	M(other)	70
Belton	S(on)	16
Fred	S(on)	15
Fred	S(on)	15

The little census card had provided nothing less than a perfect statistical description of the photo itself. I had been right about the approximate date of the photograph; and now I knew the name and identity of the older woman. She was Rolan's own mother, my great-great-grandmother; and her name was Caroline. I grinned.

I remained in Montgomery for another night; and the next day I carried the census search farther back—all the way to the 1870 census—by looking for Rolan as a child in a household and then reading up to see who was listed as its head. In this way, I came to discover for the first time the name of Caroline's husband and my great-great-grandfather, Gabriel.

The date was June 28, 1990. Later that day, arriving back in Birmingham, I stopped by first at Uncle Lamar's house before going home. He met me at the door. With a broad grin, I said to him, "Her name was Caroline, Uncle Lamar." He peered off into the distance as though garnering up his memories. Then he slapped his knee in delight and almost screeched his response: "Yeah, baby! You sho is right. Her name wuz Caroline. Um-hum, Caroline. Sho wuz!" It was a good exchange between uncle and niece—private, warm, and welcoming. So, I thought relishing the moment, this was doing family history research. It seemed like it was going to be a good thing.

Yet as the steady, plodding work continued, there were also incredibly low periods. There were times when I could do little more than sob—sometimes for days on end—as I found slave kin in the pages of old courthouse ledgers only to see them lost again, sold away from their families, on white men's whims, to pay off debts. The work itself was hard enough, but the emotional strains were much harder to bear. It all had to do with the fact of slavery, and with its legacy.

To begin with, though U.S. census materials have been available since 1790, blacks were not mentioned by name until the census of 1870. This was so because prior to 1870, blacks in this country were mostly the property of slaveowners, and as such they were considered to be non-persons. Thus, rather than find names of possible kin, I found only tallies of slaves, listed by their age, sex, color (that is, "B" for Black, or "M" for Mulatto), or specific infirmity ("blind," "idiot"). There were some exceptions. For example, some blacks were free people of color and so were listed as such, and by name, on earlier census records. And if a slave somehow lived past her or his 100th birthday, that slave was listed by name, even on the earlier materials. One of my ancestors, a woman named Sarah Hough, was listed by name on the 1860 census as having attained the ripe old age of 120! But again, these blacks represented the rare exception.

At the Federal Census Archives in Waltham, Massachusetts, I developed a rather intimate relationship with rolls and rolls of microfilmed census materials. Then, after the preliminary charts were completed, I headed to the records rooms of county probate offices throughout the Southern states. My great-grandparents, their parents, and their children had lived in those counties before and after the Civil War. Even this assumption was a gamble, for some ex-slaves, following emancipation, had left the counties of their enslavement. And who could blame them? Other slaves had stayed put but changed their surnames. Gabriel Willis meant Gabriel who belonged to the slaveowner Willis. Often, as I surveyed the microfilm reels, I watched, through tears, as newly freed slaves changed their last names to "Person" or "Worthy" or even "Self." Others took the name of their earlier masters, ones who had been, presumably, kinder than their last one. In order to keep my own search going, I made the assumption that my ancestors had stayed in the same counties after emancipation and that they had kept the last name of their last owner. And in my case, these assumptions proved to be true.

So off I went, in my rental cars, to various Southern probate county seats. Sometimes my sister accompanied me, and other times I took along my teenage nephew, Jason. He was big for his age, and his size gave the feeling of safety. But often I rode through long stretches of barren, rural countryside alone. Though I was sometimes afraid, I was not going to be deterred. As I drove down those desolate roads, it seemed that the melancholic land itself called to me and told me that it was my home, too. From a deep, soulful place, I felt its mournful cry. I envisioned myself and my people here, toiling under brutal conditions, yes, but also making their lives, raising their kids, and forging a life and a community against all odds. Often, in the shadows of evening's dusk, I thought I saw groups of huddled slaves silently waiting to cross a river or creek. Sometimes the shadows congregated under some large oak. I felt these figures communing with me, saying, "Yes, we were here." With my heart, I recognized and greeted them. And I drove on.

Having reached those county probate offices, the search for my kin became one that, quite often, turned itself over into the hands of pure luck. Yet often luck was with me, and I found my kin, listed in the wills and probate inventories of white slaveowners, with monetary values next to their names: "Gabriel, a man slave, $700." "Adam, a man slave, $400, and his wife, Little Mary, and 2 children, $300." The anger that fueled my searches more often than not turned miraculously into exhilaration as I found a relative. My own family of kin was expanding, and the cruel-hearted slaveowners melted away into oblivion.

Since the publication of Alex Haley's *Roots,* many African Americans wanted to trace their roots all the way back to Africa by going solely after the father's single line. I had, from the beginning, determined to trace all *eight* lines of my great-great-grandparents. I wanted to gain insight into the breadth of lives that flowed into my own. Eventually, what I had sensed, and what older family members had known or suspected all along, became clearly evident to me: six of my family's lines threaded back through black slaves; and two of them, generationally quite near to me, led directly to white slaveowners, or to white men who lived more recently.

Finding and reclaiming my black kin was hard, but it was a labor of love. Locating my white kin presented problems of another kind. From the beginning of my earliest sojourns to county probate offices, I had talked with a number of white local historians. All were white Southern women whose families had lived in those areas for many generations. Their passion was genealogical research, and they knew the family lineages, both black and white, of their respective locales as well as they knew the backs of their hands. I had, for instance, been talking with Becky James, local historian of Marengo County, where my mother's people had lived, for almost four years. Whenever I walked in to that probate office's record room, James was always there. Once, when I was there with my sister, San had called me aside and whispered disapprovingly, "Dean, why are you talking with that woman? Can't you see from her eyes that she doesn't mean you any good?" But I figured James might be able to help me with my search. That's how research worked, I told San. Then the fateful day arrived. I knew that my mother's father's father had been a white man, and I suspected that Becky James might know who he was. When, finally, alone, I mustered enough courage to ask her about it directly, she just said, "Um-hum. Well, everybody says that your granddaddy's daddy was Gaius Whitfield." She had known that information since the first day we'd met. But now she wouldn't leave me alone; wouldn't let it go. She added, "Yeah. I expect it's true, too. He was a very smart man and very well educated. Now I can see where that intelligence of yours comes from." She pronounced this last sentence slowly, with a sneer on her face, and in a tone that indicated mostly disdain and contempt. For four years she had been waiting for me to ask that one question. And now she could tell me, like a devil, licking her chops.

I gathered up my things and hurried out to my rental car in the parking lot. There, for almost an hour, I sat, tightly gripping the steering wheel, while my body shook, and shook, and shook. My sister had been right. Becky James meant me no good.

Still, I persisted. In that records room and in numerous others, I continued to track down my kin. "Where was I from?" I was from *right here,* via Birmingham and Connecticut, and I was staying until I reclaimed all of my family, whole. "Where was I from?" I was from a smoldering storm of fury too long stymied. And like a black bull, I was ready to destroy all the neatness and propriety of this white china shop.

I could do this work, in part, because I was returning from the North, because I had lived for most of my life among whites and looking them in the eyes had become second nature to me, because my scholarly training had given me ways of ferreting out hunches, and because—in a word—I *did* know my place, and that place was *quite okay.*

A LAMA-HIT

ᖇ

B y the fall of 1995 I was heavily into the family history project, and I'd suffered another psychic blow from Becky James. In the county courthouse in Linden, Alabama, attempting to silence her overly eager interest in my research, I grabbed a volume from *Miscellaneous Records,* set it down in front of her, turned to a specific page, and, pointing to a record of sale, said to her, "You see this man, Adam? Adam was my great-great-grandfather. He was sold one day, away from his family— just like that!—to this man, David Compton."

"Um-hum," she responded. Then, looking right at me, she said, with a smile and with pride in her voice, "Well now, David Compton was *my* great-great-grandfather!" With that remark, I was almost completely undone. This woman was evil, and you could see it in her eyes. As she proudly announced her historical ownership of my ancestors, I saw, in her eyes, profound enmity and pure, unadulterated hatred. For the first time in my life, I began to consider that hell might actually exist and to wonder whether compassion and goodness were any match for its evil. Back in Connecticut, these considerations continued to take their toll. I could neither sleep nor eat. For about ten days, I felt myself being slowly consumed by dread and anger.

As always, friends sought to help ease my pain and offered various forms of consolation and encouragement. One night on the phone, Randy in California suggested: "What you need, babes, is a Lama-hit!" by which she meant a direct meeting and a frank discussion with a spiritual guide. "I hope you get one soon."

Lama Yeshe had died in 1984, but as merciful fate would have it, that "Lama-hit" was not far off. Some months before heading South I had agreed to speak at a two-day conference at Brandeis on "Tibetans in Exile and the Jewish and Tibetan Buddhist Connection." I would speak briefly about the pivotal role of present-day Tibetan nuns in the outlawed demonstrations for Tibetan independence and about their tremendous courage in the face of Chinese retaliation. Of course, I longed for such courage and strength myself. My heart soared when, only minutes after finding my way to the correct Brandeis building, I looked up to see the smiling face of an old friend, Lama Pema. He, too, would be speaking at the conference, and he had driven up from his center in New York City to do so.

His gentle face was like a vision. I approached him right away and told him that I was in great need of his help. With accustomed generosity, he responded: "Well, if you think I might be able to be of help, I will try."

Lama Pema quickly greeted a number of other conference participants, then excused himself and came over to join me. We sat at a round table and began our discussion over paper plates filled with traditional Tibetan foods specially prepared for the conference. I told him that I was doing some family history research. Then I told him about my last encounter with James and ended with the statement that looking into her eyes had scared me to death. Lama Pema listened attentively. At the height of my tale of desperation and anger, he quietly shook his head, as if completely attuned to my suffering. Then, with characteristic calmness and insight, he began to advise me.

"Well, first you must know that you would not have recognized such intense emotions if these were not a part of your own mind." He said this without the slightest trace of judgment or blame, but his pronouncement caught my attention. "This deep hatred is in *me*?" I asked, preparing to defend myself. "But Lama Pema, seeing that stuff frightened me to death. I wanted to run away from it. I don't want any part of it!"

"Yes, I know. It's very terrifying. But then, you should also know that all such emotions are empty. They come from the mind; but they come and go. You need to let them just go." I sat silently, trying both to take in what he was saying and to remember his words for later deliberation. Then he continued: "You are doing important work. You have important work to do. You can't let this encounter stop you from doing that. You should just think of this lady like spit." Not quite sure I had heard him correctly, I asked, "Like *spit*?"

"Yes, like *spit*!" Then he motioned with his mouth in imitation of spitting. "If someone spits, you know, on the ground, it would be silly for that person to stand there and contemplate that spit, or to wish to suck the spit back into his mouth. You just spit, and you go on. So, think of the meeting with this lady and the bad emotions that came out of it as spit. Spit it out, and keep going!" His spitting gestures as he told me this made me laugh aloud.

I thanked him for his instruction and told him that I would certainly think more about it. Before excusing myself and heading off to the ladies' room, I reiterated his advice, "Like *spit,* eh?"

LIGHTNING FLASH

ᏋᎥ

Though my confidence had been strengthened over the years, some problems still remained. One of these had to do with my old fear of lightning.

I suppose my father just didn't know about lightning rods. Nor did the planners of Docena deem them necessary features of the frame houses they constructed. But lightning was certainly a very real feature of Southern weather. In spring and summer, it posed a constant threat. We also knew that if thunderstorms became severe enough, tornadoes, too, might be in the offing. At least twice when I was quite young, lightning struck our house.

Whenever violent thunderstorms came up, my family observed a rigid routine. If the storms occurred during the day, all activities ceased immediately. Whatever electric appliances were in use at the time were quickly turned off and disconnected, whether radios, lights, or later, our television. Then we were reminded to move away from the windows, to sit down, and to be quiet while God was doing His work. These precise movements always struck immediate terror in me. And the enforced silence and stillness demanded of us only served to focus my complete attention on the incomprehensible magnitude of the power and danger that were now present.

Often, as we sat and watched the lightning flash and crackle and felt the thunder rumble through earth and sky and shake our little house, my heart raced and rumbled inside me as my limbs went weak with fear. Such storms during the daytime hours were scary enough, but often they came at night.

Once when I was about five years old, a severe thunderstorm struck during the night. In our one bedroom, the four of us—my parents in one bed, my sister, San, and me in the other—lay with eyes wide, waiting and listening, while God did His work. Everything was pitch-dark. The winds swirled around the house, and the rain pelted down so furiously we thought the windows would soon come shattering in on us. No one said a word. The lightning and thunder danced and crackled loudly and with ferocity. Then, for a moment, there was a deathly lull. In that instant it seemed quieter than before Creation. It was as if all of the world was suddenly holding its breath; just as inside that tiny house, the four of us certainly were.

Between our bed and our parents' was an old dresser. The dresser's mirror partially covered one of the two bedroom windows. Atop the drawers, on the side nearest my parents' bed, sat a clock and our telephone. Suddenly, interrupting the lull, came a faint buzzing sound. It seemed to be coming from the phone. The buzzing started to grow in intensity. The lightning wanted in! Before any of us could utter a sound, a thin sizzling streak entered through the window, lightly touched the phone, and then traveled through and across the room and into our new bathroom. Next we heard a loud crackling explosion. We all reared up together, like boards on a spring. It had struck something. An electric smell and a soft cloud of smoke started to fill up the bedroom.

"It hit something!" my father yelled. "Get up and get some clothes on!" He jumped up first and grabbed his flashlight. Outside the wind was howling louder than ever. My sister and I started to yell and cry. My mother was almost hysterical. She screamed, "O.J.! What're you going to do?" and then, "Don't go in there!" Daddy was heading for the bathroom.

"Get the children dressed, Red, and go on over to Mama's. Y'all better get outta here!" Fumbling around in the dark, we were all like crazy people. My sister and I scrambled for shoes while my mother bundled us up in robes and herded us toward the front door. The smoke was getting thicker; but more than anything, I did not want to go outside into that violent night.

"Go on!" my father yelled through the smoke. I looked toward him, squinting my eyes. For a moment there was a bright glint of light. From somewhere he had grabbed our axe and had climbed up on a chair or bench. Over my shoulder, I saw my father swing the axe, hard, up into the ceiling just before my mother pushed me through the door. He thought there was fire up inside the roof. That fleeting sight, of him desperately wielding an axe amid lightning and smoke and ozone, remains one of my most terrifying memories. I didn't know if we would ever see him again.

Then the three of us were out into the night, blindly making our way across to Grandmama's. The rain fell in big cold and vicious drops. The wind roared in our ears and lashed us like whips. We reached the back stairs of my grandparents' house and held on to the banisters to keep from being blown away, screaming the whole time. My grandfather Belton met us with his flashlight and then continued past us to go and help Daddy. Inside, my grandmother had lit a kerosene lantern. There in her kitchen my mother, though still hysterical, peeled off our sopping clothes, and Grandmama wrapped us up in her warm handmade quilts. We dropped to the floor, huddled in fear while God, with a vengeance, continued His work.

"Nothing for us humans to do," my grandmama said, meaning to comfort us, "but watch, listen, and wait. The Lawd's working now!"

Dawn was slower than ever in coming. But the storm lessened, and when daylight made its first appearance there was only a steady, but now softer, rain falling. All four of us headed over to the house. Inside there was still lots of smoke and that electricky smell. Daddy had chopped holes in the ceiling of the bedroom closet and in the top of the bathroom.

The iron pipe behind the toilet had a big gash in it that ran all along its length. The lightning had come into the house, past the phone, across the room, and then had run along that pipe down underneath the house. My father suspected that the underground pipes were busted, too; and his suspicions proved true. But there was no fire in the ceiling wiring, so the house hadn't caught on fire. The smoke had come from the asbestos insulation around the pipe.

It had been a terrifying experience. But we were considered blessed not to have been harmed. We were "blessed" again shortly after that when lightning struck our big apple tree, severing it at its base, for it fell away from the house, its biggest branches crashing down and crumpling our wire fence out back but missing our bedroom wall by inches.

Today some of my friends think my fear of lightning is exaggerated, or at least unfortunate. It spoils their enjoyment of what they think is an exciting show of nature's power. But there was no satisfying me about lightning. From the days of sitting perfectly still and quiet while God did His work, to that night when our house somehow got involved in and touched by that work, I had had an inconsolable fear of lightning, one which no amount of comforting talk or gentle encouragement had been able to appease.

But then lightning, especially for Southerners, is real. Its dangers are chronicled yearly in our newspapers—"273 died this year after being struck by lightning." "300 die from lightning." I grew up hearing such figures. Yet I didn't need the papers to know the awesome power of this natural phenomenon. I had direct experience.

I do not think I was ever actually struck by lightning, though I am not exactly certain of this. I marvel to read about people like Gretel Ehrlich who have been struck by lightning—even twice—and who have survived it. But I do know that I have always been very sensitive to it and to the electrical changes and shifts that occur during severe storms. The hairs on my skin stand up, and I experience throughout my body a heightened sense of something akin to soft, fluttering static. It's as though the electrical charges in the atmosphere dance and flicker throughout my nervous system.

No matter where in the world I've been, lightning seems to follow me. Once, when I was living in the house in Maharaj-ganj, Nepal, lightning erupted violently again to intrude on my world. My house sat back away from the road that was a major thoroughfare through this upscale neighborhood in Kathmandu. About twenty yards behind my house, the land abruptly fell away, leaving a sandy cliff that dropped perhaps a hundred feet. Below, rice fields spread out like a shimmering green carpet, soft and alive. The view from my backyard was, in a word, stunning. However, the electrical power for the entire neighborhood was routed through thick, bulky power lines that ran the length of the cliff face.

While living in this rather luxurious house with its great views, a monstrous thunderstorm came up. Kanchi had left for the day, and Lakshman, who rarely returned to his village some miles away, had decided to go that day. I was left home alone in my two-story house. The sky had been steadily darkening since noontime, and by early afternoon it seemed already as dark as night. I had been shuddering most of the day in anticipation and was fevered by the time the first crackles began. I told myself that I would be okay, that the house was constructed of bricks laid over with concrete. Nothing would catch fire.

In a matter of minutes, the huge droplets of rain that had been whipping against the windows became electrical sparks pelting them. Downstairs I watched as the three- to four-inch sparks literally banged up against the windowpanes. It seemed, once again, that this lightning wanted in. It wanted me! I decided to go upstairs, where, for a time, I sat cringing in a corner of my bedroom farthest away from the windows there. But the house had numerous big windows, a feature that in calmer times flooded everything with light and made it a cheery place.

The sparks continued to clang against the windows. It occurred to me that it might be prudent to shut off my fuse box. Amid roaring thunder, howling winds, and the pelting sparks, I began my terrifying journey down to the first floor. The fuse box hung on the wall just at the foot of the stairs. I had perhaps three or four steps to go. I had gotten so close, in fact, that I'd actually reached out my arm to pull down the handle that served as the box's switch when, right in front of my face, the box exploded. I saw red and blue sparks shoot upward and downward. A smoldering metal form was all that remained. For a moment my knees collapsed and I fell back against the stairs.

The next day I learned from the repair crews what had happened. Apparently, all the power voltage that normally supplied that section of Maharaj-ganj and that ran behind my house had suddenly been diverted into the cable line that entered into my house. If I had touched that fuse box, my body would have received all that voltage directly. As it was I had been only inches away from putting my hands on a charge as powerful as the lightning itself.

A couple of years after my Nepal experience with lightning, a fierce storm came up while I was in Birmingham visiting San. Unlike me,

San never developed a fear of lightning. She was in the middle of cooking while she also had a wash going in her utility room that sat out from the house on her back porch. It was raining lightly. The Weather Channel was reporting the approach of a severe thunderstorm. My body began its familiar dance.

"Sandy, this is going to be a serious storm," I said, but she paid little attention, continuing her cooking and her trips out back to load and reload the washer and dryer. I saw that her back porch was collecting small pools of water. I didn't want her to be standing in one of those pools with lightning around.

"San, I really think you need to stop going out back. It's a powerful storm."

"Oh, Dean. Try not to worry so much. It probably won't even come this way!" She knew how nervous I was about lightning, and she would not allow my fears to stop her activities. Understandable. But this was no ordinary storm, and I knew it.

Sharp claps of thunder soon followed the rain. Sandy headed once again out back, but I ran to the door and grabbed her.

"Uhm-uhm," I pleaded in desperation.

"Oh, Dean. Okay. I'll sit awhile with you, but I only have a little time and I want to get dinner finished."

I was glad she'd agreed out of compassion. I tried to still my racing heart but it was pounding harder and harder. The lightning crackled through the air. Sandy sat opposite me on the corner of the couch in her den, a kitchen towel in her hands. Suddenly all the power in the house went off. Everything just stopped. All we were left with were the bright bolts of lightning flashing outside the window.

"Try to stay calm, Dean," she said. "Everything will be okay."

"Yeah, I'll try," I answered. "Still, I'm glad you're not out back."

"I guess I'd better check the fuses," she said after a few minutes.

"Please *don't,* San. Not right now." Giving out a long sigh, she let me be. I silently uttered protection mantras.

The power was off for about half an hour. The storm began to lessen. Suddenly, everything started up again all at once: the lights in the kitchen and throughout the house, the washer and dryer, the tiny digital clock on the VCR.

"Okay," San said, as though released from her prison, "maybe now I can finish my cooking." She gave me a kind look and returned to the kitchen, asking me on her way to turn on the television again. When I did, there was a news bulletin. A raincoated and hooded news reporter was standing with a microphone raised to her lips. "Behind me, you can see the most incredible sight," she was saying. As the camera panned away and behind the woman, there came into view the smoldering tail section of a passenger plane. The plane, brought down in the fierce storm, had crashed into two homes located about a mile and a half from San's. The strong rains had helped to keep the various fires in check, but people in the plane and on the ground had died.

It was not the time to say "I told you so." People not very far away from us had lost their lives, and still more bodies might be recovered from the debris. Turning up the volume, I called San in to watch the story. Shaking our heads in sympathy, I said, "I knew this was a really bad storm. I could *feel* it!" San let the "I-told-you-so" comment go.

Later that evening, however, after the day's storm was well past and all was quiet, San came and sat next to me. "Dean," she began, "you really have to do something about your fear of lightning. I hate to see you so scared. And you know, weather is always here. You can't do anything about that. So you have to learn to deal with it." I knew she was right.

"Don't you know anybody in Connecticut, any therapist, that can help you? I mean, maybe hypnosis or something. You need *help!*"

Well, I did know several therapists. San was right, I knew, and maybe this was the time to try to do something about it. Here I was, a grown woman, petrified whenever lightning flashed, whenever the skies turned dark.

Back in Connecticut, a therapist friend smiled broadly when I asked her if she could hypnotize me to help with my fear. She said she didn't practice hypnosis but that she had had some success with a procedure called EMDR. Telling her I was ready to try anything, we set up a series of four sessions.

During our first session I learned that the letters stood for "Eye Movement Desensitization Reprocessing." The therapy had been developed in the late 1980s by a woman therapist, Francine Saphiro, who'd discovered it quite by accident. She had found that certain movements of the eyes, in conjunction with visualizing a traumatic experience, helped to re-process that experience. She, and subsequently other therapists, had tried out the procedure with clients and had found it to be of help in re-processing specific traumas. It had proven especially helpful, for example, in cases of post-traumatic stress syndrome among Vietnam veterans and with victims of rape.

Okay. I was game. I found the therapy to be easily administered. It was noninvasive, and I could control the tempo of the procedure by saying at any point that I wanted to stop. Two levels were measured throughout the sessions: the first, on a scale of one to ten, was to be a ranking of my level of fear, one being lowest and ten being highest; the second was a gauge of what overcoming the fear would feel like—an affirmation regarding how I would feel to be completely without the fear. This latter positive imaging had a ranking of one to seven, one being still frightened and seven being completely fearless. We began.

The therapist asked me to actively visualize being terrified during a lightning storm. I chose my early childhood experience when lightning had struck our house. Then while I held that visualization in my

mind's eye, I was instructed to follow, with my physical eyes, the movement of my therapist's fingers, as she moved these from right to left
about three feet in front of me. At certain points, she would stop moving her hand and ask me to rank my level of fear, from one to ten. She
also asked me to describe, in just a word or two, any other associative
visions or ideas that had come up. Then we began again—me visualizing the lightning storm, her moving her fingers in front of me. It
struck me that this technique was akin to many forms of Buddhist
meditation in that when one really meditated one sat right down in
the middle of one's problems and spiritual wounds, welcomed them in,
and then looked at them squarely and directly with focused yet relaxed
concentration. As a result, one could come to discern the true cause
of the problem and, thereafter, set about healing it.

The EMDR sessions moved along smoothly but unimpressively, or
so I thought. I did, however, begin to notice a sort of distancing of myself from the frantic feelings of fear. More and more, I began to be able
simply to watch the frightening scene in my mind's eye as if it were a
movie on a screen. I could observe it, but I was less and less drawn into
it and thus less and less overcome with fear. At the same time, my positive affirmation of myself, as a person who was unafraid, gradually
began to grow stronger.

What had happened, almost imperceptibly, was that I came to understand why my fear of lightning was so overwhelming in the first
place. This realization grew directly from the brief moments during
the sessions when I described the various images and associations I had
when visualizing myself seated right in the midst of my fear. I described the great cosmic chaos of the storm, its being a sort of dooms-
day event for my family as well as myself, with gigantic dark clouds
rolling and crashing. Then, surprisingly to me, I described the fear
and sense of dread I had experienced when I watched the movie *The
Chamber* and saw the young naive white lawyer from the North drive

up to a Southern KKK camp event. And then the key association: I described the lightning as very similar to the flaming embers I had seen fly up into the night sky when, as a young girl, the Klan had burned a cross in front of our house. That was the image that did it. With the help of my therapist, then, I could at last make sense of things. I had managed to connect in my mind those embers from the cross-burning and those hateful people and all the dangers they represented for my family in particular with every lightning storm I'd ever experienced.

Perhaps the EMDR sessions would allow me to break the connections between certain synapses in my brain that had become entangled. If so, I might actually be able to loosen the powerful hold these images had on me and to see lightning as a far less threatening though, of course, still dangerous, natural event. Even so, after only four sessions, I did not know for sure how I would react or feel when the next real storm came up. A few weeks went by. One evening a pretty serious storm arose. Rather than retreat furtively to the safe nook upstairs in my house, I picked up a book, stretched out on my den couch, and read it. My only thought was "There's a storm, but it's not after me."

CHURCH WITH DADDY

❧

Daughter, tomorrow is 'casual day' at the church, so I'm calling to invite you to join me at worship service." He probably sensed my hesitation and silent groans, but I didn't want to refuse him. And now, given the church's new open-door policy, I no longer had any excuses. My dad and I had often argued about this point. I argued that a church should welcome anyone who wanted to attend, regardless of what people wore. No one, I contended, should be barred from attending because of their clothes. I did not like getting dressed up. But dressing for church was part of the black church tradition.

"Oh, well. Okay," I consented. "What time?" We made the arrangements.

The next day I was surprised when Dad showed up for me wearing slacks and a short-sleeved pullover. *I* was more dressed up than he was, even though I was just wearing my latest pants suit and loafers. He beamed and complimented me.

"Thanks," I blurted out. "Let's go."

When we got in his car, he gave me a little hand-scrawled note.

"See if all this is correct. I want to give it to the secretary." The note read: "Dr. Jan Willis, daughter of Deacon Rev. Oram Willis, is visiting from Middletown, Ct. She is currently head of Religion at Wesleyan University there." It was then that I knew he intended to have me introduced to the congregation.

"Augh . . . Daddy," I mildly protested. But secretly I was happy. He was proud of me. I made some slight emendations to the note, penciling in "religious studies department," while the car raced on and, handing it back to him, said "okay" as he brought the car to a halt in the church's parking lot.

Inside the impressive building, my father led me through a host of corridors, past offices, classrooms, a dining hall, and several long hallways crowded with folk. He had always loved being a tour guide. This church was not like St. Matthew's or Mt. Ararat, with congregations small enough so that one knew everyone by name. Sixth Avenue Baptist boasted a membership of some five thousand folk. When Dad saw someone he knew, he energetically greeted them and then introduced me. There were throngs of people. The earlier service had just ended. Some were leaving as others, like us, flooded in, making our way to the sanctuary.

Rounding one hallway, we spotted Mr. Satisfield, my former high-school physics teacher, talking to a group of young women. My father admired him. He had told me that Satisfield headed the educational programs at the church. We approached, respectfully, and I tapped him on the back. "Hello, Mr. Satisfield." He turned, feigned great surprise, and said, "Janice! How good to see you!" He introduced me to the group of women and leaned near to ask, "How many books have you written now, young lady?" "Four," I responded. My father beamed. For a moment, I flashed on the fact that both Lama Yeshe and my father called me "daughter." It had been from Lama Yeshe that I had first heard it as a term of true appreciation and endearment. Though my father had probably meant it all along this way too, it was only now, after years of my own hard struggles and practice, that I could hear it from him in this way. It was a startling revelation. In response, I looked to my dad and beamed back at him.

At the entrance to the main sanctuary, an usher stopped us. The choir had just entered and was finishing up the first hymn. There was a crush of people in the foyer still awaiting entry. My dad gave the usher his scribbled note and told him to make sure that Mr. Hewitt, the church secretary, got it right away. Then suddenly we were allowed in and quickly taken to a seat in the second row. As we were led farther in, past the hundreds of seated congregants, I realized for the first time that my dad had clout here. He was a deacon at this large church, and deacons sat up front. I was accompanying *him,* as his guest.

With a wave of his hand, the usher silently requested those already seated on the row to slide over, making room for us. I moved in and sat. I had expected that my dad would sit, too. But he did not. Instead, he stood, swaying and clapping his hands, as the chorus finished its second song. Glancing quickly around, I noticed that besides the male chorus, my dad was the only one in this great crowd standing. For a second, this fact embarrassed me. Sixth Avenue Baptist was noted for being the "dicty," most cultured, and snootiest black church in Birmingham. Besides having the largest congregation, it had always been associated with the upper-crust blacks of the city. Blacks at this church normally did not stand. Cultivating an air of refinement, they seldom gave way to the emotionalism of most black congregations. But none of this deterred my father. He stood, swayed, and gently clapped until the choir finished its song. I found myself suddenly deeply touched by this defiant gesture. I was also moved by my father's independent spirit and by his genuineness. I knew, too, that he had the many pressures of my mom's Alzheimer's on his shoulders, and it was perhaps only here that he could gain some release. Tears welled up in my eyes.

I looked away from him and toward the front. On the podium sat three young adults, two men and one woman. These were the associate pastors of Sixth Avenue Baptist. Next to them, and just slightly out of my clear view, sat Reverend John T. Porter, the head minister of the church. I had met Rev. Porter on a previous trip to Birmingham, when he'd come into a bookstore where I was autographing my book *Enlightened Beings.* I don't believe my father had told him about the signing. I think he had not wanted his pastor to see me signing a book about Buddhism. Even so, upon seeing me in the bookstore, Rev. Porter had smiled a deep smile, congratulated me, and said, "Well, young lady, either the Lord or the Buddhas sent me here today!" I liked this broad-minded man immediately. On a subsequent visit, he had graciously taken me out for lunch, where we'd shared a wide-ranging and engaging talk about his life's journey and my own. After lunch, he'd told me that Sixth Avenue Baptist would keep me in its prayers, and I had thanked him for the new mantra that he had taught me: "Lord, have mercy." It was only later that I learned that Porter had been an assistant pastor with Martin Luther King, Jr., in Montgomery, in those early and trying days. Now, I managed briefly to catch Rev. Porter's eye. We winked at each other.

Behind the ministers, and flanking both sides of the stage, stood the male chorus. Three rows deep on either side, the choir included fully fifty men, all standing proudly and looking great, dressed in black pants and white shirts like ones I'd only seen worn with tuxedos. They wore no ties—it was casual day—but each of their collars was closed with an elegant circular ebony pin.

I had not attended a Baptist service in almost twenty years. Except for the chapel at Wesleyan, I'd not set foot inside any church. As a child, I had argued against the hypocrisy and money-grabbing of preachers. As an adolescent and wise-acring college student, I'd rejected the whole of Christianity as the white man's way of subjugating all blacks and of denigrating our African cultural and spiritual roots. In a more thoughtful mood, I had granted that there were noble—even radical—sentiments expressed in some New Testament passages. But I believed that it was one thing to say "Love your neighbor" and quite another to know how to do that, especially in the South, where you grew up knowing that your white neighbor did not love, or even respect, you.

It was through Buddhism that I had first encountered a tradition of meditation that offered a way to instigate positive spiritual change. Still, getting older told me that Buddhism had no exclusive rights to such methods. Sitting in Sixth Avenue, with some decades and life experiences behind me, I began to see this environment differently. It was a place of solace for my father. It was a place that welcomed me and allowed my tears. It was a joyous place. The Spirit moved and breathed here because it was holy ground. That *same* spirit infused Buddhists, too.

Though the singing was most outstanding, I enjoyed the whole of the service. The chorus had marched in to the hymn "God Is Good All the Time." Then, everyone stood together and sang "Joyful, Joyful, We Adore Thee." The associate minister sitting next to Rev. Porter rose and came to the podium. He was an attractive young man, well dressed and with a quiet, dignified demeanor. His job was to give the invocation. When he opened his mouth, I was immediately impressed. That young man, perhaps only in his twenties, uttered a thoroughly uplifting prayer that proceeded flawlessly from his mouth without stammer or stutter. His deep and melodious voice sounded like that of an angel. With my head bowed I inwardly beamed, not only at the message but also at the sheer eloquence of the messenger. An attractive, intelligent, articulate young man, in the service of the Lord. I thought, "Praise the Lord for this young one who praises You so well!"

The church's secretary, a slim dark man in casual but neat clothing, walked over to a second podium on the other side of the raised platform. Speaking into a microphone, he welcomed the congregation and proceeded to read announcements and to introduce visitors. There would be two large family reunions; one was having its Sunday dinner in the church's dining room following the service. A group of perhaps thirty-five people stood en masse, then a second family group stood. Almost before I knew it, the secretary was saying something about my father, and I realized that *I* was being introduced. Since Dad and I were already up front, we first faced the altar. I bowed to Rev. Porter, and we both turned briefly to face the rest of the congregation. Then, just as quickly, the two of us were seated again. The secretary asked the church to extend to all of us warm greetings. There was general applause. When the room fell silent again, the woman associate pastor came to the podium nearest Rev. Porter. She offered another prayer that was this time shorter but still quite eloquent. I smiled as I thought, "Good for you! And good for this church to have a *woman* associate pastor."

A man from the chorus moved toward a microphone at the edge of the choir stand. He began the hymn "He's An On-Time God" in a wonderfully rich falsetto singing voice. I thought the song's refrain was simply marvelous. It went:

> *He's an on-time God, yes He is*
> *He's an on-time God, yes He is.*
> *Job said, "He may not come when you want Him,*
> *But He'll be there, right on time."*
> *He's an on-time God, yes He is.*

The congregation was clearly moved. I could hear members all around saying "Go on, boy. Sing the song!" My father stood up again. This time, I stood with him.

My father's voice was a deep, strong bass. He would have made a good addition to the choir. We clapped our hands and sang along: "He might not come when you want him, but he'll be there, right on time!" Soon, individuals and then small groups of people began to stand. Rev. Porter stood, too, and began to clap. This was a celebratory moment. The music was good, the message even better. The sheer power of the song's words got people on their feet. There seemed to me to be a groundswell that had been initiated much earlier when my father had first stood there all alone.

By now my own floodgates had completely opened up. Here, in this sanctuary, you could let your tears stream forward. Everyone had seen tears before. Here you were part of a community of worshippers; a community of people who knew about hardship and, at the same time, knew that it did not last forever. Here joy, too, was present. This group knew that misery and joy can stand side by side. Indeed, it is this very knowledge that black people call "the blues."

Rev. Porter ascended to a podium, higher than the two others, and center stage. His sermon was quick, pointed, and well-delivered. He began by saying, "Lots of people nowadays are depressed and despairing. Despondency *spreads* over the land. There are people right here today who are depressed and despairing, who think that their own individual trials are just too heavy to bear. Let the church say 'Amen.' But," he continued, "there *is* a *solution* for that despair. *Jesus* knew what the solution was." He paused, and then added, "And because of Him, so do I!" He asked, "Do *you* know what it is?"

"What is it, Reverend?" the congregation responded as if one voice. Porter raised his hand and made the gesture of counting as he said: "Count your blessings!" and the church moaned in agreement.

Like a skilled teacher, Rev. Porter began again, taking a different tack this time. "Lots of people sing about the blues. B.B. King sings about it with his guitar. Francine, is it?" Of one accord, about half the church members yelled back, "No, Reverend. It's 'Lucille'!"

"That's right, 'Lucille." He chuckled. Everyone joined him in laughter.

"How do you count your blessings? How do you do that? Well, you just *do* it! Every day. In the midst of whatever misery, count your blessings. At the end of every day, count your blessings!"

In the course of his exhortations, Porter fleetingly mentioned a biblical reference, and my father reached for his Bible. After a minute he whispered to me, "It's not Second Thessalonians. He must mean First Thessalonians." Quickly flipping to that book, he showed the text to me: "Now, we exhort you, brethren, warn them that are unruly, comfort the feebleminded, support the weak, be patient toward all men. Rejoice evermore. Pray without ceasing. In everything give thanks. . . ."

Rev. Porter descended his podium and began to walk toward the congregation. He came to the first row, middle aisle. In a teacher-disciple kind of call-and-response, he asked, "What do you need to do in order to hear God's words? In the Bible it says that the voice of the Lord comes *not* . . . how?" "Not in a whirlwind," my father and several other members answered in unison. This went on for a few more exchanges: "And *not,* how?"

"Not in an earthquake . . . not in a fire."

"But how?" Porter had moved closer to us and was looking directly at my dad. And my dad and he said in one voice, "It comes in a *still, small voice.*"

The two men were communicating. My dad could quote scripture with the best of them. I was proud of him. Rev. Porter wound down his sermon. "So in order to hear Him, what must you do? You must take yourself aside, to a quiet space. Count your blessings, take yourself apart, and wait for God's response."

The sermon had lasted only about ten minutes, but it had said a lot. I was amazed at how similar so much of it sounded to what I knew from Buddhism. Porter could have been talking about Buddhist meditation. The teachings, at least as interpreted by these African Americans, were about overcoming suffering, about patience, strength, and the cultivation of true love. And they were delivered with compassion. The great Buddhist sage Shantideva had not said it better, only differently:

> *There is no evil equal to hatred,*
> *And no spiritual practice equal to forbearance.*
> *Therefore, one ought to develop forbearance*
> *By various means, with great effort.*

The message was universal: *Practice patience. Think of others always with compassion, and as for yourself, count your blessings. Give up everything to hear that still, small voice.*

I liked very much what I had heard that morning and what I had, myself, experienced with my dad and with my people. I knew that at this point in my life, this was the right place to be. In this black Baptist sanctuary I, an African American Buddhist, had come home.

MAMA

൭ൟ

Leaning against a large stone planter, I looked out over the bustling street to the multidecked parking lot across from the hospital's main entrance. I had been here six days but only now, as I was preparing to leave, had I discovered this third-floor patio where staff and others in the know came to have a quick cigarette. All other times San and I, or I alone, had made the trek down to street level and walked around the massive brick structure that comprised this section of UAB, Birmingham's state-of-the-art medical complex.

Upstairs on the eighth floor, my mother lay unconscious, her frail sweet-smelling body dwarfed by various tubes and bags—I.V., pulse monitor, and catheter—attached to and invading her tiny body.

Seven days earlier, San had phoned just before midnight.

"Hey! What's up?" I'd answered, trying to be upbeat while all the time knowing that she wouldn't have phoned this late if there weren't a problem.

"Dean, Beebee fell today. She missed one of the back porch steps. We thought she'd broken her hip at first, but she didn't. They did a scan and discovered that she has a small bleed in her brain. We've just gotten back from the hospital; been there since around three this afternoon."

"Oh, *no*! A bleed? Well, what does *that* mean? Should I come? I don't know about getting a reservation, but I can start driving right now." I tried to sound calm, but I wasn't.

"No! No. Whatever you do, please don't drive, Dean. It's too far and too dangerous. Look, they're going to do another brain scan in the morning. I'll call you then. For now, just pray and do your mantras."

"Okay. Try to get some sleep. I'll start praying. I love you, San."

I put the phone down sweating, my heart pounding.

My mother had Alzheimer's. She'd been diagnosed with the disease almost six years before, though when any of us really thought about it we knew that she'd probably had it for a couple of years before that. Besides her early and frequent bouts with paranoia—her unrelenting fear that my father was plotting to kill her, her screaming fits, her seeing ferocious predators where none existed—we'd watched as her body began slowly to melt away until a once robust woman had become a mere wisp of her former self.

Luckily, we'd managed to get a first-rate neurologist at the very beginning. Dr. Herrell had assembled a fine team of supportive staffers, and my mom had responded well to the drug therapy she had prescribed. Within three weeks of beginning the anti-psychotic drugs, the threatening voices that plagued my mother's mind were abruptly and completely silenced. Herrell had prescribed appetite stimulants as well, and for a time, my mom began to gain back some of the pounds she'd lost while her mind was overwhelmed. Still, in spite of the valiant efforts San had made throughout to ensure that she ate well, my mother now weighed only eighty-four pounds.

I had seen Beebee just a week before when I was home for the Christmas holidays. Generally she seemed happy; chuckles came easily to her. Unlike some other cases of Alzheimer's patients we'd heard about, Beebee never screamed or cursed at us. Instead, she laughed and tried to participate. For this sweet and gentle attitude of hers, we all felt truly blessed. Though she clearly made attempts to communicate with us, her speech was usually all but undecipherable. We began conceding to most of what she said with brief responses like, "You're right about that!" or "You don't say?" just to make her feel a part of things. I sometimes had trouble with this technique. Still, Mama seemed to be aware of whatever conversations were going on. Sometimes, to our great delight, she added her own comments, in short sentences that rang clear as a bell.

As with most Alzheimer's folk, she maintained clear memories of very early events in her life. Most evenings just around dusk, for example, she'd grab hold of one of our hands and say, clearly and definitively, "Come on. Let's go!" Eventually we came to realize that what she wanted was to go home; that is, to her childhood home. Like any other child, she knew that this—above all—was required by her parents: Be home before dark! The phenomenon is apparently called "Sundowner's syndrome." It always took some ingenuity on our parts to get Beebee past the fifteen or twenty minutes each day when this vivid memory dominated her.

And my mom still had a wonderfully touching side. Though she often couldn't speak clearly, she could still sing. And if we started one of the church songs she'd sung in the choir, she'd join right in. "Amazing Grace" was a favorite with her and also "Pass Me Not, Oh Gentle Savior." In quiet moments we sometimes heard her humming these old spirituals. And I thought to myself at those times that were she to die right then, what a blessing to have such sentiments in her mind. At Christmastime we'd discovered that there were other songs as well that Mama could still sing: "The Hokey-Pokey" and "Hit the Road,

Jack!" To sing along, and to watch the sparkle in her eyes as she joined in with her soft voice, her tongue cooperating, brought us great joy.

But the many years of drug therapy had taken a pretty stiff toll: her tongue continuously and forcefully moved in and out and from side to side, her body continually jumped and lurched even when she was seated, and she now walked with a decided arch in her back, so that her slight form looked like the letter "C" bobbing backward. This tentative posture made us fear that at any second she might topple over. And that fear always kept us hopping, following closely along with outstretched arms in case she began to fall. And that is what had eventually happened. She had fallen the height of two steps from the back porch onto the concrete and brick walkway below.

After talking with Sandy I sat on my couch, alone except for the fevered and heart-thumping fear that this might actually be the moment of my mother's death. A bleeding in her already atrophied brain might be fatal. Now that the talking was done, my tears came. What was I to pray for? And how?

I peered at my Tibetan *mala*—my prayer beads—lying on the table. Then I put my hands together.

"God, please help my mother," I thought. But the words did not ring true. I felt like I needed first to apologize for not having called His name more often. I switched next to Jesus, thinking that He was probably the best intercessor. Again, I first apologized. It was not that I didn't believe in Them, or in Him, for to Christians the two are one and the same; it was just that I was not used to this form of prayer. I next thought of Lama Yeshe and Lama Zopa. Calling them clearly to mind, I prayed, "Please, help my mother now!" Next the Buddha of Compassion came to mind and I began saying his mantra, *Om mani padme hum, Om mani padme hum, Om mani padme hum*. The two traditions, Baptist and Buddhist, began to clash in my mind. I felt flushed.

I was scared; nothing was clearer than that. Now, when there needed to be some clarity, when I needed to know what to do, I was stuck, almost frantic. My mother was probably dying. What should I be praying for?

What I needed was not to fret over *which* tradition or which ritual to employ. What I needed was to calm down and locate the true "object of meditation," as Buddhists would say. None of this was about competition; it was not about pleasing me, or my sister, or my father. This was about my mother. *She* was the central focus now. I found myself saying, "Whatever is best for her," and then, "for *you,* Mama, let that be so." The rest just quietly flowed: "May you have peace, Mama. May you be free from pain. May you accept what is happening. May you relax and let go." For the first time that night, I felt calm. *Whatever is best for you, Mama, may that be so.* That was the mantra I needed. My heart felt a bit lighter.

I arose before my alarm went off and headed down for a cup of tea before calling San. On the way, the phone rang. It was 8:00 A.M.

"Dean, they've done another scan and the bleed is larger."

"Oh. Bless her heart. Okay. Now I think it's time to come."

"Yeah. I think so. See if you can get a flight, and call me when you know the details so I can pick you up."

That was it. I put down the receiver, grabbed my wallet, and picked up the phone again. The Delta reservations person, a man named Reed, was gentle and respectful with me. He understood the problem and calmly went about helping me, even through my sobs. There was a flight I could make at 11:50 A.M. I called a limo service and arranged to be picked up at 10:15. Then I called Sandy to tell her I'd arrive in Birmingham at 3:07 P.M.

I had two hours to get ready, which meant to pack, gather the garbage, leave a note for the postman to hold my mail, shower, and call a few friends to let them know what was happening. I fully expected, now, that my mother was dying and that the more thoughts and prayers that went her way, the better.

The two connecting flights went smoothly, but the trip seemed long. I kept up my new mantra, "Whatever is best for you, Mama," and extended it to include, "We all love you very much." Sandy was there at the gate. She looked tired but gave me that familiar smile and a hug. We headed straight for the hospital.

Pushing open the wide door to my mom's room, I spied her lying in what seemed a massive bed, tubes and monitors everywhere. But she looked the same, her hair freshly done up by San into a little bun atop her head. To my surprise, her eyes were open, and they grew wider when I entered. She knew that I had come, that I was there.

"Hi, Beebs!" I said cheerfully, reaching over the bed rails to give her a kiss. "Hi, Sweetheart! I came because you had a fall. I'm here now. See? We're all here with you." She kept her gaze on me, but she was unable to speak. My dad was there. He and San had been keeping a round-the-clock vigil. I hugged him. "Hey, Daddy. You okay?" Two nurses came in, Sandy introduced them to me, and for the first time, the three of us—Daddy, Sandy, and I—stepped outside the room to talk.

Later that evening, we all met together with the doctor who had cared for my mom since she arrived by ambulance the day before. He was an intelligent and sensitive young man who took time with us and who willingly answered my questions even though he'd probably done so before for San and my dad. I liked him. He did not think that a third scan was necessary since the family had already determined, and I'd added my assent, that no extraordinary means should be employed to keep my mom alive. The only way the doctors had of doing anything about the bleed was to perform surgery, a craniotomy, to suction it out. But in her weakened condition, even the anesthesia might kill her. He agreed with our decision against surgery and added that if it were his mom he would choose to do likewise. There was a slim chance that the bleed might resolve on its own. There was even a chance that *because* of her Alzheimer's, the blood might find its way to an atrophied spot of her brain and simply settle there. But these, we were cautioned, were unlikely scenarios. All we could do was wait, watch, and pray. Thus began what would become a weeklong family gathering—inside Beebee's room and outside her door.

Sandy stayed all night at the hospital, and I went to her house later that evening with the task of notifying all the relatives about my mother's condition. Sandy wanted her two sons—Michael, living in Atlanta with his new bride, and Jason, away at school in Montgomery—to know and to make plans to get there to see their grandmother. I called my mother's sister in Mobile; my dad was to phone her other sister in Detroit. The close friends I'd managed to call that morning began phoning me at Sandy's house from as far away as California, Connecticut, and Holland. These conversations completed, and after speaking with Sandy, I finally turned in.

It is so good to have a nurse in the family! I cannot imagine what other families do in such situations, without that kind of close and knowledgeable ally. Sandy could explain things to Daddy and me; and she could ask the right questions of the doctors and the nursing staff who cared for my mom. It was San who took charge and orchestrated the family's coming together. I was her ally; and I did what I could to lessen the pressures on her.

I had told San earlier that I thought it was really important to tell Mama the truth about what was happening to her. I had tried that afternoon, but with no real privacy in my mother's room, I'd felt unable to shout into her ear. San had said that though she could almost certainly still hear any message we might have, the Alzheimer's would probably prevent its making much sense to her. Still I wanted to try it. When I left San at the hospital, I asked her to try and tell Mama these words: "We are here and we love you. You have been a wonderful mother to us and we are really glad, and proud, to have had you as our mother. Now, since you have done all you had to do, just relax and let go. We'll be all right. Just relax and let go." I wanted my mother to be able to die a peaceful death.

The next morning when I phoned Mama's room, Sandy was crying. During the night, she told me, Beebee had slipped into a coma. Her eyes no longer opened. The doctors called it, euphemistically, an "unresponsive state." As it turned out, my mother never awoke from that coma. She was brought to Sandy's and remained in that state for another two weeks. I returned to Connecticut and work. The first thing I had asked San that morning, after trying to comfort her a bit, was whether she'd managed to tell Mama what I had asked her to.

"Yeah," she said, softly through tears, "I told her."

MAMA WORE RAINBOWS

ତ୍ର

On the twenty-third day of the Month of Miracles . . . the great Gyelwa Ensapa dissolved his coarse bodily form into the Dharmadhatu. During his funeral ceremonies, many remarkable events occurred that struck the minds of everyone with great wonder, such as the appearance of a myriad of rainbow canopies and a continuous rain of flowers that fell from the sky as if showered down by the gods.

— Nam-thar of Gyelwa Ensapa

At the age of eighty-four, the great Master Milarepa passed into Nirvana. Over the region there appeared widespread and wonderful signs . . . . In the firmament above them an inconceivable variety of offerings from the gods, such as rainbows and five-colored clouds, formed themselves into parasols, banners, canopies, bunting, and billowing silk.

— Nam-thar of Milarepa

For the rest of her life the mother worshiped the tooth with total belief and devotion as if it were a true tooth of the Buddha. From the tooth miraculous signs appeared, and at the time of her death a myriad of rainbow lights arched over her body as a sign of high spiritual attainment.

—Story told by Paltrul Rinpoche

"A myriad of rainbows dotted the skies around Birmingham this afternoon." That's what the weather anchor of a local news channel reported the evening of my mother's funeral. I was struck by his description. Not only was I surprised by his use of the word *myriad*; I was absolutely sure that his words were true. I breathed a long, contented smile.

Always an avid weather buff, on the way to the gravesite, riding in the first car, I had remarked on the changing skies: bright sunlight one minute; dark, heavy clouds the next. "There are *rainbows* somewhere," I'd said aloud, *"right now."* It was the only contribution I made— before my final outburst—to the various conversations going on inside our limousine as it followed the hearse that carried my mother on the long, meandering journey to Elmwood Cemetery. No one besides me, it seemed, appreciated the significance of such rainbows.

My temper was still short because, in spite of the fact that my mother had just died, so much of the talk, the busyness, and the *business* of the last few days had focused on her physical appearance; on how her shell of a body looked—for the living.

It fell to my sister and me to decide upon what Mama should wear as she lay in the casket. Sandy had said, "Tomorrow, we'll have to go to the funeral home and choose a shroud." When my mother was only a child of nine, she went with her aunt Ann to pick out a shroud for her mother, Sadie. She'd been too small to see over into the casket, so someone had had to pick her up and hold her so that she could have a final look.

As my sister and I were talking, my aunt chimed in, "No, baby. They don't do that anymore. No. People wear what they liked to wear and look good in. Now, you *know,* when *Dorothy Willis* went to church, she walked in there *looking good!* That's how she ought to go this time. Um-hum." Aunt Nate usually didn't speak much. When she did, people listened.

So, next morning Sandy, Jason, and Aunt Nate had gone shopping. They'd bought a stylish eyelet beige suit, beige sequined gloves, and now were off shopping for a hat. I was confused. Why couldn't my mom look like she looked now, just before her death? Why couldn't she wear something that she'd actually worn? I knew she'd lost weight, but what was wrong with that? Sandy and Aunt Nate meant well, but it seemed to me as though Mama's petite, Alzheimer's-ravaged body might be an embarrassment to the community.

When I'd first arrived home, I knew immediately that I'd gotten there too late when I saw all the cars lining the street and pulled up into Sandy's yard. I had driven more than eleven hundred miles through dense fog and heavy downpours. Still, arriving around ten o'clock in the evening, I was told that my mother had passed away earlier that afternoon. I was really sad to learn that her body had already been taken from the house. Why take her away so quickly? Why can't we see her, be with her, just for a little bit, while she's still warm? But the house was already full of people communing, keeping vigil with the grieving family, bringing tons of fried chicken and huge hams and potato salads and soft drinks. I couldn't show my distress about not having seen my mother.

Daddy took me with him into Sandy's bedroom, where my mom's now-empty hospital bed stood in the center of the room. He held my hand and told me how it had been those last hours, when he and San stood on either side of her, each holding one of her hands, listening as her breaths became more labored and finally ceased altogether. Hearing his dignified but tearful narration, I shed tears with him. Then quickly I wiped them away and re-entered the rest of the house with its throng of people, to greet them and thank them for coming.

Except for Aunt Nate, a true friend and warrior to my family throughout my mama's long battle with the debilitating disease, I hardly knew any of the older people who were there. I did spot, however, a few of my other relatives. My mom's pastor was there, too, along with his wife. As far as I knew, he'd never visited my mom, though she'd been sick so long. I felt that I had to push down my anger about all this, so I swallowed hard and tried to make small talk. Sandy, through tears from the stress of it all, said we would see my mom the next morning.

Entering Robert's Funeral Home was like entering a luxurious, fake mansion. Soft carpets and elegant furniture gave an air of spaciousness, refinement, and repose. But in its back interior rooms, that dread process of embalming was carried on, right there on the premises. When the soft-spoken, suited young man beckoned us around the corner, we saw Mama for the first time since they'd taken her from the house. She was stretched out on a gurney, covered only by an old and tattered flowered sheet, her head lying on a wooden prop, her fine-textured wavy hair hanging straight down. I moved in closer. This was not my mother. This was only her used-up material body. No life was left here. Her spirit was gone.

Asking for a few minutes alone, I carefully removed from my bag the small Buddha statue that His Holiness the Dalai Lama had given to me. Wrapped in a silk *khatta*, I touched it to the crown of my mother's head as I whispered into her ear, "Mama, you've done *great* by all of us and we will be okay. We all love you very much and we'll love you always. Now you have a journey to make. *Go on!* It will be all right. Don't worry about anything. Go on your journey, and travel well!" I returned the statue to my bag and softly chanted some mantras. Then I kissed her cold forehead and left.

In retrospect, I am sure this viewing of my mom's body at this stage, in so unkempt a fashion, was done in order to heighten the family's dependence upon and gratefulness to the funeral home. For the next time we would see our mother, she would have been made "just a little fuller in the cheeks." She would be dressed, wearing makeup, earrings, gloves, the whole works, each item carrying its own individual pricetag. And she'd be looking good. Ten years younger and sharp, like old times.

That night, after seeing my mom's body, I had performed a simple meditation of my own. Seated on a pillow on the floor, I had first called to mind Lama Yeshe. He appeared immediately above my head, radiating a very broad smile. I found his joyfulness immensely soothing; it silently confirmed that my mother was okay. Under Lama's smiling face I then envisioned the Buddha, also floating just above my head. Both images appeared bright and steady. I brought to mind my mother's gaunt and tiny body, lying cold and alone in that funeral home. What next appeared, completely without discursive thought of any kind, was a bright stream of white light. The light began with Lama Yeshe, flowed downward through the Buddha and into me, and then turned the corner and flowed from my heart, across space, and into my mother's form. This transit of light continued for several minutes in the darkened stillness of the room. When I broke off the meditation, I felt at peace.

All the emphasis on how Mama would look was certainly added to by the fact that just a few days before, Miss Blackledge had died, and she had been "funeralized" at the same church on the previous Sunday. And whatever else might be said about Miss Blackledge, one had to admit, "She looked *good,* girl, in that coffin! Yes, Lord, *she looked good.*" In the old days, back when my mom was up and around, Mt. Ararat Baptist had been blessed with three "stone fashion queens": my mom, Miss Blackledge, and Jennelle Martin. Only the latter woman was still alive. Though I certainly admit to bias, I think my mom won those fashion shows. Like the other two, my mom never wore the same outfit twice; she wore mink stoles with mink hats and alligator bags with matching alligator pumps. She'd put them on layaway and pay for them for months, but in the end she sported them proudly. My mom's outfits were classy, stylish, and sophisticated.

The day of the funeral, loads of people gathered at Sandy's house. The procession to Mt. Ararat began from there. It being a Tuesday, we wondered whether the church would be filled; most people worked, and a mid-week funeral was hard to make. Still, when the two limousines for family arrived, along with their police escorts, a procession of fifteen or sixteen cars slowly made their way up to Mt. Ararat. Arriving at the church, there were so many cars already there that we had to wait until extra space could be found for the rest.

When the ushers guided us in, we saw that the church was completely filled. My mom had center stage lying in her casket, surrounded by plants and flowers and flower sprays. Just above her was the podium on which sat Rev. Bry, Rev. Porter, and my cousin Ronnie, now Rev. Willis. About a quarter of the church's pews were reserved for the family. We were led in last, down the center aisle and to the casket itself. There, my dad became tearful again. Sandy almost lost her footing. Each had leaned over and kissed my mom before taking their seats. I did likewise, whispering to her again, "I love you, Mama. Have a good journey."

We had planned a brief service, and all the proceedings went off smoothly. Of all those gathered there, it was Jason who could not contain his sorrow. Though he was now a senior in college, he was the baby of the family, and he and Beebee had been very close. My mom had put him on her lap when he was about three and showed him how to drive her car, something that had frightened us a great deal at the time. Perhaps as the result of that, Jason and my mom drove everywhere together. They were road partners. Whenever she needed company, he was always at the ready; he'd even taught her new routes to get to places. One might run into the two of them anywhere in Birmingham. And when his granny had gotten down with Alzheimer's, he'd remained close and patient; and she loved to lean against his sturdy, soft body. They'd shared something very special, and now she was gone. He had written a poem remembering their bond, and we put that in the program, too. He called it "A Grandmother's Love":

> *There were so many times*
> *That you brightened up my day*
> *You brought sunshine out of rain,*
> *Made a way out of no way.*
> *You were there for me*
> *Whenever I was down*
> *You put a smile on my face,*
> *Took away the frown.*
> *You were a beautiful butterfly*
> *With your wings spread wide*
> *Little did I know*
> *That you could no longer bide.*
> *God has picked you now*
> *To fly in His flower garden*
> *I will always miss and love you*
> *Have a safe journey, "road partner."*

While the congregants silently read the details of my mother's life, Jason's sobs became more and more uncontrollable. He was led out to the foyer, where his heartfelt wails continued to echo throughout the church.

There was a light rain falling outside. It was brief, and soon we were back in our cars, heading for the cemetery. That's when the skies were alternately dazzlingly bright, then dark and menacing. Various subdued conversations began in our limousine: The service had gone well. The church had been full. Why had Mama wanted to be buried in Elmwood? They'd not wanted blacks buried there before! Wasn't that hate-filled "Bear" Bryant even buried there?

It was the Bryant comment that finally pushed me over the edge. "Could we just all be quiet for a while?" I blurted out. I was sad and stressed out. I didn't want to talk. I wanted to think about Mama, about how sweet she'd been, how loving.

The casket, covered in flowers, was already at the gravesite when our limo pulled up. The clouds were getting darker and more threatening; the wind had picked up. A great number of people gathered under and around the tent set up at the site. The spot we had managed to secure for Mama was quite beautiful. It lay just a few feet away from a gorgeously tall and wide-branched tree that gave the place the feeling both of protection and peace. Nature would look after her.

My cousin Ronnie read a scripture; Rev. Bry another. It got very dark. My aunt Nate, seated next to me, whispered something about getting back to our cars because a storm was coming. Seated here in front of Mama's coffin, I didn't notice at all the vivid streaks that slashed the sky and came right down to the earth quite near to us. My father, Sandy, and I just sat there. People started to file by us, giving us hugs and shaking our hands.

Funerals bring people together. Though they focus on a specific individual, they really serve as times when people think about themselves and their own mortality. Surely, many of those present at my mother's funeral offered compassionate prayers for her. But mostly they cried about their own losses and pains, their own sorrows and fears, as they themselves confronted the great mystery of death. I did not fault them for this. We were all only human. Still, my emotions were conflicted.

I asked the limousine driver to drop me off at Sandy's. I did not want to go back to the church for the dinner. Daddy, I think, was annoyed with me for this breach of etiquette.

At Sandy's, I poured myself a Pepsi and took a seat in the den, alone. It was then that I heard the weather man say, "A myriad of rainbows. . . ." In all the varied traditions of Tibetan Buddhism, the appearance of rainbows at the funeral of a saint is a sign of their special holiness. It was not exactly that I was thinking of my mom as a saint. But I thought of her great kindness, of her joyful countenance throughout her long ordeal with Alzheimer's, how laughter and chuckles came so easily to her, how she'd brought us all together around her and given us the chance to say our good-byes, how she had loved and cared for us till the end. And it was as though the world—as though Nature itself—was confirming her goodness and was letting me know that she was in safe hands. So, when the question comes up about how Mama looked in the end, I know it's not the suit, the gloves, and the hat she wore that matters; what matters, at least for me, is that *Mama wore rainbows.*

TEACHING AS MY PRACTICE

೧౨

At different times both my parents had visited with me while I was teaching. They each had come separately while I taught at UCSC, and they had come together for a visit during my year at the University of Virginia. They had come to Wesleyan as well. My mother actually sat in on a couple of my classes at the various schools. So I was surprised—and tickled—to overhear her say one day to one of our neighbors in Birmingham, "You know, it's just incredible! Dean gets paid all this money for only four hours of work a week!"

Even more amusing, my dad had come along to correct *her* misunderstanding by saying, "Now, Red. They don't pay her for what she *does*. They pay her for what she *knows*!" Neither of my folks seemed to have any idea of what teaching actually involved. They could not see the long hours of thinking and planning that went into each class, the preparation that preceded each lecture or discussion. For them, it was enough that their daughter had a good job, was a professor, and made a good salary.

The Sixteenth Karmapa of Tibet once explained, very simply and directly, what we, as Buddhist practitioners, must do. He said, "We have to *do* what we *know.*" Within the guild of American academia I am known as one of the first American scholar-practitioners of Tibetan Buddhism, and that recognition has its drawbacks as well as its perks.

Academia is justly suspicious of people who would use the classroom as a pulpit to advance their own private, sectarian views. Those of us who teach in religion departments are especially scrutinized and, in some cases, especially vulnerable. I have always tried to take care not to preach in my classes, and I certainly have no interest in converting my students. At the same time, however, I know that it would be quite impossible to teach Buddhism, and especially Tibetan tantric Buddhism, without having some idea of its inner workings, some experience of its actual practices, and this involves acquaintance with meditation.

Rarely has a student in one of my Buddhism classes failed to inquire of me, "Professor Willis, do you *practice* Buddhist meditation as well as teach it?" Seeing myself as a teacher, I first attempt to guide this question to another one: "Why do you wish to know this? Is it a question that you would typically ask of your physics or psychology professor?" After allowing the student to ponder the point, I then admit to knowing something about Buddhist practice, to having practiced various forms of Buddhist meditation, and to have learned something from my practice experience. But I then remind them that I do not teach classes in Buddhist meditation but, rather, classes in Buddhism—in its historical, philosophical, and cultural developments and variations. Students, unlike some university administrators and colleagues, seem to be able to appreciate this response, and we then get on with the business of investigating the broader subject.

However, some students do come to my Buddhism classes expecting more than just an academic investigation of the materials. I once had a young student who, after taking my "Introduction to Buddhism" course, decided to abandon college and become ordained as a Buddhist monk right away. That student's father, a columnist for a large urban newspaper, contacted the school's administrators and threatened to sue. I managed, actually with the help of Lama Yeshe, to dissuade that particular student from pursuing his stated course. Not only was he seeking ordination for misguided, personal reasons; he seemed oblivious to the fact that prospective monks and nuns must have the permission of their parents to enter the order. That student went on to finish college and then to follow his other dream of playing in a rock-and-roll band—no doubt equally distressing to his father.

Still, most of the time, it is a wonderful occupation. And like any serious teacher, there *are* things that I do wish to convey to my students. I want my students to appreciate that we human beings are, all of us, human beings: we all wish to have happiness and to avoid suffering. I want them to develop the ability to identify, and therefore to empathize, with other human beings, to be able to practice standing in another's shoes. In almost every class I teach, one writing assignment requires that they attempt this. I ask students to *imagine themselves* as a sixth-century B.C.E. Indian woman (whether young or old, daughter, wife, widow, etc.). One day a Buddhist nun appears in your village or town teaching the Buddha's doctrine and inviting you to join the Order. What would be your response? Why? When I offer a course on African American religion and rebellion during the antebellum period, I also have students attempt to imagine themselves as but one of the millions upon millions of Africans captured and transported to the New World. For each African captured, there was a story, a family, a human being's life. *Imagine yourself as one such African. Imagine your experience of being captured and of the middle passage. What do you see, smell, taste, feel, and think?* I want everyone to be able to reflect on the life and world of another.

I do not think it's my place to preach to students. Yet I believe that if they can come to appreciate others and to lessen their clinging solely to thoughts of themselves, to that extent they can become better human beings and realize their true humanity. Twenty years down the road, students may not remember the specific dates of a given Buddhist dynasty or school, they may not be able to define key Buddhist terminology, or even to recall exactly the Four Noble Truths. But maybe they will remember that Buddhism stresses overcoming suffering through understanding how we play a part in constructing it, and that compassion and wisdom go hand in hand. These are lessons about being human. They are simple things, though difficult to actualize. If students try to learn this, I believe I have performed a valuable service.

WOMEN'S LIBERATION

⚭

When I reflect upon the fifteen years during which Lama Yeshe was my teacher, it seems clear that his personal mission with respect to me was to build my confidence. He wanted me to realize and understand that, like everyone, in my innermost core I was pure, intelligent, compassionate, and powerful. He sought to help me manifest that understanding. Lama Yeshe often said that low self-esteem and lack of confidence were the main traits he observed among the hundreds of Western students that flocked to him. I was not only one of Lama's earliest students; I was one of the ones that fit that bill perfectly. Some of the reasons are clearly cultural and racial: being a black American, a woman, from the South, and an African American woman interested in Buddhism. There are lots of reasons why, when I first met Lama Yeshe at the age of twenty-one, I was a less-than-confident human being in the world. Throughout the course of my relationship with him, I see his primary efforts as having been directed toward having me manifest the qualities of confidence, pride, strength, and capability that he knew I possessed.

Lama Yeshe used to tell me that I should not hide so much. He'd say, "You should be *beautiful* in the world, and *strong!*" I vividly recall taking him to hear a lecture by Angela Davis once when he was visiting California. She was speaking at the University of California, Santa Cruz, in the outdoor amphitheater on campus. Lama Yeshe was visibly excited to see and to listen to Davis speak. Several times during her talk, with clenched fists, he said aloud, "This is how one ought to be: strong and confident, like this lady!" He absolutely loved her. And for a number of weeks after that, he would say to me—never as a put-down but just as a *reminder*—"You should be strong, like this woman! You should show *your* beauty and *your* strength to the world!"

Lama called me daughter. I assumed that he called any number of other single women daughter as well. But I know that he thought of me, in some way, as being special. His mission was to make me feel that specialness, too, and to teach me to trust my own power.

There is a vast gulf between "different" and "special." My mother had seen me as being different; Lama Yeshe saw me as being special. And special means loved for one's self alone, for one's core, which is ultimately pure, wise, compassionate, and powerful. Lama Yeshe knew this about me, as he knew it about *all* beings. And this is what genuine teachers do: they love us without reservation because they truly see us as precious, each in our own right—as nothing less than Buddhas. The wonder is that if someone whom you trust and admire views you in this way, even *you* begin to feel that way; and with continued reminders, you begin to see *yourself* in this way.

In my case, several reminders were necessary. Sometimes they came in the form of embarrassing public episodes; other times, they came in private moments of validation that touched me deeply.

When I was in Nepal in 1980—now as Professor Jan Willis—Lama Yeshe asked me to give a lecture one evening to a group of Westerners gathered at Kopan for the annual monthlong retreat course there. I gave a talk on the life and philosophical views of Asanga, the fourth-century A.D. founder of the Yogacara school of Mahayana Buddhism. In the course of my remarks, I mentioned that some texts say that Asanga's mother had been cursed to be born a woman. Immediately following my talk, a group of women attending the retreat bombarded me. One said, "We *heard* that—that she was cursed to be a woman! And we hear that there are some other Buddhist texts that say we can't attain enlightenment in a woman's form. What do you say about all of this?" I responded, "Oh, come on, now. Just look at Lama Yeshe; look at your own experience. Have you ever experienced that?" But the rumblings I'd stirred up must have continued.

Some days after that, Lama Yeshe and I were having lunch together and having a discussion about the set of life stories I was then translating. At some point we walked out together onto the upper deck of the monastery. From that vantage point, we were looking down onto the front courtyard, where we could see the entrance to the *gompa* as well as Kopan's library and the mailroom down below. There were a number of Western students milling about in the courtyard, on a break from the day's activities. Suddenly, Lama Yeshe grabbed my arm and began calling out to all of them below. In a booming voice, he called, "Look, all of you! Look! Look! You want to see women's liberation? *This* is"—pointing at me and patting me on the shoulders—"this *is* women's liberation! *This is* women's liberation!"

Now, for me, this was both a very wonderful moment and a very awkward and humbling one. I was bending down and trying to get away from everyone's gaze and from Lama Yeshe as he held me there, patting me on the shoulder and telling all of them that I was women's liberation. As he was bellowing my accomplishments, I was saying, "No, no, Lama, please no, don't say this; please don't say this!" And he was smiling the whole time. Even though that particular occasion was embarrassing to me, it seemed to cause Lama Yeshe a good deal of happiness; and it also seemed to make everyone else feel good.

While Lama's claim about me was pure hyperbole, his pride in me was genuine. Thus, his showing me off was completely unlike those moments I'd experienced when I'd been paraded in front of and made to perform before white superintendents at my all-black elementary school, occasions that left me only with feelings of anger and resentment. As a child, I had been shown off because I was smart; but when Lama Yeshe showed me off it was a loving way of helping me to heal a long list of old wounds: my mother calling me evil, the white superintendents' amazement at a black child's intelligence, the sense of the dire mistake I'd committed by solving my sister's math problem, the humiliation I'd later suffered because I couldn't spell, going to college amid Klan threats, and the bogus idea that universities were lowering their standards in order to let in black students. It was as if Lama Yeshe were saying, "Let the old wounds go, daughter. Let them all go." Standing there with him, for the first time in my life I began to feel that I could let them go; let them all go and embrace my true self, which was, like the true selves of all other beings, clean, clear, capable, loving, and lovable. At that moment, confidence arose strongly in me, and I knew that everyone ought to feel this way.

From the very beginning, Lama Yeshe had pointed out and celebrated my intelligence. During that first year when Randy, Rob, and I lived and studied with him at Kopan, he would sometimes say to me, "You see. I tell you one thing, and immediately you make five!" Unsure of his meaning initially, I asked, "Is that bad, Lama Yeshe?" "Of course not!" he responded. "It is very *good*! It means that your mind is quick! That is very good, dear." After that, to make the same point, he would hold up his hand and spread his fingers for emphasis. Because I so admired Lama Yeshe's own intelligence and because when I'd first met him I already considered myself to be quite a serious student of Buddhism, this kind of validation was especially important to me. Lama Yeshe continually encouraged me that it was okay to be smart. In fact, over the course of the fifteen years that I was his student, he treated me more like a colleague.

Two years before I gave that talk at Kopan, Lama had privately given me his seal of approval in a way that was so powerful it still moves me today. I had been offered a visiting appointment at Wesleyan for the academic year of 1977–78. Lama Yeshe and I had been discussing this when he mentioned to me that he would himself like to try out the university experience. Though the University of California, Santa Cruz, where I had been teaching had never had an enrobed lama on its faculty, as it turned out, it was a fairly simple matter to have them hire Lama Yeshe to replace me for a quarter's term. He would teach only one of my courses, and it was, appropriately, "Tibetan Buddhism." So, during the academic year of 1977–78 I taught at Wesleyan while Lama Yeshe taught at UCSC during the spring quarter. Now, the academic year at Wesleyan ended before the spring quarter at UCSC, so Lama Yeshe invited me to come out and to give a guest lecture in *his* class during the last week of the term. Though I had given lots of guest lectures in numerous settings, that particular occasion will forever stand out in my mind.

Lama Yeshe briefly introduced me to the class, then took a seat among the students. I gave a lecture that compared the sacred life stories (called *nam-thar* in Tibetan) of two of the most famous Buddhist yogis, Naropa and Milarepa. I began by first writing the term *nam-thar* on the blackboard in Tibetan. The students seemed impressed by the beauty of the script as well as by my general remarks concerning how such spiritual biographies work to impart, in narrative and aesthetic form, the essence of practice. I proceeded to narrate each of the yogis' lives—with all the facial, hand, and body gestures that I am famous for—and then to compare and contrast certain details of the stories. The time flew by; I was in my element. When I finished, the hundred or so students gave me a standing ovation. Just before the class's question-and-answer period, Lama Yeshe beckoned me over to him. He was beaming like a proud father. When I leaned near to him I could see that tears were streaming down his cheeks. Lifting his robe to partially cover his face, he whispered to me, "Lama is *so very proud* of you!" I thought my heart would burst wide open. It seemed at that moment that *this* was the assurance I had been waiting for all my life.

Another story that stands out in my mind is Lama Yeshe's asking me to teach him Western philosophy. Sister Max, an African American woman who took nun's ordination in the 1970s and became his special aide, called me early in 1983 and said that Lama wanted me to arrange a brief course for him. When I asked, "Why me?" Max said, "Because Lama knows you've studied Western philosophy as well as Buddhism and he knows you're a great teacher!" I was flattered no end. It was decided that we would have to conduct the private tutorial in the summer after Lama had completed teaching the monthlong retreat course at Vajrapani Institute in California.

That particular trip turned out to be Lama's last teaching tour in the States; he died early in March of the next year. What happened during our mini-summer course together was absolutely remarkable. Lama Yeshe set aside one month in which just he and I met each day for three hours—from 9:00 A.M. till noon—six days a week, and I led him through a course in Western philosophy.

He had asked me to prepare a short anthology of selections for him. He wanted to learn about key Western philosophers and their major ideas by actually reading their works directly and then discussing them. In keeping with his request, I prepared a little booklet that contained important arguments from the giants of Western thought, selections of roughly four to five pages in length, all in English. I called the booklet "From the Pre-Socratics to Wittgenstein."

I had done my best to design a good, short survey course for Lama. But once we actually started, *he* did most of the work. He carefully read each of the selections and then responded to them with a mind that was so quick and so incisive I simply marveled.

For example, I would have provided Lama Yeshe with a passage from Plato that discussed his notion of ideal forms. For the *next* day, there would be a piece by Aristotle, wherein Aristotle refuted Plato's claim. Most Westerners know about this famous philosophical debate. Namely, Plato made a claim for ideal forms, what we later came to call "universals." But Aristotle subsequently pointed out, in rebuttal to Plato, that universals did not exist in the world but could only be demonstrated in, and through, particulars. Therefore, Plato's concept of ideal forms was, logically speaking, erroneous; universality is only an ideal construct that lacks logical proof; only particulars manifest in the world. Now, *before* ever having read Aristotle's response, in our morning discussion of Plato, Lama Yeshe began right away by saying that he strongly objected to the argument. And in explaining his reasons for doing so, he argued *precisely* in the way that Aristotle did. As soon as he had understood what these philosophers were saying, he could immediately see the faults in their arguments. And I got to witness a demonstration of his incisive philosophical acumen day after day after day. The fact that Lama Yeshe wanted to spend hours studying Western philosophy—at a time when his health was so rapidly failing—was amazing in its own right. He believed that if he understood the philosophical underpinnings of Western thought, then he'd understand where his students were coming from and could better communicate with and teach them.

That summer was also great because, for a solid month, there was just Lama Yeshe and me working together—one to one—every morning. Afterward, we would be joined by Aye, Lama's Danish personal attendant, for lunch. After our three hours of discussing philosophy, Lama Yeshe would go out to his garden—he always gardened wherever he was—and pick some chives, onions, or other vegetables and then come in and cook lunch. It was a time of incredible closeness.

As our monthlong tutorial neared its end, one extremely touching moment occurred which I alone witnessed. One morning when I arrived for our class, Lama was lying on the couch. He appeared totally exhausted. Aye was off that particular day. When I entered, Lama raised his arm with effort and held out a set of keys. By this time, his heart condition was getting a great deal worse. Though none of us knew it then, he would be with us only a few months more. He said to me, "A lady stopped by earlier this morning, a generous older student. She has a house on the ocean down south. Please take me there."

He had already packed a tiny knapsack. When I helped him to his feet, he handed me a scribbled map to the house.

We drove south for fifteen or twenty minutes before turning right onto a dirt road that headed off directly toward the ocean. We found the woman's house and with her keys entered it. The house was gorgeous, a two-storied structure covered in bougainvillea, tucked away behind palm and Japanese coastal trees, private, quiet, and serene. It stood just above the cliffs overlooking the blue ocean. Her living room walls, on two sides, were constructed completely of glass. The view was breathtaking. It appeared that Lama Yeshe had been here before. He told me that he was going upstairs, to "his room," to lie down and that I should call him at lunchtime.

After a couple of hours went by, I pulled together a meager lunch with the vegetables and fruits I found at the house. Then I tiptoed up the outside steps that led to the room Lama Yeshe had entered. I really didn't want to wake him; I hoped that he was getting some rest. But I thought he might also need some food. I tapped lightly on his door. No answer. Then I began to wonder whether he might be meditating or, worse, really sick. I tapped again. No answer. I pushed open the door.

What I witnessed then was at the same time a great relief and a searingly poignant moment. Lama Yeshe hadn't heard me knock because he was already up and in the bathroom washing up for lunch. That was a relief! Then I noticed the room. In the foreground was Lama's bed, which was set against another wall of glass overlooking the ocean. On it was his tiny knapsack, opened; and on one of the pillows of the bed was the little philosophy booklet I had prepared for him. It was turned to the selection on Feuerbach that we would be discussing the next day. Lama had been reading and underlining key passages with a yellow marker.

I have been fortunate indeed to have had such a close relationship with Lama Yeshe for almost fifteen years, to have received incredibly profound teachings from him and, near the end of his life, to have enjoyed such a special time with him. He was a true master of *empowerment,* not just of the formalized rituals lamas perform, but of genuine empowerment. Though we all possess innate purity, clarity, strength, and potential to be infinitely wise and compassionate beings, still we need *someone* to encourage us and to show us how to manifest those qualities. Lama Yeshe directly helped me to do this in ways great and small.

I have also been fortunate in other ways. Though my own family was poor, my parents, my sister, and I were close-knit and loving. In spite of that memorable and damaging remark, I know that my mother loved me without bounds, as most parents love their children. My father still refers to me as "daughter," with pride. In my case, however, it took a gentle Tibetan lama who also called me "daughter"—and who lived thousands of miles away from Docena, Alabama—to help me to understand and appreciate the preciousness of familial love. Both Lama Yeshe and my mother have now passed away. Yet because of their love, I now know that spiritual liberation is a true possibility.

A BAPTIST-BUDDHIST

❧

It was the kind of slow-motion thing that you see in movies. My car was skidding, swerving out of control on the slush and ice of a highway recently plowed—but not recently enough. I was returning from Boston, trying to get back home to Middletown before the big snow-and-ice storm forecasted for later that afternoon arrived. Now I knew that I should have taken my hosts' advice and stayed in Boston.

The storm had been the delight of weather forecasters for days, and I did not want to be caught in those treacherous driving conditions that had been their theme all week. Leaving Boston on the Mass Pike around 7:00 A.M., things had seemed all right. I put on some music and applauded myself for making the right decision. After driving for about an hour, the flurries began. It was a beautiful thing, snow; and I'd soon be home. By the time I turned off onto I–84, the roads were getting bad. Attempting to calm myself, I determined that if I slowed down, keeping ample space between my car and the ones in front of me, I'd still make it okay.

Just after passing Hartford, the snow got really heavy. I cut off the music and gripped the steering wheel a bit tighter. At least now there were only three lanes to worry about, not the five that had led into the Hartford area. Traffic slowed but was moving. I told myself, "Only twenty minutes. Then home." I tried to keep focused on the cars ahead and the tracks they were making. "Follow in the tracks," I told myself. "Keep inside the tracks. You'll make it." I was scared.

Then suddenly I saw things from the perspective of an observer. The car was spinning out. It turned almost sideways then, suddenly, righted itself. Then it began to slide toward the center guardrails. I silently mused, "So, this is how it is. Just like that, one's last moments." Images of my father and sister flashed by. No time to say anything to them. I saw the guardrails rushing toward me. The car would hit them in the next second and that would be it.

A booming *OM MANI PADME HUM!* woke me up. I was screaming the mantra at the top of my lungs. I saw myself leaning forward, clutching the steering wheel so tightly that my knuckles were white. My car had moved back into the tracks of the middle lane. I don't know how it got there. In less than a split-second, it had simply jumped back into the tracks of the lane, as if some giant invisible hand had snapped it up and placed it down again.

I looked to my rearview mirror. Behind me, cars were braking and swerving. They had been attempting to stop as they saw me careening into the guardrail. I said another few *OM MANI*s for them while I held tightly to my steering wheel.

As I continued on, now moving very slowly, I thought more about that near brush with death—how quickly our treasured selves can be extinguished; how fragile life really is. And I thought about how surprisingly that booming *OM MANI* had come out of me, in what I thought was my last moment of this life. It is the mantra of Avalokitesvara, the Buddha of Compassion. I regularly intoned it whenever I passed a dead animal on the highway, to wish it peace and blessings.

Perhaps in those compressed seconds I saw myself as a dead animal. The best I can figure, however, is that it was the shortest prayer I knew. What went along with it, I think, was the wish not to be separated from Lama Yeshe in whatever future rebirth. Perhaps I was a Buddhist after all.

Once, when I was teaching at UCSC, the car I was driving suddenly stalled less than a foot from a railroad crossing. The next second a speeding train roared by, its warning horns blaring, while my car trembled and shook as though it would fly away. Then, I had not called out the mantra. At least I didn't think I had.

And, returning one night to Hartford's Bradley Airport, after two lovely Christmas holiday weeks spent with my family in Alabama, another thoroughly frightening event took place. I was, as usual, flying on Delta Airlines. The company's biggest hub is Atlanta; they fly hundreds of flights into Birmingham and their pilots have a first-rate flying record. Hence, for most of the flight into Hartford, I was feeling pretty relaxed. However, temperatures all up and down the East Coast were pretty frigid, and this caused a good deal of turbulence. As we bumped along, dipping and rolling in the rough air, there were more than a few white knuckles in evidence. Buckled in at my window seat, for most of the hour-and-fifty-minute trip I tried to maintain a relaxed attitude, trusting in our pilots to steer us safely in. Still, as Bradley's airfield came into view, I found myself being more than a little relieved.

From the window, I could see the lights of the tarmac. Like most others on this particular flight, I let out a giant sigh of relief. Seated beside me were an older woman who had seemed frightened for most of the trip and a young girl who was, presumably, her grandchild. I smiled encouragingly before I spoke, "Okay! See, there's the runway! It won't be long now."

We were no more than a few feet above the tarmac. The plane's landing gear was down, its headlights illuminating the field. Then things abruptly changed. In an instant, the plane veered steeply upward. It went into a climb that was almost perpendicular. We were like astronauts, our heads pressed back against our seats, our bodies feeling the G-forces of lift-off. My own knuckles went white. Papers from somewhere started blowing through the compartment. Overhead doors snapped open. Oxygen masks dropped. Some people started to scream. I started to pray, at first aloud and then silently, but speeded up, with urgency. I called on both my guru, Lama Yeshe, and upon Jesus. "Lama Yeshe!" I screamed, "may I never be separated from you in this or future lives!" Gripping my armrests in silence, I continued, "May you and all the Buddhas help and bless us now!" Without pausing, I then fervently intoned, "Christ Jesus, please help us. Please, I pray, bless me and all these people!"

That plane climbed straight up for almost four minutes. My prayers became continuous mantras. Finally, the engines' roar lessened and the plane began to level off. The pilot's voice came over the speakers. He sounded nervous himself but tried to speak reassuringly, "Ah-h, ladies and gentlemen, I'm sorry it's taken so long to get back to you. It seems that just as we were landing we hit one of those stiff wind shears and we had to get out of it. We're going to try this landing again, this time from the east." A collective sigh went up from all of us.

I call myself a "Baptist-Buddhist" not to be cute or witty. I call myself a "Baptist-Buddhist" because it is an honest description of who I feel I am. When I was on that plane, racing straight upward through the frigid night air, I did not feel as though I were simply hedging my bets. I felt sheer and utter terror, and I called on both traditions for help. Long ago, Kierkegaard had argued that one doesn't know what one really believes until one is forced to act. That climbing plane showed me what I believed.

Most times, actually, I think of myself as being more an African American Buddhist. When I seek to make sense of things or to analyze a particular situation, I am more likely to draw upon Buddhist principles than Baptist ones. But when it seems as though the plane I'm on might actually go down, I call on both traditions. It is a deep response.

About this dual description, my folks seem, generally, accepting. Though one day while telling me that she thought my years with Lama Yeshe hadn't caused me any harm, my mother did let me know, in subtle and not so subtle ways, that she worried for my soul and its salvation. Many others, who've had occasion—or taken the license— to comment on it, have stridently voiced disdain and disapproval: "Either you believe in Christ, our Lord, as your sole and only savior, or you're lost!" A young, well-educated, and articulate black man who was visiting Wesleyan once told me exactly this. To this vociferous attack by a newly reborn Christian, and to others like it, I can only say, "Well, I trust that Jesus Himself is more understanding and compassionate." The Jesus I knew from the Gospel stories was the Jesus who had ministered to women, to the poor and downtrodden; and He was the Jesus I knew personally, because He had ridden with me on that bus ride to Cornell. Moreover, it seems to me that those who see a disjuncture in my being a Baptist-Buddhist haven't spent any amount of time reflecting on what, or who, a Buddha really is—or a Christ, for that matter. As always, in matters of faith and of the heart, a little concrete experience and practice usually takes one higher, while at the same time sets one on firmer ground.

If I have learned anything about myself thus far it is that in my deepest core I am a human being, graced by the eternal truths espoused both by Baptists and by Buddhists. And more than that, I am aware that it is not any particular appellation that matters. For ultimately, what I have come to know is that life—precious life—is not a destination. Life is the journey.

DREAMING ME, V:
THE LIONESS'S ROAR

ை

Again, *I find myself tenuously balanced on a branch of the tree in our backyard, a tiny twig as weapon in my hands. Encircling the tree below me a pride of lionesses prowls. The thought occurs to me that Sandy and my mom are someplace safe.*

Every so often, one of the lionesses raises up and swipes at my feet. I find the courage to look down at the animals. I see their upturned faces. Surprisingly, none of them looks menacing. Though their mouths bear traces of dried blood, they do not appear to be malicious or to threaten me.

There is a singular, great lioness among them. As she approaches the tree, the others part, making way for her. With her gigantic paw, she swipes up at me. Her face is powerful but gentle. She actually seems to be smiling at me; her furry soft paw beckons me. Slowly, my hand releases the tiny branch. It drops away silently, and I begin climbing down.

When my feet touch the ground, the other lionesses have all disappeared. Only the great lioness remains, standing some distance away. I feel inexorably drawn to her. I trust her. She stands, motionless, peering at me. A flash of light-

ning streaks the sky. I recognize it as a sign of power, and I am not afraid. As I come nearer to the lioness I see reflected in her eyes, my own. My hand goes out to touch her. Reaching for her I seem, suddenly, to see the world as though through her eyes. I feel a deep rumble building in my chest, and rearing my head, I roar.

LIONS

⚭

When a professional astrologer first did my chart and announced that I was a Leo rising, you could have "bought me for a ha' penny," as the old folks say. *Me? Leo rising? No way!* I'm much too timid, too afraid, to have Leo anywhere in any of my determinants, astrological or otherwise. But Leo rising I am. There is a *lion* in there somewhere. And for most of my life, my spirit has been nudging me to let it out and let it roar.

Leos are strong, sure of themselves, ambitious, and powerful. I don't see that as part of my nature. But sometimes friends have advised: "Just look at all you've done, all that you've accomplished. That stuff took desire, ambition, fortitude, and strength." But how often do any of us really take the time to reflect upon our accomplishments or, to put it another way, actually to count our blessings?

I know that I have been extremely *fortunate* in this life. Looking back now, I'm very glad that I didn't join the Black Panther party back in 1969. If I had, who knows what might have happened? I might have been shot and killed; I might have been incarcerated and, as was my father's biggest fear, had my spirit crushed. I also might never have returned to India, where I met the Tibetans and, ultimately, Lama Yeshe, who helped to show me how to make life meaningful.

Buddhist tradition says that there are two professions that are superior to all others: medicine and teaching. Being a physician is superior because one can directly benefit beings by lessening their physical sufferings. Being a teacher is superior because one can help beings to understand ways of benefiting themselves both now and in the future. As can be imagined, it considers the teaching of Buddhism as the best of professions. The Buddha is revered because he is seen as having been the greatest of teachers.

I have been a teacher of Buddhism for more than twenty-five years. This has been a good job for me professionally—I've been paid to practice, and to think about, a philosophical and religious tradition that I greatly admire. How fortunate can one be, to get paid for doing what one loves? And I've had the opportunity to help to shape young minds; to get young people to pause and think about what is truly meaningful in life, about what being human entails.

Over the course of those twenty-five years, I have taught—in the classroom—perhaps six thousand students. Through my books, I imagine, I've reached a few thousand more. So, in this way, I have had some impact, I hope for the good. I believe I have certainly had a more positive impact in this way than I might have had I joined the Panther party. Former students still write to me or call me and tell me this is so.

I also believe that the stage upon which I work, the university classroom, is enriched by my presence. Just the fact of my being an African American woman teaching at a place like Wesleyan, or UCSC, or the University of Virginia, offers a positive role model not only to African American students but to other students of color as well. I have also been told that it offers a positive image to women students, and to women generally. All this is, I think, a good thing.

Life takes funny and often unforeseeable turns. Mine certainly has—from that moody child in Docena, Alabama, to physics, philosophy, and now, professor of religion and buddhist studies at Wesleyan. Though Lama Yeshe repeatedly told me that at my core my center was calm, clear, and intelligent, I thought of myself as fearful and shameful. In spite of low self-esteem, I pushed on. Some part of me must have been brave and strong, though it never quite seemed that way from inside. Inside there was a constant duel between pride and humility. This duel must be true for all human beings. Yet I think it is true in a special way for most African Americans and most people of color. We persist, we survive, we live on in spite of forces that seem at times to wish our complete silence, if not our annihilation. That has been our history.

I wake up every morning in black skin. This fact brings with it, for me, a sense of responsibility. I feel that I have to go out into the world being an example, an embodiment of strength and confidence for the race, even when, inside, I don't always feel that way. It is, sometimes, a heavy burden. Heavier still is the blanket objectification that all blacks, by virtue of their skin alone, endure.

But we do not do it alone. We do it with the power and strength of the ancestors, with the kindness of friends, in the care of angels, with the Buddhas' and God's love. We live and we contribute. I am happy to have been able to contribute.

During the past years, and especially when I first began doing family history research in the South, I began having a series of recurrent dreams about lions. Sometimes frightening, but always awe-inspiring, the lions invaded my dreams and my psyche. They clearly wanted in, though I tried for a time to repress them. I believe the lions are me, myself. Perhaps they are my deepest African self. They are the "me" that I have battled ever since leaving Docena and venturing forth into a mostly white world. I believe it is time to let the lions come to the fore and to make peace with them. For making peace with them is making peace with myself, allowing me to be me, authentically.

Lions are strong and magnificent. In Buddhism, the lion's roar is the mark of the eloquence and power of the Buddha's speech. His eminent disciples, too, are often referred to as his lions. They carry on and embody the Teachings. With the help of some of these lions—especially Lama Yeshe—I have begun to make peace with my own inner lions.

In the end, the most profound lessons of life are the simplest, and I try to remind my students of these: We are all human beings. We all wish to have happiness and to avoid suffering. Take the time to imagine yourself in another's shoes. Count your blessings. Try as much as is possible to practice loving-kindness. At the very least, try to avoid harming others.

Every now and then, a lion must roar. It is part of her nature. If my life's story is of some benefit to others, that will be a *fine roar*.

Acknowledgments

On my life's journey, I have had numerous helpers. I could not have reached the place where I am now without any one of them. The list must begin with my parents, Dorothy and Oram Willis, who raised me up and cared for me even though I was such a moody child, and who encouraged me as best they could even when they might have feared for, or doubted, the future outcome; and continue with Sandy, who was always more than just a sister to me but my best friend as well. My teachers in elementary and high school, all fine African American educators themselves, would have to be included, as well as the young white Harvard student who volunteered to teach me Schrodinger's equation and its meanings; Bea MacLeod, who came down to encourage me and who managed to get me up to Cornell for the Telluride Summer Program; Allen Wood, my Cornell advisor, and his wife, Rega, who opened their home to a fledgling student and were not afraid to show me their own early efforts at, and fears about, teaching; Norman Malcom, who respected my intelligence, taught me chess, and showed me that one could do philosophy not just to engage in abstruse analyses but to reflect on the importance of living a good and decent life; Calum Carmichael, who arranged for me to get a Cornell Traveling Fellowship and thus return to Nepal as an alternative to joining the Panthers; Ed Dirks, who as head of the Danforth Foundation corresponded with me while I was in India even before I officially got a Kent Fellowship; Barbara Stoler Miller, Sanskritist and poet, the model of good teaching and a supporter throughout the entirety of my work; Herman Blake, who put time into recruiting me to teach at the University of California, Santa Cruz, and who, after offering me my first job there, served as a kind of teaching mentor himself; Josie King, whose tireless care for students and warm friendship with me provided a model of compassion and helped sustain me during those early teaching years; Alex Haley, who not only gave the country *Roots* but appreciated my input about oral traditions in India, and opened one of his homes in Jamaica to me and my family for a glorious holiday. And truly good friends: Randy and Robbie Solick, Vera Schwarcz, Elea Mideke, Ashraf Rushdy, Deborah Muirhead, Julia Lowe, and Marlies Bosch. I couldn't have been luckier! I might not have made it without any one of these compassionate souls. I owe particular thanks and love to Marlies. Without her, the book you have just read might not have come together as it did. For in addition to her considerable talents as a ceramist and photographer, Marlies is also a skilled journalist and a wonderful editor. During the three years of writing this book, it was Marlies who read every line of every draft and who at key moments said, "Stop. *Tell* me. Now, *this* is what's important!" or "No, no. Begin *here!*" My thanks to her are immeasurable.

It was not my idea to write a memoir. Trace Murphy at Doubleday first suggested the idea, and it was he who encouraged me to get an agent. Here, I was even more fortunate, since John Taylor "Ike" Williams, of Palmer and Dodge, agreed to accept me as a client. Ike is a lion of a man, graced with wisdom, integrity, and abundant good humor. To him, I offer sincere and heartfelt thanks. In the final stages of writing, Amy Hertz at Riverhead Books gave shape and form to the text, often forcing me to sit and think about connections in my life I had never consciously seen. In the end, she read and reread more versions of the book than I had hoped to write. But from this vantage point, her efforts and assignments for me to "tweak it just a bit more" were worth it. I am grateful to her.

About the Author

JAN WILLIS is a professor of religion at Wesleyan University and the first African American scholar-practitioner of Tibetan Buddhism in America. In addition to earning a master's degree from Cornell University and a Ph.D. from Columbia University, she has studied with Tibetan Buddhists in India, Nepal, Switzerland, and the United States for more than three decades and has taught courses in Buddhism for twenty-five years. The author of several books, including *Enlightened Beings: Life Stories from the Ganden Oral Tradition* and *The Diamond Light: An Introduction to Tibetan Buddhist Meditation,* she has also published numerous essays and articles on Buddhist meditation, hagiography, women and Buddhism, Buddhism in America, and Buddhism and race. She lives in Middletown, Connecticut.